THE WORLD WE FOUND

THE WORLD WE FOUND

The Limits of Ontological Talk

Mark Sacks

Duckworth

First published in 1989 by
Gerald Duckworth & Co. Ltd.
The Old Piano Factory
43 Gloucester Crescent, London NW1

© 1989 by Mark Sacks

All rights reserved. No part of this publication may be reproduced, stored in a retrieval system, or transmitted, in any form or by any means, electronic, mechanical, photocopying, recording or otherwise, without the prior permission of the publisher.

ISBN 0 7156 2237 4

British Library Cataloguing in Publication Data

Sacks, Mark
   The world we found : the limits of
   ontological talk.
   I. Title
   111

ISBN 0-7156-2237-4

Photoset in North Wales by
Derek Doyle & Associates, Mold, Clwyd
and printed in Great Britain by
Unwin Brothers Limited, Old Woking

Contents

Preface		vii
1.	Locating a Philosophical Issue	1
2.	Focussing a Philosophical Perspective	25
3.	Brains, Vats and Putnam's Internalist Approach	56
4.	Goodman: Final Focus of the Philosophical Perspective	94
5.	The Need for Global Ontological Talk: The Ontological Fallacy	117
6.	Examining Global Ontological Talk: Verificationism	136
7.	The Terms of Global Ontological Talk	157
8.	Conclusion	184
Bibliography		189
Index		195

To my parents

Preface

This book runs its course, in a relatively straight line, from beginning to end. In so doing it belies its origins. It is in fact the product of an effort to unravel, in part, certain thoughts which for a long while seemed stubbornly indifferent to the needs and benefits of systematic, critical exposition. I hope that something of the initial conception has survived, in something approaching clarity.

It might be useful, by way of providing a general orientation, to indicate a perspective which to some extent structures the enquiry. There was, and to a degree still is, a tendency, common to certain exponents and critics of analytic philosophy, to regard such philosophy as having little to do with metaphysics. While this clearly captures something of the mood of early analytic philosophy, there seems to be a growing awareness that we can now see analytic philosophy most rewardingly in its relation to the larger concern with metaphysics, against which it was conceived to be a reaction, and from which it constituted a retreat.

The perspective afforded by placing central works of the analytic tradition within the larger setting of metaphysical concerns, brings to the forefront a certain discontinuity which resulted from the abrupt analytic turn away from metaphysics. The following pages show how as a result of this discontinuity certain long-standing metaphysical issues, even though still potent and unresolved, have been allowed to go largely unattended. The aversion within the analytical tradition to certain metaphysical excesses which purported to answer questions about our knowledge of the external world still seems entirely appropriate. Yet the spirit in which the concern with the underlying issues was avoided now appears to be somewhat dogmatic. We seem, consequently, to be left with unsettled metaphysical problems lurking in the wings. This suggests the possibility of turning back with the benefit of hindsight to address matters from which philosophical discontinuity might temporarily have diverted our attention.

The attempt to confront these issues involves examining a particular conception of the independence of the world from experience, upon which the positions of realism, idealism and scepticism rest. There are of course various ways of construing both realism and idealism, and scepticism. This book focusses on one particularly basic form of realism and idealism, which is described as *ontological* realism and idealism. These positions involve a specific form of what I call, broadly, 'ontological talk'.

The first chapter provides a description of ontological relations in general, and of the particular conception set in terms of them which is common to the positions of realism and idealism. The particular kind of sceptical problem which ensues when that conception is assumed to be coherent is outlined in very general terms.

The second chapter then enters the relevant historical terrain, drawing from Kant and contemporary Anglo-American philosophy. Chapter 3 offers a close examination of Putnam's recent work, showing that while it presents a case against metaphysical realism it cannot defuse the sceptic's worry. Chapter 4 discusses Goodman's ways of worldmaking. These three chapters together establish a perspective which poses the central challenge, and at the same time clarifies the framework within which that challenge is to be discussed in the present enquiry.

A sharp distinction is drawn between local ontological talk, in which ontological dependence and independence relations function unproblematically, and global ontological talk, upon which realism, idealism and scepticism (in at least one of its forms) turn. As the preceding chapters show, such ontological talk is assumed to be coherent, and has indeed implicitly been given a place within philosophy from Kant down to the recent work in the analytical tradition. Yet, as long as such global ontological talk remains acceptable, there will be room for the sceptic to ask how we know that the real world is as we experience it to be. (This particular sceptical question functions as a philosophical compass at various junctions in the book; the fact that it is still there to be asked, prompts the discussion on to the next stage.)

The question arises whether there is reason to introduce global ontological talk at all. Chapter 5 takes up this issue in some detail, attempting to examine the different grounds upon which the introduction of such talk might be thought to be necessary, and concludes that in fact an internalist account which avoids global ontological talk is quite adequate. After thus showing the extent to which global ontological talk can be relieved of philosophical duties, the way is left open to proceed with an examination of its coherence.

Chapters 6 and 7 consider possible arguments to the effect that global ontological talk is in fact not coherent. Chapter 6 considers Carnap's verificationist argument and weaker possible modifications of it. It is contended that such arguments in their more doctrinaire forms are unacceptable, while in their acceptable forms they are too weak to deliver the conclusion required to meet the challenge. The fact that the sceptic remains unscathed is evidence of this.

Chapter 7 therefore attempts a different line of argument which, drawing on various earlier strands, turns directly to the conception involved in any form of global ontological talk. The success of this argument would undermine all global ontological talk. It would, however, be unreasonable to regard the argument as conclusive. Certain objections are raised, and possible counter-objections are offered, but the overall aim is only to have offered an opening step — one which certainly leaves room for, but which I hope also merits, further consideration.

The final chapter anticipates, very roughly, the kind of position with which we would be left if, either on the basis of the argument in Chapter 7, or perhaps merely on the grounds provided in previous chapters, global ontological talk were to be rejected. It is suggested that much would in fact be left unchanged by the move to an internalist position entirely devoid of such ontological talk. No detailed elaboration is attempted, however; the book sets out to enquire how the ground might be cleared with a view to possible construction, not to commence that construction.

I have not, as will be obvious, attempted a comprehensive account of the vast literature relevant to this concern. In particular, I fully realise that it is, in a sense, both arbitrary and unfortunate to have restricted myself to discussions of relatively modern philosophy. The modern perspective promises to highlight the relevance of the central issue to our current philosophical concerns. The issue is not, however, confined to this modern perspective. The latter merely provides one way into a long-standing issue which could well have been approached by a variety of different routes. Thus, the early sceptic's and, for example, Plato's concern with the relation between appearance and reality, world and Forms, would have been relevant to a more broadly conceived version of this book. My excuse for structuring the book around a single perspective to the practical exclusion of all others is that it was dictated by considerations of length and clarity. I can only hope that the reader will generally be sufficiently aware of the relevance of such discussions to make their absence less damaging.

I am grateful to Simon Blackburn and Edward Craig for detailed comments on an earlier version of this book, to Anthony Grayling for his extensive comments on a later version, to Ross Harrison who commented on an early draft, and to Hilary Putnam for his detailed consideration of the third chapter, which concerns some of his own work.

For their encouragement during my stay at King's College, Cambridge, I am grateful to G.E.R. Lloyd, who also commented on an earlier draft; to Rob Wallach; and in particular to Tony Tanner. I am similarly indebted to David Heyd, whose intellectual example has remained constant for many years; and to Lydia Goehr, Leah Rosen, Barry Smith and Lucy O'Brien for their comments, stimulation and support at various stages from the genesis of this project to its conclusion.

Special thanks are due to Bernard Williams, who supervised the doctoral dissertation on which this book is based. Without his uncompromising stance, particularly in the earlier stages of research, it would certainly have exhibited even less rigour than it does.

I am grateful to the following institutions which provided support during the course of the research: King's College, Cambridge, the British Council, the Israel Zangwill Trust, and the Leo Baeck Scholarship Committee (London); and to Dr. Ernst W. Leffers.

My thanks also to the members of the Department of Philosophy at Sheffield University where I spent a pleasant year as a Research Fellow. The time afforded by this Fellowship made possible the preparation of this manuscript for publication.

Finally, my very special thanks to John G. Ferrari. Discussions and friendship with him over a long period of time combined, somehow, to render philosophy and recreation almost indistinguishable. From beginning to end he was a vital source of encouragement, geographical distances notwithstanding.

University of Liverpool M.S.
June 1987

1. Locating a Philosophical Issue

1. Introduction

In the following pages I intend to investigate 'ontological talk'. In particular I wish to examine the notion of something either being, or not being, real. The term 'real', notoriously, is one of the more elusive items in the philosopher's lexicon. The first part of this chapter will therefore be devoted to elucidating the sense of the term relevant to the present investigation. The remaining part will be concerned to explain a related philosophical problem.

An attempt will then be made, particularly in the following three chapters, to map the philosophical terrain in relation to which this problem has been formulated. The map is in no way intended as a comprehensive enquiry into the history of this philosophical issue. My aim is rather to establish a perspective within modern philosophy which emphasises the relevance of the present enquiry.

1.2 Clarifying the terms of ontological talk

The following distinctions all play a crucial role in almost any account of our experience. We distinguish between *physical* and *non-physical* objects; between *non-fictional* and *fictional* objects; between *actual* and *merely possible* objects. We also talk of *existing* as opposed to *non-existing* objects. I do not mean to undermine any of these distinctions, or indeed others which could be added to the list. There is, however, a further distinction, between real and non-real objects. This is a vague distinction; it is used loosely in a variety of contexts, even within the context of philosophy. In many of these uses the distinction is perfectly neutral. But there is one central philosophical use of it which I wish to examine in this book: the use relevant to the notion of reality upon which the idealist, the realist and the sceptic base their disagreement. The point of this examination is to explore the possibility of applying an Ockham-like razor, not merely to specific putatively real entities, but indeed to any ontological assumption of there being – or not being – something real.

I do not suggest that this is an entirely new line of investigation: it is partially foreshadowed both by Carnap and by contemporary internal or empirical realism in some of its forms. The extent to which this is so will become clear in the course of what follows.

Were it to emerge that there is need to dispose of all talk of objects being or not being real in this sense, quite evidently either the other pairs of concepts listed above would collapse, to the extent that they are dependent on this distinction, or we would have to disentangle them from it. In other words, in order to maintain these other oppositions, it would be necessary to provide an account of them in a way that does not rest upon, or in any way presuppose, the notion of real or non-real objects. The idea would be to show that these distinctions require only a local, internal perspective, whereas the notion of real or non-real objects requires a completely different, global, mode of discourse. A complete account of how these distinctions can be maintained in the absence of the ontological notion will not be attempted here; I mention it merely to point out in advance the kind of concern with which the present line of enquiry could leave us.

1.2.1 The term 'real'

To proceed it is necessary to define precisely the intended meaning of the term 'real'. It is advisable to start by setting aside a common meaning of 'real' which is definitely not the one with which I am concerned.

Austin notes[1] that often we talk of a real x – say, a real duck – where what we mean to say is that it is not a fake. Thus we distinguish between a real duck and a decoy duck; between real turtle and mock turtle. This is an utterly neutral distinction – and has nothing at all to do with the ontological notion with which I am concerned. To see this it is sufficient to point out that the notion of reality with which this book is concerned can be applied equally to the real duck and to the decoy duck. We can talk both of a real real duck, and of a real decoy duck. The sphinx-like thing floating on the lake is only a decoy duck, made of plastic, and although it is not a real duck like those swimming on the Cam, it, as much as anything else, might nevertheless be considered to be real in the relevant sense.

The sense of 'real' in which the decoy is thought *not* to be real might be better captured by a contrast between being a mere decoy and being a *genuine duck*. In contrast, the sense of 'real' which is relevant to the present discussion is not one which can equally well be captured by

---

[1] In *Sense and Sensibilia*, OUP, 1962, chapter 7, pp. 62-77.

1. Locating a Philosophical Issue

talk of genuine as opposed to fake objects.

The difference between these two senses of 'real' is, however, more substantial than the above has revealed. Geach, discussing the concepts of 'good' and 'bad', draws a distinction between attributive and predicative adjectives.² An adjective is (logically) predicative if in a sentence 'x is an A B', where 'A' is an adjective and 'B' is a noun, it is possible to split up the predication into a pair of predications – 'x is a B' and 'x is A'. Otherwise the adjective 'A' is (logically) attributive. Thus 'big' and 'small' are attributive adjectives: 'x is a big flea' does not split up into 'x is a flea' and 'x is big', nor does 'x is a small elephant' split up into 'x is an elephant' and 'x is small'. For, as Geach says, if these analyses were legitimate, a simple argument would show that a big flea is a big animal and a small elephant is a small animal (ibid. p. 33). The same applies to the adjectives 'forged' and 'genuine'. In contrast, in the phrase 'a red book', 'red' is a predicative adjective in the logical sense defined (although not in the grammatical sense), for 'is a red book' logically splits up into 'is a book' and 'is red'.³

In many of their uses the terms 'real' and 'not real' too are attributive adjectives. Indeed this is essentially the point that Austin was making. Austin, having said that 'real' has many and diverse uses in many diverse contexts, goes on to 'mention under four headings what might be called the salient features of the use of "real"', granting that not *all* these features are equally conspicuous in all its uses.⁴ He proceeds to say that 'real' is (1) *substantive-hungry*, (2) a *trouser-word*, (3) a *dimension-word* and (4) an *adjuster-word*. What Austin means by a word that is substantive-hungry coincides with what Geach calls an attributive adjective. Thus Austin says:

> 'These diamonds are real'; 'These are real diamonds'. This pair of sentences looks like, in an obvious grammatical respect, this other pair: 'These diamonds are pink'; 'These are pink diamonds'. But whereas we can *just* say of something 'This is pink', we can't *just* say of something 'This is real'. And it is not very difficult to see why. We can perfectly well say of something that it is pink without knowing, without any reference to, what it *is*. But not so with 'real'. For one and the same object may be both a real x and not a real y; an object looking rather like a duck may be a real decoy duck (not just a toy) but not a real duck... That is, we must have an answer to the question 'A real *what*?'...⁵

---

² P.T. Geach, 'Good and Evil', in Analysis, 1956, pp. 33-42.
³ Geach holds that 'good' and 'bad' are always attributive, not predicative adjectives. He does not ignore the fact that others, in particular moral objectivists, have maintained that there is also a predicative use of the terms 'good' and 'bad' (ibid., p. 35). He rather attempts to show that this is an unacceptable view. This, however, is a separate issue.
⁴ ibid., p. 68
⁵ ibid., pp. 68-9.

Now it is true that in many of its uses 'real' does function in this way, as a substantive-hungry, or attributive, adjective. This is indeed the case when 'real' is used in the sense of 'genuine' as opposed to 'fake', or 'natural' as opposed to 'artificial'. But it is not clear that all the diverse uses of 'real' are of this sort, i.e. substantive-hungry or attributive adjectives.

Indeed there are uses of 'real' in which it is employed rather as a predicative adjective, one which is not substantive-hungry. Where 'real' is taken as substantive-hungry, as for example in the case where it means 'genuine', Austin is right in saying that 'we can't *just* say of something "This is real"'. But Austin does not in fact show why 'real' must always function as substantive-hungry (or as an attributive adjective). In some cases it does, but this does not show that it always will. Indeed it often does not. And in this book I am concerned with other such uses of 'real', as a predicative rather than an attributive adjective. When 'real' is taken to be a predicative adjective, it is indeed possible to move from 'x is a real B' to 'x is a B', and 'x is real'.

However, since there could well be more than one sense to 'real' even as a predicative adjective, it still remains to say what the relevant meaning of 'real' is in the present concern.[6]

Some unsatisfactory suggestions might help to point the way towards a more satisfactory answer. I might suggest, following common practice, that for x to be real is for it to be a mind-independent entity. However, even if acceptable on all other grounds, this would seem to imply that minds are not the kind of things which could be said to be real. Yet clearly minds could be so regarded. Thus it would only be permissible to say that 'real' refers to that which is independent of minds if it were allowed that minds too could be mind-independent. This immediately begins to seem like an unnecessarily convoluted way of introducing the notion, even if in other respects, which have not been examined, it was satisfactory.

The idea of something being real is sometimes also put somewhat poetically in terms of what there is from an external god-like point of view. The idea is that what is not real exists only insofar as it is directly or indirectly observed, or generally experienced in some way, whereas what is real would inhabit the world quite apart from all such observers. This way of putting the matter does indeed capture something of the ontological sense of 'real', but unfortunately the poetic trimming spoils the acceptability of even this partial picture. After all, God seems to be just another observer, just another – perhaps rather broadminded – bearer of experience. But the initial idea was to

---

[6] It is, in fact, not altogether clear that the distinction between attributive and predicative adjectives can ultimately be defended but, since I use the distinction here for expositional purposes only, this matter can be left aside.

1. Locating a Philosophical Issue

say that what is real, as opposed to what is not, would be there even in the absence of all such experiencers, however divine they might seem to be.

Also, there is perhaps a suspicion that it is not possible to talk of God or of anything else as having an *external* point of view. That is, it might seem that no point of view can possibly be external. For if a point of view, call it God's, were external, how could it then be a point of view directed at this world? Whereas, if it is a point from which this world can be observed, it cannot be external – accessibility renders it a point of view which in the relevant sense is internal rather than external to the world. However, the operative words here are 'in the relevant sense'. The exact sense of the word 'external' has yet to be clarified – it is not clear whether the divine external point of view is epistemically, causally, socially, physically or ontologically external. And until this is clarified the force of the objection remains difficult to assess. But its assessment is in any case peripheral to the present concern, and might well be left aside.

I suggest that the entire introduction of the poetic element, of God's point of view, derives from the insight, valid in itself, that *saying* what is real requires that we have some form of experience, and so, since we want to transcend our own to talk of what is real independently of it, and yet cannot do so without introducing some form of experience, we rather obscurely try to appropriate a God-like point of view. The entire attempt is in fact confused. It is of course true that some experience is required to *say* of anything that it is real. Nobody would rightly wish to deny such truisms. But the present concern is with the notion of something which is real in the sense of being such as would inhabit the world independently of all experience, and of all desire or inclination or indeed ability to *assert* that it is real. The idea is of something which is independent of all experience, not merely of mine or the Martian's, but even of that somewhat obscure divine being's experience. It is for this reason that the introduction of God, although picturesque, will not help to capture the sense of 'real' which is in question. It is only once this poetic feature is discarded that the relevant sense of the notion can be intimated.

In saying that something is 'real' we mean to say that it inhabits the world independently – in some sense yet to be clarified – of all experience, even of experience different from and somewhat more 'divine' than our own. Thus the statement 'This is a real heater', where 'real' is used, as it will be here, as a predicative adjective of ontological import, is supposed to indicate that x is a heater, and that x is real: that is, is such that it exists independently of all experience.

It should perhaps be mentioned, before proceeding to clarify this point, that another feature which Austin attributes to the notion 'real' is that it only makes sense to say that something is real if we can make sense of what it is for it *not* to be real. 'That is', in Austin's words,[7] 'a definite sense attaches to the assertion that something is real, a real such-and-such, only in the light of a specific way in which it might be, or might have been, *not* real.' Austin is speaking here of 'real' as substantive-hungry, as an attributive adjective, as is shown by the qualifying clause 'a real such-and-such'. However, this remains true when we come to view 'real' as a predicative adjective. To say that something is real, is to contrast it with some opposite which it might have been. Corresponding to what we have said about 'real', we might therefore say that something is not-real, if it is not independent of all experience, if it only exists as dependent upon experience, in such a way that in the absence of experience it would not be around in the world.

The above definitions might be sufficient to indicate very loosely the use of the terms 'real' and 'not real' which is in question in the present enquiry. A somewhat more precise analysis is needed, however, in order to set up a framework for an investigation into the coherence of such ontological talk. It is necessary, first, to explain the notions of independence and dependence as they are used in saying that what is real is *independent* of all experience, or that what is not real is *dependent* upon experience. Later it will be necessary to say more about the use of the term 'experience'.

1.2.2 Dependence and independence relations

Dependence and independence are most naturally understood as n-place relations (where n is greater than 1) which hold between objects.[8] 'Objects' here is taken as broadly as possible to cover any item which may function as the referent of a properly referring term. We can refer to the letter-box; and can refer to its red colour; both items are therefore objects, albeit very different kinds.

Dependence and independence relations hold between any such objects. Any objects referred to will be either independent of one another or dependent upon one another. Dependence and independence relations are thus contradictories, on a presuppositional view of contradictories. It is a presupposition of statements expressing dependence and independence relations being either true or false that the referring terms involved in them do in fact refer. Wherever the referring terms involved refer successfully, from the falsehood of an

[7] ibid., p. 70

[8] In what follows I will, for convenience and without loss, consider these relations in their simplest form, as two-place relations.

independence claim we can infer the truth of a dependence claim between the same referents, and *vice versa*. Granted successful reference to *x* and *y*, it cannot be false both that *x* is independent of *y*, and that *x* is dependent upon *y*. The fact that the one is false suffices to assure that the other is true. In cases of reference failure, however, neither claim will be either true or false.[9]

However, this still leaves unclear the precise nature of these relations. It is necessary to distinguish between different kinds of dependence and independence relations before they can be employed in understanding the relevant use of 'real' and 'not real'. For consider the possibility of someone contending that not merely trees and stones, but also tables, chairs and perhaps even thoughts are real. We have said that what is real is being considered to be independent of all experience. Yet, in a very obvious sense, thoughts are not independent of us. Neither are chairs and other such artifacts. To some extent the inclination – where it exists – to say of these latter things that they are nevertheless real can be explained by making a distinction between ontological and causal independence/dependence relations.

Talk of something being real turns on *ontological*, not *causal*, independence. The two kinds of relations are similar enough to be easily run together; yet they are different enough for their confusion to be misleading. Without altering the above characterisation of dependence and independence relations in general as holding between objects, we might now add a more specific definition of ontological dependence and independence: *x* is ontologically independent of *y*, iff *x* could exist even in the absence of *y*; *x* is ontologically dependent upon *y* iff *x* could not exist without *y*. In contrast causal independence/dependence are taken as saying that *x* does not/does come about as a result of *y*. To take a clear example, consider the case, already introduced, of an extended object and the colour of that object. The redness of a letter-box is causally independent of its being extended. However, the redness of that object is not ontologically independent of its being extended. It could not in fact have been that, or indeed any other, colour if it were not extended.[10] Thus we see how causal and ontological relations might diverge. Here we have a case of (a) ontological dependence and causal independence. It is equally easy to

---

[9] I would not wish to settle the question concerning the semantics of such sentences in cases of presuppositional failure. Strawson in 'On Referring' argued that in cases of presuppositional failure sentences cannot be used to make assertions which are either true or false, and yet he attempted to avoid the claim that the result is a statement which is neither true nor false (i.e. has some third truth value), or that the sentence is simply rendered meaningless. This raises complex issues, an adequate discussion of which lies beyond the scope of this book (see section 7.1 below).

[10] On this, see Berkeley, *The Principles of Human Knowledge* (London, Fontana, 1962), Introduction, section 7.

see that we could have cases of (b) coinciding ontological and causal dependence, or of (c) coinciding ontological and causal independence. Indeed causal and ontological relations are so easily conflated precisely because causal dependence (or independence) relations often coincide with ontological dependence (or independence) relations in these ways.

To illuminate the present difficulty regarding thoughts or artifacts which are clearly dependent on us in some sense and yet could be said to be real, i.e. independent of all experience, it might be helpful to consider the fourth possibility, of (d) ontological independence in conjunction with causal dependence. That is, it might be that even though as a matter of contingent fact x comes about as a result of y, and so is causally dependent upon it, some z would have caused x in the absence of y, so that x would exist even without y, which renders x ontologically independent of y, even though being causally dependent upon it. Thus the crack in my window this morning is causally dependent upon one particular stone from among the many that the builders left loose on the scaffolding before going home for the evening yesterday, but the crack is not ontologically dependent upon that particular stone, to the extent that even in the absence of *that* stone, one of the others that cascaded down in the course of the night would have done the job.

Of course what is doing the work here is the fact that causal dependence is defined as a merely contingent rather than a necessary relation. On a Kripkean account, based on the necessity of origins, it could be said that if the crack in my window had come about as a result of some other stone, it would not be the *same* crack, even if it was in exactly the same place, of the exact same length, shape and disposition to worsen under pressure, weather conditions etc., and had come into existence at precisely the same time as this one did. It would not be the same crack simply because it would then have resulted from stone B rather than stone A. But it does not seem right to insist that, if this crack in the window is causally dependent on the falling of stone A, it is necessarily dependent on the falling of stone A. Insisting that if it had been caused by stone B it would be a different crack, even if in all other respects it was identical with the present crack, would seem to result in what Salmon calls trivial essentialism.[11] It is not even clear, in the face of forseeable developments in genetic engineering, that Kripke is right in seeing the causal dependence of a person on his or her parents as a necessary causal dependence,[12] unless again this amounts to a trivial form of essentialism. However, this is not to deny that in some

---

[11] Nathan Salmon, *Reference and Essence*, Oxford, Blackwell, 1982. Salmon argues, most convincingly, that nontrivial essentialist theses regarding origins and substance cannot in fact be derived from the direct theory of reference.

[12] Kripke, *Naming and Necessity*, Oxford, Blackwell, 1980, pp. 110ff.

1. Locating a Philosophical Issue 9

cases a causal dependence relation might be necessary rather than contingent.

Now the suggested compatibility of causal dependence and ontological independence between two objects turns on the presumed contingency of the causal dependence involved. Cases of *necessary* causal dependence between C and A preclude ontological independence between those objects, since in these cases it is true not only that C comes about as a result of A, but also that C could not come about in any other way; so that C could not exist in the absence of A, which amounts to ontological dependence.

We should pause here to consider that what follows from this is only that the absence of necessary causal dependence between objects is a necessary condition of their ontological independence. It does not follow from this that only two objects linked by contingent causal dependence can be candidates for ontological independence. Ontological independence can obviously hold between causally independent objects. Nor does it follow that ontological dependence just is necessary causal dependence. Necessary causal dependence is only one particular form of ontological dependence. Ontological dependence can hold equally well between objects which are causally independent of one another (as in the case of an extended object and its colour). It would thus be wrong to slip into thinking, on the basis of the immediately preceding discussion, that ontological dependence and independence were themselves merely particular forms of causal dependence relations, to be adequately unpacked in terms of those relations. We have merely seen what happens in the case of overlap between these two different relations. One of these cases of overlap is particularly relevant when we now turn back to the main thread of the discussion.

Consider the causal dependence upon us of thoughts, or of artifacts. In contrast perhaps to the two examples considered above, here we do seem to have a clear case of necessary causal dependence. And to the extent that this is so, without qualification, thoughts will indeed be ontologically dependent on us. It is possible of course to consider thoughts as objective Platonic objects occupying some third realm; such that we latch onto them but do not cause them, bring them about, at all. Such thoughts will not stand in any (either necessary or contingent) causal dependence to us, and this perhaps provides a sense in which thoughts could be said to be ontologically independent of all experience. But on the usual view of thoughts – or at least of thought tokens – they do appear to stand in necessary causal dependence to us. This is quite clearly so if 'us' is taken broadly, to mean all conceivable experiencing beings. If 'us' is taken more narrowly, however, to mean us-humans, then in the case of these thoughts a Berkeleyan God could perhaps be said to entertain them even in our absence, in which case their causal dependence upon us might not be necessary. And such thoughts – whose *causal* dependence on human experience was merely contingent – could then be thought to be *ontologically* independent of all human experience. (Of course whether this kind of ontological independence of all human experience is enough on its own to merit considering thoughts to be *real* remains to be seen. This will require examining the notion of 'experience', to establish *exactly* what it is that real things are said to be ontologically independent of.)[13]

But even on the narrow reading of 'us' it would still remain clear at least in the case of artifacts that their causal dependence upon us is necessary. That is just what it is to be an *artifact* – artifacts would not exist if we humans did not bring them about. (Moreover, there does not seem to be room to say that artifacts might be dependent on us, but independent of our being the sort of things that have experience. The things that are dependent upon us but not in virtue of our having experience, such as the skin-dust we produce, or the footprints unwittingly left behind in the sand, are hardly to be considered *artifacts*. Artifacts, it seems, have a necessary causal dependence not just on the biological systems that we are, but in particular on the *experience* through which we produce them.) In view of the necessity of this causal dependence, we will not be able simply to appeal to the distinction between causal and ontological relations, claiming that certain things – artifacts – which are dependent on our experience for their existence are only *causally* dependent, and so can nevertheless be said to be *ontologically* independent of all experience, i.e. to be real. The necessity of the former dependence entails the contradictory of the latter.

However, the fact that their ontological dependence derives specifically from their necessary causal dependence, and that this is only one particular route to ontological dependence, might finally suggest an explanation of why it is that we so readily tend to regard certain artifacts as real, despite the fact that they are ontologically dependent upon us in the way we have just seen. Their necessary causal dependence on us means that they could not be brought into existence without us; where this is so only to the extent of entailing that they are ontologically dependent on our *creative* experience. Now some artifacts approximate to what we might call maximal artifacts, which permit only of such creative experience of them. And in such cases there will accordingly be little inclination to regard those artifacts as real. Their ontological dependence on our experience will be straightforward and evident. But the matter is more complicated in

---

[13] See section 1.2.3 below.

the case of material artifacts such as the Eiffel Tower, or the more mundane artifacts such as tables and chairs. Once they have been brought into existence, these artifacts permit of a cognitive experience of them, with respect to which they are like any other ontologically independent object. This is not to deny that any adequate hermeneutic understanding of these artifactual objects might require taking into account their necessary origins in human creative experience and their consequent ontological dependence upon that experience. But insofar as we concentrate solely on the simple cognitive experience we have of, say, the Eiffel Tower, we will find reason to regard it as being ontologically independent of all *such* experience, just as any other physical object is, and on these grounds might think of it, once it has been created, as being among the independent furniture of the world.

Whether this is in fact the kind of ontological independence that is required to show of anything, either artifactual or natural, that it is real in the sense with which this book is concerned is however a separate question. Here we confront again the need to proceed to the second task mentioned at the end of the previous section (1.2.1). So far we have attempted only to unpack the kind of relations relevant to ontological talk. It remains to be more specific about what we are to understand by the term 'experience', and in particular by the qualification intended in talking of '*all* experience' when it comes to talk of something being or not being real.

1.2.3 The terms 'experience' and 'all experience'

Throughout the following, even where I omit the cumbersome qualifying phrase, I will use the term 'experience' to mean experience which is characterised, at least in part, by intentionality: *object-directed* experience. And here, again, I use the term 'object' in the broadest possible sense, to range over any item to which we can refer, from a twinge to a tree.

By stating that I am using 'experience' to mean object-directed experience I intend merely to unpack the term, without suggesting that the intention is to set it apart from experience which is not object-directed. It seems, on the contrary, that intentionality is a feature of any conceivable form of experience; that ultimately we can make sense only of object-directed experience, however rudimentary the object domain. Even the kind of self-reflexion described by mystics is comprehensible only insofar as it is thought to involve intentionality, object-directedness (perhaps of the form aRa).[14]

---

[14] This will be seen more clearly in section 4.3 below.

Accordingly, in talking of x being real if it is independent of all experience I mean independent of all object-directed experience. It remains to clarify the force of the qualifying phrase 'all'. In using this qualifying phrase so far I have merely tried to indicate in loose terms that being real involves independence of experience only in a certain limiting sense. It is now time to take a step towards developing a more technical but precise statement of that limiting sense. It will emerge more fully in later chapters.

The phrase 'all experience' will not be taken to mean all bearers of experience, or the totality of their experiences (be they of one kind or another). 'All experience' is intended rather as a colloquial shorthand for 'the *form* of all experience'. Thus embedded, the force of the qualifying term 'all' is to explain that I do not mean the form of conscious life which is unique to members of the human species as opposed to the form of experience had by members of some other groups. The idea is not to contrast one local 'we' with another, to talk of one cultural form of life, human, as opposed to some or indeed all other conceivable forms of life. Rather than this, in talking of the form of all experience I mean to talk generally about that which all these different empirical forms of life share in common; i.e. the logical form of experience which applies to *us* in the very widest Wittgensteinian reading of 'us',[15] i.e. as including any conceivable experiencer, however different his experience might be from our-human form of experience (including, for example, Wittgenstein's talking lion whom we could not understand at all).[16]

This clarifies the wide range indicated by the phrase 'all experience'. The idea is to pick out the logical framework or structure of experience which is common to all conceivable groups of experiencers, however different they may be; to isolate the minimum, the lowest common denominator, in terms of the structure of experience that we – in that broad sense – all share between us. This might be clearer if, instead of talking of the form of all experience, I were to talk of all experience being of a certain form. I have avoided this formulation because it is suggestive of an objectual reading, as if all experience is *of*, i.e. directed towards, that form. Since this would seem to be false, I have preferred to talk of the form of all experience. In view of what was said above about the sense in which I understand the term experience, it will be evident that I take one central feature of the form of all experience to be its object-directedness.[17]

---

[15] See Bernard Williams, 'The Truth in Relativism', and 'Wittgenstein and Idealism', both in *Moral Luck*, CUP, 1981.

[16] Wittgenstein, *Philosophical Investigations*, Oxford, Blackwell, 1953; third edition, 1967, p. 223.

[17] See section 4.3 below for discussion.

1. Locating a Philosophical Issue

This clarification should suffice for now to explain what was meant by the term 'experience', and by the qualification introduced in 'all experience'. I will continue in places to use the phrase 'all experience' as a colloquialism for the lengthier but more accurate 'the form of all experience', in order to avoid cumbersome repetition. Further discussion of the *reasons* for appealing to this form of all experience must await the fourth chapter.

1.3 The terms 'real' and 'not real' again

The above clarifications, both of the nature of ontological relations of independence and dependence, and of the phrase 'all experience', suffice to enable us finally to be more precise in stating what is meant by the notions of 'real' and 'not real'. We can now say that x is real iff x is ontologically independent of the form of all experience. Conversely, x is not real iff x is ontologically dependent upon the form of all experience. It is then a merely intentional object, i.e. only a feature of the object-directedness involved in the form of all experience.[18] Thus trees, for example, are real if they are not merely presented as objects in virtue of the form of all experience, but are ontologically independent of that form. As I have just indicated, the primary motivation for employing this limiting sense of experience in explicating ontological talk of something's being real or not real will emerge only in the course of later discussions.

This completes the more precise, even if still introductory, analysis of the intended content of the terms 'real' and 'not real'. We have moved gradually from dependence and independence relations in general to ontological dependence and independence relations in particular, and from that on to the specific nature of those relations in talk of being or not being real. In doing so we have become clearer about the content of such talk, but have left aside the formal characteristics of the relations involved.

We said of dependence and independence relations in general that they were n-place relations (where n is greater than 1) which hold between objects, so that a presupposition of statements purporting to express such relations being either true or false is that the two (or more) referring terms involved do in fact refer successfully. Nothing was said further as to whether the referring terms must refer to

[18] Note that an advantage of the present analysis is that it makes clear that there is no reason to think of merely intentional objects as essentially private. If physical objects are said not to be real, i.e. to be ideal, as they were by Berkeley, they are being said to exist only as dependent on the form of experience structured on object-directedness – they will then be merely intentional public objects.

different objects, or might refer to one and the same object. This was left open because dependence and independence relations differ on this score. Some but not all such relations admit of a dependence relation between an object and itself (aRa).

Ontological dependence and independence relations might well be defined as reflexive relations, since it does seem arbitrary to rule out the trivial ontological dependence relation which holds between any object and itself; i.e. to say that it could not exist in its own absence.[19] Thus we might say that it is true of every object that it is ontologically dependent upon itself, and false that it is ontologically independent of itself. Consequently the application of such relations presupposes only that the terms involved refer, whether or not they refer to different objects.

However, this is altered when we narrow our interest specifically to the ontological talk involved in asserting that something is or is not real. Regardless of the precise identification of what it is that something must be independent of if it is to be considered real in the relevant sense, it is quite clear that it must be something other than itself. Conversely, something could not possibly be said to be not real simply because it is dependent upon itself, and could not exist in its own absence. If that were allowed, we would have a ready proof that nothing is, or indeed could be, real.

Thus when it comes to the application of ontological relations involved in talk of what is or is not real, we need to specify that those particular relations presuppose, not merely that the terms involved are successfully referring terms, but that they do not refer to one and the same object. That is, in these cases we must confine ontological relations to relations between objects x and y where x is not the same as y.[20] In these special applications ontological independence and dependence still continue to function as contradictories on a presuppositional view; it is merely that there is an added presupposition that must be met.

Where both these presuppositions are met, 'real' and 'not real' will be coherent contradictories. Where only the first presupposition is met, ontological relations can still function coherently as contradictories, but they will not be sufficient to allow the ontologial talk involved in something's being or not being real to get underway. And of course where neither presupposition is met, ontological dependence and

---

[19] It seems much less obvious to allow reflexivity in the case of general causal dependence, since it is only in most unusual cases that it is right to say that an object comes about as a result of itself. For the most part the dependence that an object has on itself will be an example of ontological dependence that cannot be unpacked in terms of causal dependence relations.

[20] There is of course an important issue, as to how we tell that two objects are different or the same. I will return to this in section 7.1.

1. Locating a Philosophical Issue 15

independence relations will not apply at all.

Having now clarified both the formal constraints and the precise content of the ontological relations involved in talk of what is or is not real, the course of the present enquiry can be made clearer.

1.4 Realism, idealism and the present enquiry

Corresponding to these two terms, 'real' and 'not real', we can formulate two opposing philosophical positions, realism and idealism. Even more than the term 'real', these two labels have enjoyed (or suffered) a wide and diverse range of application and interpretation. It is therefore desirable at this stage to appeal to the foregoing as the basis for my intended use of these labels. This intended use does not aim to coincide with any of the accepted uses of these terms. Rather, the aim is to define some fundamental tenets in terms of which the various positions which pass under these labels can be analysed.

For any domain, any position which accepts that that domain is real, i.e. ontologically independent of the form of all experience, will be in this respect a position of ontological realism. Any position which denies this and asserts that that domain is ontologically dependent upon the form of all experience will be in this respect a position of ontological idealism.

I have added the adjective 'ontological' to distinguish these basic kinds of realism and idealism from epistemological realism and epistemological idealism. These positions are not usually distinguished, a fact which contributes to the general confusion in the discussion of these matters. The distinction between the two might be understood in the following way. Epistemological realism claims that the real world is accessible, that we can have knowledge which presents it as it is. Epistemological idealism denies this, claiming that what we know is not the real world as it is in itself. However, both these positions share in common the assumption that there is some real world, some world which is independent of all experience. In this way epistemological realism and idealism are both positions identified *within* the range of positions which are to be called ontological realist positions.[21]

This explains one sense in which Kant could well deny that he was an idealist. He is not a thoroughgoing ontological idealist. He accepts that there is an ontologically independent world, the thing in itself, and in virtue of this is an ontological realist. However, he says that

[21] It is in fact possible to see someone like Berkeley as an ontological idealist who is nevertheless an epistemological realist. The philosophical sense of this marriage will emerge in the discussion of Kant in section 2.1 below.

that real world, independent of the form of all experience, is not the world as we know it, and this is the epistemological idealism which runs alongside his ontological realism. (This distinction is related to, but is of course not identical with, Kant's own distinction between empirical realism and transcendental idealism. It could, indeed, help to explain that Kantian distinction.)[22]

It should be noted that, insofar as epistemological realism and idealism are positions which both involve ontological realism rather than ontological idealism, this latter distinction is the more fundamental of the two. It is only once the commitment to ontological realism over idealism has been made that the other commitment to either epistemological realism or idealism will be able to get underway.[23] The latter depend upon the acceptability of the former. This provides good reason for holding the two apart, and concentrating on ontological realism and idealism.

It is however important to point out that, as defined, ontological realism and idealism differ from many positions that are traditionally called realist or idealist, and that this is not merely the effect of introducing the separation between ontological and epistemological readings of realism and idealism. The intention has not in fact been to construct a description which coincides with any of those traditional positions, but rather has been to provide a precise and simple basic definition of such ontological talk, in terms of which those traditional positions can be further analysed. The fact that ontological realism and idealism have been defined here in terms of independence and dependence of experience merely in the limiting sense, of the form of all experience, assists in this analysis.

Most obviously, ontological idealism on the above definition is different from empirical idealism. This difference is important, and is effected precisely by the fact that ontological realism and idealism have been defined here in terms of independence and dependence of experience merely in the limiting sense. Empirical idealism would claim that the world is ontologically dependent upon, and perhaps is in some sense constructed by, us, experiencing beings, taken more or less narrowly – most narrowly as first person singular empirical solipsism. Ontological idealism as defined here need not endorse any such extreme and highly untenable views. Ontological idealism, unlike empirical idealism, leaves room for saying that the world (however identified) is indeed independent of us and of other experiencing beings. It asserts only that the world (however identified) is dependent on the form of all experience. Similarly, and for the same reason,

---

[22] See below, section 2.1.
[23] Generally speaking, this is so. We will see the Kantian exception in 2.1 below.

ontological realism as defined here is different from empirical realism, insofar as it asserts not that the real world (however identified) is independent of us (a claim which is allowed to the ontological idealist as well) but that it is independent of the form of all experience. The fact that the former claim is allowed to the ontological idealist as well is intended to ensure that we do not make matters easy for ourselves by taking on a form of idealism which is untenable to begin with. We will return to this in later chapters.

But even allowing for this difference regarding empirical readings of realism and idealism, the suggested definition of ontological realism and idealism still cuts across the various traditional formulations of realist and idealist positions. This results primarily from the fact that ontological realism and idealism as defined above are indifferent to the specific identification of that which is said to be or not be independent of all experience. Consequently the traditional idealist view that the material world is a construct of mind will be a form of ontological realism on the present view, to the extent that mind is itself said to be real. To put it differently, mentalism and materialism are sometimes called idealism and realism, but for the present purposes both would be forms of ontological realism insofar as they identify either the mental or the material as being independent of all experience.

Thus ontological idealism would differ both from Berkeleyan idealism and from Descartes' essentially similar problematic idealism held after the *cogito* in the Second Meditation and before the proof of God's existence in the Third.[24] Both those forms of idealism seem to be committed to the view that only minds are real.[25] In view of the limiting sense of experience involved in ontological talk of what is real it is possible to explicate the sense in which the traditional idealist might hold that the self, minds, souls or egos are real. Clearly they are not mind-independent, or indeed independent of thought, since they are for the most part defined as thinking substances. The point of saying that such thinking substances are real would, presumably, be to say that they are more than emergent roles sustained by, and dependent upon, the object-directedness of experience. Even in the total absence of the form of all experience, of which object-directedness is one feature, they would still exist as pure thinking substances; not independent of their own thought, but independent of that thought's being object-directed. If talk of something's being real is coherent at all, this would seem to be an acceptable way of accommodating a somewhat tenuous view concerning the reality of minds or souls (or, indeed, of thoughts).

[24] R. Descartes, *Meditations of First Philosophy*, (trans.) Haldane and Ross, CUP, 1931.
[25] Some qualifications regarding Berkeley will be introduced towards the end of this section.

Minds could thus be said to be independent of (a) being taken as intentional objects, or (b) taking themselves as intentional objects (i.e. self-reflexion), or (c) their being related intentionally to any other object, or indeed (d) there being an object-directed form of experience at all. The self-reflexion of Descartes' *cogito*, incidentally, does not show the self to be dependent on taking itself as an object. Even if such self-reflexion does involve taking oneself as an object, and it is not at all clear that it does or indeed could,[26] it does not follow that the existence of the self is thereby shown to be dependent upon such self-reflexion. All that follows is that such self-reflexion provides proof of the existence of the self, which is not to say that it could not exist in the absence of such proof. (Even if the *cogito* is seen as a performance rather than as an inference,[27] it still follows only that proof of the self's existence is dependent on an intentional relation to its activity, not that its existence is. (But in any event, there is little reason to attribute this particular view of the *cogito* to Descartes.))

The relevant point here is that, on the present account, the specific claim of traditional idealists that minds are real would place them among the ontological realists, rather than the ontological idealists. The other claim of such traditional idealists, however, that the material world is not real, would constitute an ontological idealist claim. The same would apply to traditional realists: in virtue of their claim that the material world is real, they are ontological realists; in virtue of their claim that the mental is not real, they are ontological idealists. Or, again, sense-data idealists would emerge as ontological realists if they were to contend (tenuously) that sensa are real, and as ontological idealists only to the extent that they claim that everything else is not real but is rather constructed in experience from those sensa. We thus see how the present employment of ontological realism and idealism cuts across, but at the same time helps to provide an analysis of, the traditional formulations of realist and idealist positions.

Most ontological realist positions with regard to some domain of objects are, as we have just seen, ontological idealist positions regarding some other domain, and vice versa – most positions of ontological idealism regarding some domain accept an ontological realist claim with regard to some other domain. However, this is not necessarily so. Following a Meinongian path to the limit, in total abandonment of Ockham's razor, we would arrive at a realist position which regarded everything as real and left no room for claims of ontological idealism. At the other extreme, in contrast to all ontological

---

[26] See n. 23 in Chapter 2 below.
[27] See Hintikka, '*Cogito, ergo sum*: Inference or Performance', in *Philosophical Review*, vol. 71 (1962), pp. 3-32.

realist positions which accept that there is something – mind or matter or something neutral – which exists quite independently of all experience, there is a possible position of radical ontological idealism. Such ontological idealism would deny that there is anything real. It would identify everything as being dependent on the form of all experience.

It is possible to provide a reading of Berkeley's idealism whereby he emerges as a proponent of just such extreme idealism. Berkeley, notoriously, held that to be is to be perceived, if not by humans then by God. The fact that God perceives them explains why trees and the like can be said to exist even when they are not or never have been perceived by any living creature.[28] Now in the foregoing discussion it was assumed that Berkeley accepts that minds (souls) and God do exist independently of the form of experience, and so with regard to this domain Berkeley was seen to be an ontological realist. But Berkeley's full view was that, to exist, something must either be perceived or be the active being that does the perceiving. And it is not entirely clear if those perceiving beings are supposed to exist independently of their perceiving or, rather, of the form of their perceiving. To the extent that those active perceiving beings do not exist independently of their capacity as perceivers, Berkeley might in fact seem to provide an example of extreme ontological idealism. He would then be asserting that what exists is, without exception, whether qua perceiver or perceived object, ontologically dependent upon the form of object-directed experience.

1.4.1 The present enquiry

We have so far seen how the distinction between ontological realism and idealism cuts across some of the traditional formulations of realist and idealist positions. Rather than converging on any one of the traditional formulations, we seem to have identified two fundamental kinds of ontological claims, different applications and combinations of which constitute those various traditional formulations of realist and idealist positions. Given that ontological idealism and realism as defined here are the fundamental constitutive elements of the traditional realist and idealist positions, it is not surprising that they

---

[28] This might seem to suggest that anything which exists totally unperceived would therefore be independent of all experience. Any such suggestion would be unnecessarily crude. There can in fact be objects which are unperceived or even unperceivable without thereby being rendered independent of all experience. For further clarification see section 5.2 below. Berkeley did in fact concede the need to allow unperceivable objects, although he did so rather unwillingly, and inconsistently with his idea that to be is to be (merely) perceived.

can be used later to analyse those positions.

Now from what we have seen here it would seem that, with regard to any given domain, ontological realism and idealism function as contradictories. They would appear to be exhaustive; that it is possible only to reject the one by embracing the other. Indeed this seems to have been the prevalent attitude in philosophy. It has seemed impossible to transcend the realist/idealist claims. For to assert that ontological realism is false – say, in the extreme case, that there is nothing which is ontologically independent of all experience – is then just to accept that everything is ontologically dependent upon the form of all experience, which amounts to extreme ontological idealism. The falsehood of the independence claim made in the former would establish the truth of the dependence claim made in the latter. It thus seems difficult to reject both realism and idealism.

It would, however, be rewarding to be able to do just this, to reject both ontological realism and ontological idealism; some further explanation must therefore be provided of an over-all strategy which might at least make this possible.

Ontological realist and idealist claims are based upon the terms 'real' and 'not real', which have in turn been unpacked in terms of ontological dependence and independence relations. Now the terms 'real' and 'not real' emerged as presuppositional (or relative) contradictories; that is, there are certain presuppositions which must be met for them to be employed at all, but where those presuppositions are met they function as contradictories. Since ontological realism and idealism are based on those notions, they must take on those same presuppositions; consequently they too are only presuppositional contradictories.

We have seen that the presuppositions of the truth or falsity of any statement purporting to assert that a given object is or is not real, i.e. is or is not ontologically independent of the form of all experience, are that (a) the referring terms of that statement do indeed refer, and that (b) in doing so they pick out different referents rather than a single common referent. Regardless of what we should say concerning the exact semantics of statements purporting to express the relevant ontological relations in cases of presuppositional failure, the point here is that in the absence of either of these presuppositions there will be no room for asserting the claims of either ontological realism or ontological idealism.

This leaves scope for a project which attempts to get us off the realist/idealist see-saw of contradictories. The strategy would be to show that the presuppositions which are necessary for the coherent formulation of such positions cannot in fact be met. Further investigation into the realist and idealist talk of what is or is not real might reveal that such talk in fact necessarily stands in contradiction to one of the formal preconditions of its coherence. To the extent that ontological realism and idealism both turned out to rest on the introduction of ontological independence and dependence into statements which necessarily fail to meet the required conditions of reference, both would have to be rejected. This rejection of realism would then not commit us to idealism, or vice versa, because these would no longer function as coherent contradictories of the required sort.

It should be clear that this line of investigation, even if successful, would not provide reason to reject the very notions of ontological independence and dependence. Ontological independence and dependence relations might be quite properly used to identify the relations between one object and some other, of whatever sort (including human beings, their mental acts, the objects thereof) within the experienced object-world. But a legitimate tool can be illigitimately applied. When it comes to the terms 'real' and 'not real', the relation of ontological independence or dependence is assumed to hold between an object-domain and the form of all experience. It is only this application of ontological talk that I wish to investigate here. The difference between these two applications of ontological talk will be further clarified in Chapter 4, where I introduce the distinction between local and global ontological talk.

I have attempted to describe some of the features of ontological relations, the formal constraints on their application in general, and in particular on their application in talk of something being or not being real, upon which ontological realism and idealism turn. It is only this particular application of ontological talk, as ontological dependence or independence of all experience, that is relevant to the present concern. The consequences of successfully undermining this particular use of ontological talk would be of some significance. In order to appreciate this, however, it is necessary to establish the need for, and the relevance of an argument against this form of ontological talk. In advance of later more detailed attention, it is only possible to present a very rough introduction to the kind of problem which results when the distinction between 'real' and 'not real' is assumed to be coherent.

1.5 A problem resulting from ontological talk

I believe that the above definitions of 'real' and 'not-real' capture a central meaning of those terms as they have been used by philosophers; although – as we will see – they have rarely been used quite so univocally. Various philosophers have, in using these terms, run together this central meaning with certain others — thereby inducing an unnoticed philosophical constraint on their conclusions. Some such constraints will be identified in what follows; but the main concern throughout this book is with the central meaning of these terms as identified above. In the absence of any specific arguments to the contrary, we may well assume that these terms, as defined, are coherent.

However, the possible practical value of this distinction between real objects and those which are not real would seem to be sharply dissipated once we realise that there are no satisfactory guidelines for its application.

How can we tell which objects are real, i.e. would be present independently of all experience, and which are not? Assuming that we can draw a coherent distinction between objects which are real and those which are not, it does not seem possible to bring it to bear on any concrete case. The main reason for this difficulty is simply that it is empirically impossible for us to transcend the form of object-directed experience so as to establish what exists independently of it.

Even in cases which on the face of it would appear clear cut, further reflection can reveal that we do not in fact have any way of establishing a fact of the case. It would, perhaps, most naturally be said that the apples projected into the space of my fruit bowl by means of holography are not real entities in the sense described above, whereas the ordinary apples in it might be. A little reflection, however, might undermine our confidence that this belief results from anything more than force of habit. The projected fruit is indeed not real fruit insofar as, say, it offers no tactile resistance or source of nourishment; i.e. it is not 'real' in the sense of 'genuine'. It is like the decoy duck not being a real duck. But nevertheless, just as the decoy duck as such might be real (in the ontological sense), so the holographic-apples, qua holographic-apples, might be real. In other words, when someone is perceiving them, should we say that the perceived items are real entities in the world, or that they are not real? Does the projected apple, while the projection lasts, exist independently of all experience; or is it a non-real entity (a merely intentional object) that exists only as ontologically dependent upon the object-directedness pertaining to the form of all experience?

Now Carnap, notoriously, argued that because empirical verification is not possible, the two relevant theses for any object-domain — realist and idealist — are meaningless. Today it is generally acknowledged that this verificationist criterion of meaning is too stringent. It might seem, instead, that we have two meaningful descriptions, between which the choice is underdetermined in principle, due to the nature of our access to the facts.

The terms real/not-real are then like the predicates green/grue, coherent but underdetermined by our experience. Except that with green-grue in particular – at least on a simplistic temporal interpretation of the problem – the difficulty of knowing which predicate to apply to a given emerald is restricted to our *present* experience – just wait until the year 2000 and then see – whereas in our case the difficulty is in principle unavoidable. We simply cannot conduct an enquiry in the absence of object-directed experience; and yet we want to establish what is the case independent of it. The difficulty seems to be that in order to be in a position to discover *that*, we would have to have given up the possibility of discovering anything.

From the impossibility of discovering by empirical investigation what is real, as opposed to what is not, it emerges that the very juxtaposition of real and non-real is empirically underdetermined. It seems intuitive to think that something, but not everything, is real. And since we cannot, by empirical investigation, *discover* what is real, and what is not, the matter would seem to be left to us to *decide*, according to our more or less systematic persuasions. As long as such talk is assumed to be coherent, it remains for each thinker to make up his mind, given the constraints of his philosophical bent. One possibility, in the face of the impossibility of empirical verification, is to employ transcendental arguments to establish what must be real. But even those who accept the legitimacy of such arguments still put them to work in various ways, resulting in a variety of different conclusions.[29]

To the extent that it is not obvious, it should be pointed out that *any* resulting demarcation of what is real as opposed to what is not will amount to a demarcation of reality as opposed to mere appearance. The distinction between non-real and real, as we have drawn it, just is the distinction between appearance and reality. Mere appearances are those things, or qualities of things, which are present only within experience, and which are nothing independent of that; while reality is the world as it is, independent of all experience. The problem seen so far could therefore be put in these somewhat different terms: There seems to be no way of discovering empirically that something is real rather than mere appearance. The nature of the distinction, in conjunction with the nature of our experience, precludes the possibility of such discovery. Yet there is no other generally accepted method for settling the issue either.

---

[29] In fact transcendental arguments are usually employed, as they were by Kant, to settle the question, not of what is real, but of what has to be taken as real. And of course, as long as the former question itself is coherent, it can still be asked whether what the transcendental argument shows we must take as real *is* indeed real (i.e. does it describe the world as it is, apart from our conceptual framework which requires us to take it as being such-and-so).

We are thus drawn into the sceptic's corner: We cannot avoid the worry that perhaps the real world is not exactly as we experience it to be. This problem is only one of a cluster of related problems which will be further understood in the light of what follows. I have introduced the issue here since it outlines – albeit very crudely – the kind of sceptical predicament which results when ontological talk of something's being or not being real is assumed to be coherent. And yet it invariably is assumed to be coherent, as will emerge from what now follows.

In the next three chapters I will provide a brief survey of some of the relevant philosophical discussions to show that, even where we might least expect it, we still find such talk of something which is real, something which is ontologically independent of all experience. It is to be hoped that the perspective afforded by this survey will vindicate the terminological setting developed in this chapter.

2. Focussing a Philosophical Perspective

The previous chapter mapped the conceptual terrain using an essentially crude grid. Specific philosophers have so far been ignored, or rather the discussion of their views has been held in abeyance. This left room for an uncluttered outline of the central issue. In consequence, however, the account provided has been both historically and philosophically impoverished (the two being intimately connected). The picture of the ontological issue has so far been simply stipulated. It is now necessary to fill in some details.

To achieve this, the above rather stark conceptual clarification will be brought to bear on some of the philosophical discussions which are central to the fabric of our philosophical tradition. This will clarify further both the issues which the present project is addressing, and its relation to the history of those issues, thus adding philosophical and historical focus to the picture.

2.1 Kant

So far, in discussing ontological talk, we have noted the impossibility of discovering in experience what is, as opposed to what is not, real. But this, in itself, although it might put some pressure on the distinction, does not count against there being anything which is real, nor against the coherence of the distinction. On the contrary, both remain highly intuitive. But if there *is* supposed to be something which is real, further problems ensue. In the first place, as has been pointed out, it follows that we can never be certain that we know this something *as it really is*. That is, even given an object which is assumed to be real – say, a chunk of rock – we can never tell of a given description whether it describes that object as that object really is, i.e. describes what that object is like independently of all experience. Without knowing whether stones *as we know them* are real, we cannot tell whether our descriptions of stones accurately depict those presumed real objects, or merely the 'outward' appearance of stones to us, the way they seem in the given context of object-directed experience. Again, the impossibility of transcending the context of experience means that we cannot in principle tell whether our knowledge is of appearances or of reality. The very definition of a real object (as independent of all experience), combined with the fact that we are inextricably bound to experience, means that we could never know that our knowledge was of reality, even if it was. *That* knowledge is forever blocked to us.

This is a tenacious problem which has always been a source of trouble for philosophers in their quest for certainty; it is the axis on which central philosophical discussions have turned.

But there is, or is commonly considered to be, a further problem. The problem seems to be not merely how we could identify a real entity and, furthermore, how having done so we could ever know that we know the real entity as it really is, but worse: how could we establish epistemic contact with it at all? How could we even interact with an entity which by its nature was *independent* of us?

In fact I am not sure that this latter remains a problem once it is pointed out that the independence here is *ontological* – and that there is no reason to suppose that ontological independence involves the absence of causal relations. (The assumption here, which will be taken for granted although it ought to be justified, is that causal connections are indeed a necessary condition of knowledge.) Nevertheless, the problem is one which has troubled some philosophers. (I will return to discuss it in section 6.2.)

Thus, if it is accepted that there is room to consider that there might be something which is ontologically independent of all experience, three distinct problems arise:

(1) How could we tell whether there indeed is a real world at all?
(2) How, even having done so, could we ever establish with any certainty that our knowledge is of that real world as it really is?
(3) How, if x is real, is it possible to be in epistemic contact with it at all?

These three questions together constitute the general question, How is knowledge possible? And with this we reach the Kantian question. Kant's answer amounts to giving up one kind of realist account of knowledge (transcendental realism) while allowing us a weaker but more defensible realist account of knowledge (empirical realism), thereby saving us from having to be idealists with regard to empirical knowledge. In other words, we avoid empirical idealism by not aiming for transcendental realism in the first place. This amounts to saying that, in the sense used above, all knowledge is of appearances. That which is *real* in the sense with which I have been concerned – the thing in itself – is pushed beyond the boundaries of knowledge. All we ever know are objects as they are for us: that is, in the context of experience.[1]

Kant's solution may be broadly described in this way: there are two senses of real, transcendentally real and empirically real. Kant acknowledges the sceptical point with regard to the transcendentally real – but thereby manages to answer the questions posed above with regard to the empirically real. In effect what he does is to protect empirical knowledge by pushing the philosophical problems beyond our philosophical boundaries – confining them to transcendent reality, and our knowledge, on the other hand, to empirical reality. All our knowledge, even that of the empirically real, is then ultimately knowledge of appearances – or, in terms of the notion described above, knowledge of what is, or at least may be, *not real*. That which is real, ontologically independent of all experience, is in principle beyond our knowledge. Thus by distinguishing the transcendent reality (thing in itself) from the empirical reality (things for us) Kant in fact concedes defeat regarding the problems raised in the above points, and yet defends our knowledge against them.

The (more modest) empirical realism is protected from the problems raised by conceding that these problems *do* apply to the transcendent reality. It is the latter which involves the present definition of real – i.e. that which inhabits the world independently of the very form of experience. The former, the empirically real, does in fact inhabit the world independently of any one person's experience, but not independently of all experience – since it is defined as that which is *intersubjectively objective*. Its objectivity arises from its being so within the context of experience, rather than independently of it. It therefore cannot be said to be present independently of *all* experience.

This distinction between empirical realism and transcendental realism has more recently been put forward as the distinction between internal realism and external (or metaphysical) realism. The one realist appeals to the way of an independent reality in accounting for truth or falsity of our beliefs. The standard opposing view avoids this, regarding it as problematic, and chooses internal realism, along with external idealism (i.e. Kant's transcendental idealism). This is to say: what we have knowledge of are inter-subjectively existing objects – objects which exist independently of us within the framework of experience. But as such they might be mere appearances relative to what is real (independent of all experience). No claim is made that the *empirically* real objects in experience are real in the sense of being independent of all experience. By avoiding such external realism (and

---

[1] Even pre-historical empirical reality, such as that which is investigated by geologists, is merely a thing-for-us. This will be explained in section 5.2.7-10 below.

thus accepting transcendental idealism) the internal realist hopes to have avoided the problems raised above which threatened to plunge us into empirical idealism. Empirical (or internal) realism – that knowledge of appearances which Kant allows us – leaves room for a form of knowledge which is immune to the problems we have raised, and so is likely to appeal to anyone who is prepared to pay the idealist price involved.

It was suggested, in the previous chapter, that the identification of what is real would depend on our philosophical bent. Certain further problems which might shape this philosophical bent have now been elucidated and have led us to the minimalist Kantian identification of what is real. That which inhabits the world independently of all experience is now pushed into the status of an unknowable thing in itself, forever excluded from knowledge, and of which no more than this can be said. This leaves us with the mere knowledge of appearances; a somewhat less ambitious, but therefore more defensible, brand of realism. This rather extreme position regarding the identification of what is real is the result not of empirical discovery, which would be impossible, but rather of philosophical problems which seem to force us into this Kantian solution. We are led this far – and stand to be led still further in what follows – by consideration of the nature of this concept of reality, along with the nature of our experience.

But even having been pushed into this position, it is clear that the distinction between real and not-real is still being assumed to be coherent. Although the distinction is under some pressure, the coherence of the notion that there is something which is real in the relevant sense has not been undermined. The fact that we are now left saying that we can never know what is real, and so also that we cannot know that what we know is what there really is, leaves entirely intact – and in fact presupposes – that there is something which is real in this sense. Indeed for Kant, if there was nothing real, it would not be possible for us to have experience of empirical reality, since the former is in some way supposed to be the ground of the latter. Kant's position thus takes the real/not-real distinction to an extreme. Even so he remains an ontological realist. What has been discarded is only the view that we either do or can *know* what is real.

It should thus be clear that Kant's transcendental idealism involves – in terms of the clarification introduced in the previous chapter – a realist *ontological* claim that there is a thing in itself, alongside an idealist *epistemological* claim to the effect that that is not what we have knowledge of. In a parallel way, empirical realism can be seen as Kant's ingenious attempt[2] to combine the converse – to apply an idealist

---

[2] An attempt which might be thought to do justice to Berkeley's central insight as well.

ontological claim regarding the empirical world in conjunction with a realist *epistemological* claim to the effect that we can nevertheless have knowledge of it. In both cases, the resulting positions are named according to the epistemological claims involved in them. Failure to appreciate this can lead to some puzzlement as to why a doctrine which asserts that there *is* some noumenal reality is nevertheless still considered to be a form of transcendental *idealism* rather than of *realism*. Transcendental realism would add to the ontological claim of transcendental idealism an epistemological claim that that was also what we have knowledge of.

It should, incidentally, also be clear that even if Kant were to *deny* that there is anything real, this, just as much as the contrary (positive) assertion to the effect that there is something real, would still presuppose the coherence of such ontological talk.

Having reached the minimalist Kantian identification of what is real with the thing in itself, it is now time to consider the merits of this move.

The main advantage of Kant's transcendental idealism and the commitment to a thing in itself, is that it at least serves to hold the sceptic at bay, if not to silence him. Kant allows for our intuition that there must be something real in a way that does not cause such acute philosophical problems of the kind that have been seen to arise where this intuition is allowed to go unchecked. He simply grants that we do not know what is real, and then confines that reality to a domain so far removed that we can retain the certainty that what we do experience is not that at all, but rather a world which is real in quite another sense (i.e. empirically real). Kant's doctrine of transcendental idealism and the related identification of what is real does not suffice to eradicate the danger of scepticism; indeed it will emerge in what follows that the sceptic cannot be silenced as long as ontological talk of what is real or not real is allowed, as it still is, however minimally, even in Kant's thing in itself. Kant grants the sceptic his claim – that we do not know the world as it is – but he at least removes the sceptic from the scene to a place where he can do no harm, so that his questions no longer threaten us with empirical idealism, with scepticism with regard to our ability to know the truth about the empirical world in which we live. This is part of the philosophical value of Kant's system.

However, quite apart from the fact that he does not finally silence the sceptic, there are problems with Kant's commitment to the thing in itself. For a start, it seems impossible to account for the nature of the connection between it and our knowledge. The reason for this is not that the thing in itself is utterly independent of us and so could not conceivably be causally connected to us – we have already warned against the confusion of causal and ontological relations upon which any such claim rests. Something *x* can be ontologically independent of *y*, and yet be causally related to it, such that *x* causes *y*. The problem is rather that within Kant's specific system it seems impossible to explain the connection between the thing in itself and our experience. It cannot, within his system, be a causal connection because the categories (of which causality is one) are limited in application to experience, and so cannot be applied to the connection between the objects in experience and the noumenal which lies beyond that experience. Kant says more vaguely that the thing in itself is the *ground* rather than the *cause* of our experience; but it seems clear, and has been pointed out by various commentators, that this answer is little more than a paper bridge over a deep crack in Kant's philosophical system. We do not seem to have any way of understanding the metaphor of 'grounding' except in terms of causation, which on Kant's view we have no warrant to do. The thing in itself thus seems to have been set up within the Kantian system as independent of us in such a way that it cannot possibly be of any effect or consequence in our experience. All Kant can do when it then becomes necessary to overcome this impossibility is appeal to metaphor – saying that the thing in itself is the 'ground' of our empirical experience – without unpacking this any further. The thing in itself has therefore come to be seen as an unnecessary metaphysical element which, since it cannot coherently serve a purpose within his system, Kant would have been wiser to eliminate altogether.

Consequently philosophers since Kant, aware of the problems surrounding such 'real' entities and in general suspicious of the metaphysical excess involved in it, have often found sanctuary in some such form of internal realism, *divorced* from the doctrine of transcendental idealism. But of course, stepping inside and shutting the door does not stop the sceptical storm from raging outside. It merely provides some sort of protection from it. This is very much the situation in which the internal realist, who has rejected the doctrine of transcendental idealism, finds himself. In the confinement of empirical realism, the philosopher provides an account of knowledge. But the question 'What actually exists in the world, independently of experience?' has not been answered. We have merely protected ourselves from it within the security of an internal realist account. And as soon as the question *is* asked – and it can only be a question of time before the critical mind turns to ask it – we are forced to step out of the internal realist sanctuary, and to turn our attention to the still raging storm.

Thus, however much progress is made within internal realism (say in the explanation of knowledge and scientific theories) there remains the philosophical issue of what is real; what inhabits the world independently of us and of all experience? Do we know the world as it independently is? The internal realist has in effect only argued the case for holding the question in abeyance, since it does not seem to be answerable. He has not, however, done away with the ontological notion we are discussing; or with the very distinction between what is real (independent furniture of the world) and what is not. Consequently the question is still there to be asked.[3]

Even if Kant's minimalist identification of what is real is not free of philosophical problems, even if transcendental idealism is an unintelligible doctrine,[4] it nevertheless remains the case that Kant's commitment to the thing in itself does at least constitute part of an attempt to allow for our having experience of an object world in the first place and for our intuition that there must be something *real*, while avoiding empirical idealism – i.e. the view that we cannot know the empirical world around us to be as we experience it to be. If Kant's account fails to provide acceptable answers – it at least suggests a strategy for dealing with the issue: at the very least it marks the important questions. By discarding (amputating) transcendental idealism without further ado, we run the risk of falling back into something like the dogmatic slumbers from which Hume is supposed to have awoken us. However much we can provide internal accounts of how empirical knowledge works, our intuitions to the effect that there must be some ontologically independent reality are then left dangling; and all the resulting problems of acute scepticism are once again left unresolved.

For my part, I do not wish to endorse Kant's transcendental idealism. The present aim, after all, is to question the coherence of ontological talk of what is real, even the minimal kind still involved in Kant's commitment to the thing in itself. But the point to bear in mind is that, as long as ontological talk *is* assumed to be coherent, Kant's strategy at least seems to offer a way of containing the sceptic.

If it is suggested that the notion of the thing in itself be dropped from Kant's system, on the grounds that it cannot coherently provide the foundations of our experience, some other account must be provided to explain our intuitive conviction that there must be something real in the world. Similarly, we must then provide some other way of dealing with the sceptic who wonders whether the world is as we experience it to be. Alternatively, we must pay the price of leaving these issues open.

---

[3] The strong connection between ontological talk and the sceptic's question which is implicitly present here will emerge more clearly in later chapters.

[4] One philosopher to have made this claim is Strawson, in *The Bounds of Sense*. I will turn to a discussion of Strawson below. He sees this feature of Kant's system as an extra wheel idly turning (*Bounds*, p. 257). Bennett too attacks this doctrine, in his two books, *Kant's Analytic* and *Kant's Dialectic*.

Evidently, until the ontological and sceptical issues which it served to answer have been either answered or undermined, Kant's transcendental idealism and the commitment to a thing in itself cannot simply be discarded without loss.

This suggests the challenge – I will call it 'Stroud's Challenge' – to undermine that ontological talk upon which the sceptic's question and even Kant's strategy for containing it both rest. The nature of this challenge will emerge more clearly in the following sections.

2.2 Quine

Some contemporary post-Kantian philosophers have, indeed, calmly turned their back on the question of what there is in the world independently of experience. They have not provided any reasons for thinking that the intuitive assumption of there being something real is perhaps *incoherent*. They simply avoid asking questions about it. The ontological notion of reality (and the related philosophical problems) remain significant, but, having rejected Kant's doctrine as incoherent on other grounds, they studiously hold the entire issue in abeyance. This cannot be an adequate answer to a philosophical problem. Rather, it is an attempted escape from one; the question is left open and unattended by these discussions. In some cases post-Kantian discussions, even some which overtly reject the doctrine of transcendental idealism, end up embracing the Kantian doctrine by default. We will see this in the course of briefly surveying some of these post-Kantian manoeuvres.

Quine is perhaps the obvious philosopher to introduce at the outset. This is not because the term 'ontological talk' which is used here is one that he too employs. Quine means something quite different by that phrase, and there are far better reasons for beginning with Quine: reasons which refer to features that are often ignored in discussions of Quine's philosophy.[5]

For Quine, ontology is subservient to epistemology. By 'ontological talk' he means what a theory says there is;[6] what objects a theory requires, quantifies over. Quine's ontological talk involves the identification of 'those objects that have to be values of variables for the theory to be true'.[7] He is interested in what things a theory assumes there to be, and it is in reply to this higher-level question that he

---

[5] A notable exception is Stroud's *The Significance of Philosophical Scepticism*, Oxford, Clarendon Press, 1984.

[6] 'Ontological Relativity' in *Ontological Relativity and Other Essays*, New York, Columbia University Press, 1969, p. 55.

[7] 'Existence and Quantification', ibid., p. 96.

2. Focussing a Philosophical Perspective

suggests we should look to the behaviour of quantified variables. As for the explication of existence itself, the general notion of existence expressed by the existential quantifier – this, Quine says, is a 'forlorn cause'.[8] It is indeed generally evident that he is interested not in establishing the nature of existence, but rather in establishing what exists on a given theory, *whatever* the nature of existence is.

Thus when Quine says that to be is to be the value of a bound variable, he is not providing the means to tell what there is in the world, but rather the means of identifying 'what a given remark or doctrine, ours or someone else's, *says* there is'.[9] This leaves room for competing ontologies; different theories have different ontologies. In each case we identify the ontology of the theory by looking at that theory's bound variables. But talk of bound variables does no more than this – it identifies (relative to a fixed background theory) what a given theory specifies or presupposes there is in the world; it cannot tell us what there *is* in the world. To answer that, Quine would say, we must *choose* a particular theory, must adjudicate among rival ontologies. In choosing which theory (ontology) to adopt – i.e. in providing our answer to what there is in the world – 'we adopt, at least insofar as we are reasonable, the simplest conceptual scheme into which the disordered fragments of raw experience can be fitted and arranged'.[10] Thus for Quine the question regarding what there is in the world is taken as the question of which theory to adopt. It is not even intended as a question of what there is in the world independent of all theories. Quine explicitly says[11] that he is talking epistemology, not metaphysics.

Given this, it is clear why Quine talks of physical objects as being posits, like the gods of Homer. The values of the bound variables which constitute the ontology of a theory are the posits of that theory. And Quine's interest in physical objects is merely in their epistemological status within the theory, as the posited ontology of that theory. The concern is with theories, and with questions of existence internal to those theories. It is in this light that we must understand Quine's saying that 'posited objects can be real ...to call a posit a posit is not to patronize it'.[12] Quine, qua apparently anti-metaphysical epistemologist, is simply not *interested* in the metaphysical aspect of ontological talk – he leaves this kind of question aside. His interest is in how theories work. And, with regard to their status within a theory,

---

[8] ibid., pp. 96-7.
[9] 'On What There Is', in *From a Logical Point of View*, Harvard University Press, 1953, p. 15.
[10] ibid., p. 16.
[11] See e.g. *From a Logical Point of View*, Foreword, p. viii.
[12] ibid.

physical objects and Homer's gods are indeed identical (although not within the *same* theory) – they are alike in being the posits of a theory, the referents of the bound variables that determine the ontology of the theory. It is only in this capacity that Quine relates to them. The further issue, as to which is *real*, in the sense defined above, i.e. which exists independently of all experience, is not one that Quine is, or considers that he should be, interested in at all.

Thus 'ontological talk' for Quine is clearly quite different from what is meant by it in this essay. Quine understands ontological talk as describing the objects into which a given theory slices reality: the concern is the ontological commitment *within* a theory. Ontological talk in the present work refers, primarily, to the use of a notion of there being some reality which is ontologically independent of all experience, and so also of our breakdown of that reality within our theories.

Nevertheless, despite this dissimilarity, there is a related point in Quine's thought which is extremely relevant to the present concern.

Quine talks[13] of raw experience upon which we impose order by means of a conceptual scheme. This conceptual scheme, or theory, is a man-made fabric which impinges upon experience only along the edges. Our conceptual scheme must accommodate this experience, but is under-determined by it. We impose order on raw experience by cutting it up into objects. There are different ways of doing this, different objects which might be posited. In ordinary common sense we posit physical objects – but even here we can conceive of alternative schemes, which cut experience up into different objects – rabbits, rabbit stages, rabbit-bushes... And of course we might choose to posit other objects: atoms, sense-data, numbers etc., in addition, or instead of the ordinary objects of our conceptual scheme. We can indeed discover which objects a given theory is committed to, by identifying the values of the bound variables of that theory – this is the ontology *of the theory*. But which theory (which ontology) we choose depends, for Quine, solely on the explanatory value its objects hold for us. This is what Quine's ontological relativity amounts to.

Yet the fact that Quine is only interested in the explanatory value of objects as *posits* leaves open the possibility that some of these objects are real; or at least that there *is* something real, something which inhabits the world independently of all experience, independently of all theories. To ignore this possibility, as Quine does, is not to defuse the underlying questions, it is at most to leave them open. In fact, however, despite ignoring the issue, Quine's views do commit him to a very

---

[13] In section 6 of 'Two Dogmas of Empiricism', in *From a Logical Point of View*; 'On What There Is', p. 16, in *From a Logical Point of View*; 'Speaking of Objects', in *Ontological Relativity & other Essays; Word and Object*, ch. 2, and numerous other places.

2. Focussing a Philosophical Perspective 35

definite position regarding what is independently real: Quine's epistemology seems to presuppose a Kantian background of transcendental idealism.

Quine talks of raw experience – not as something that is constituted by our conceptual scheme, but rather as something that impinges upon that scheme. He talks of conceptual schemes with their different ontologies as ways of ordering raw experience. Indeed that experience can conflict with our conceptual scheme, forcing us to make changes in it. It thus seems that our raw experience is not itself the result of conceptual schemes with their posited ontologies, but is rather the consequence of something beyond or independent of all those schemes, to which various schemes with their ontologies variously bring some kind of order. In other places (e.g. 'Epistemology Naturalized') Quine talks similarly about 'external stimuli' (p. 81) or of sensory or experimental 'input' (p. 83). Such notions strongly suggest that, beyond the various theories with their different postulated ontologies, Quine presupposes some kind of noumenal reality. Beyond the different ways of cutting the cake, there is the cake itself, or at least the base of it. At the very least, beyond the ontological talk within theories, indeed beyond the theories themselves, there is raw experience, sensory input. But precisely because he has not defused the central notion involved in (what I have called) ontological talk, and has chosen rather to avoid examining what he considers to be a 'forlorn cause', it is difficult to see what option there is (going only by the lights of his own approach) other than to identify that sensory input which is independent of all theories as resulting (presumably in a causal sense) from some kind of Kantian noumena, upon which those theories impose order. Indeed in places Quine talks of imposing order not on raw experience but on *reality*: for example, on p. 1 of 'Speaking of Objects':

> We persist in breaking reality down somehow into a multiplicity of identifiable and discriminable objects...

It thus seems that, although Quine's epistemological interest leads him to focus on ontological talk within a theory, this involves an implicit commitment to the other, metaphysical kind of ontological talk. The idea still seems to be that there is some kind of independent noumenal world which different theories with their different ontologies cut up into objects in different ways. Quine's exclusive concentration on what given theories say there is amounts to a form of empirical realism (plus relativism) which assumes some unknown noumenal world as that which lies beyond all theories. It is in this sense that Quine seems committed to transcendental idealism and, consequently, to the sceptical doubt that the real world is not, or at least may not be, as our theories describe it.[14]

It should, however, be emphasised that Quine's 'raw experience' is obviously not itself that which is real, independent of all experience. 'Raw experience' still refers merely to *experience*, albeit in its most rudimentary, primitive, form. And it might in fact be suggested that Quine's raw experience is not meant to pick out some ground which lies outside all theories, but rather is meant to be regarded as part of the required ontological commitment – a basic posit – of any adequate theory.

This will not do. In the first place, Quine would then even more clearly be leaving entirely unanswered the issue of what there is beyond all empirical theories. Stroud makes a similar point, pointing out that despite Quine's more scientific orientation, he might be in the same boat with G.E. Moore insofar as neither emerges from the confinement of the empirical domain to answer, or even to ask, the philosophical question concerning the world external to it.[15] This confinement would in itself, without further ado, strongly suggest an implicit commitment to transcendental idealism. But in any case it does not seem right to describe raw experience as itself being part of the basic ontology posited by any theory. To make sense of the objects which a theory quantifies over being *posits*, we must be assuming something which is not a posit. Davidson makes essentially the same point in discussing Quine:

> It is reasonable to call something a posit if it can be contrasted with something that is not. Here the something that is not is sensory experience – at least that is the idea. (p. 193)[16]

Although Davidson ultimately rejects the idea, he recognises that Quine's sensory experience is meant to serve as something which awaits organisation by the various theories bent on organising it. It is

---

[14] For a similar reading of Quine see a brief comment in the introduction (p. xiii) to Putnam's third volume of collected papers, *Realism and Reason*, CUP, 1983. For another somewhat similar reading of Quine see pp. 289-90 of Stroud's paper 'The Significance of Scepticism' (cited below). Stroud emphasises the scepticism rather than the transcendental idealism to which Quine is committed. I have chosen to emphasise the transcendental idealism rather than the scepticism, since it seems to be the more basic point. This scepticism is such that it is inherent – albeit tamely – in any view which involves transcendental idealism. The scepticism results, as we shall see, from the implicit acceptance of ontological talk.

[15] Barry Stroud, *The Significance of Philosophical Scepticism*, OUP, 1984, pp. 230; 253-4.

[16] Davidson, 'On the Very Idea of a Conceptual Scheme', in *Proceedings and Addresses of the American Philosophical Association*, 1973-74, vol. XLVII, November 1974, pp. 5-20. Reprinted in *Inquiries into Truth and Understanding*, Oxford, Clarendon Press, 1984. All page references are to this latter publication.

supposed to function as external and neutral ground relative to the various theories.

Given that Quine's acceptance of raw experience thus places it beyond all theories, where does this leave him with regard to reality? When we turn to consider what gives rise to this raw experience in the first place, or how we make sense of the 'sensory bombardments' from which Quine would have theories start, we seem to encounter an implicit acceptance of a reality independent of all experience. Quine's merely epistemological approach does not broach these questions, and would, by default, seem at *this* point to fall back on some ontological notion of a noumenal reality beyond all experience, which itself sustains that raw experience which is the matter from which theory construction begins. The alternative answer would be extreme ontological idealism, which is hardly feasible in view of the fact that in places Quine actually talks of reality rather than of raw experience as that which confronts our theories.

From the discussion so far Quine emerges as accepting, or at least probably having to accept, the existence of something which is independent of all experience, even though he does not confront the issue directly. Other post-Kantian philosophers have been more explicitly concerned with the noumenal; particularly, in the analytic tradition, philosophers have been concerned to discard the commitment to the thing in itself. However, this is usually done without sufficient argument, and in a way that leaves the associated philosophical problems unanswered. It is to some of these discussions that I will now turn.

2.3 Putnam's internalism

One such discussion is provided by Putnam in his more recent works, in which he rejects metaphysical realism and opts for internal realism.[17]

Since I shall be discussing Putnam's *Reason, Truth and History* extensively in the next chapter, I will concentrate discussion here on his 'Realism and Reason'.[18] In this paper Putnam first declares his rejection of his own previous position of metaphysical realism in favour of internal realism. In particular I would like to clarify what Putnam's

---

[17] I refer mainly to: (1) 'Realism and Reason' in *Meaning and the Moral Sciences*, London, Routledge, 1978; (2) *Reason, Truth and History* CUP, 1981; (3) 'Why There Isn't a Ready-Made World' in *Synthese*, May 1982. [Reprinted in Putnam, 'Realism and Reason' *Philosophical Papers*, vol. 3, CUP, 1983.]

[18] All page references in this section will be to this paper, unless stated otherwise.

position is, following this recantation, with regard to the existence of an ontologically independent reality. While Putnam's new position of internal realism is presented as avoiding Kant's transcendental idealism, it is not quite clear that he does not in fact end up with an empirical realist view resting on a background of just such transcendental idealism.

In places, where he is stating his view very generally, Putnam rejects the idea of there being a noumenal world (for example, in the Introductions to both *Meaning and the Moral Sciences* (p. 6) and *'Realism and Reason' – Philosophical Papers*, volume 3). However, as we shall see, in other places his own discussion seems to presuppose a noumenal world, or at least to allow for the presupposition of some such reality. I believe that light might be cast on this unclarity by considering the nature of Putnam's argument against metaphysical realism.

In 'Realism and Reason' Putnam introduces metaphysical realism as that theory or model which purports to be 'a model of the relation of *any* correct theory to all or part of THE WORLD' (p. 123). This world is said 'to be *independent* of any particular representation we have of it' (p. 125). I assume, although Putnam says no more about it, that the independence intended is *ontological*. A consequence of the metaphysical realist view is that even the theory which appears ideal by our lights might fail to describe the independent WORLD as it is. A theory might be complete and consistent, and might correctly predict all observation sentences as far as we can tell, and still be false in the sense that it might not describe THE WORLD as it independently is. It is this feature of the metaphysical realist position that Putnam wishes to show is incoherent.

Putnam offers two kinds of argument in 'Realism and Reason'. The one involves verificationism: given an ideal theory, what constraints could show whether it might be either a false or a true description of (reference to) the way the world *really* is? Since there are no such constraints, Putnam claims that the 'supposition that even an "ideal" theory (from the pragmatic point of view) might *really* be false appears to collapse into *unintelligibility*' (p. 126). However, this conclusion does not follow. All that follows is that we cannot *tell* whether an ideal theory does indeed describe the way the ontologically independent world is. It does not follow that it is *unintelligible* that the ideal theory *might* be false. It might well be that we are simply in the rather uncomfortable predicament of not being able to reveal the fact of the matter. The argument shows why the metaphysical realist is indeed committed to such scepticism, to not knowing whether the world is as the ideal theory describes it – but for all this, it would seem to remain coherent to think that there nevertheless is a truth of the matter. (But see further discussion of Putnam's view in *Reason, Truth and History*; Chapter 3 below.)

Putnam's second argument involves relativism: the real world, i.e. THE WORLD, allows for different yet individually complete descriptions. Various descriptions, each entirely adequate, can be mapped onto the real world. One adequate theory might deliver as true sentences which are false on another equally adequate theory, and yet neither theory need be incompatible with the world. Any such sentences express properties of the world which are merely theory-relative. One description might identify one unique set of things, another might identify another unique set of things – and not only can both equally well be mapped onto the world, but each can be mapped onto the world in different ways. Since the world allows for all these different projections, no one theory can capture the world as it is; or at least, we might say, any theory that does this by accommodating all others within it will be so general as to have nothing to say about the way the independent world is, other than that it allows all these different mappings. In this Putnam is following Quine (ontological relativity) and still more obviously Goodman (see Chapter 4 below). And like Quine and Goodman, Putnam does manage to go some way towards establishing a case against the metaphysical realist, insofar as this realist assumed that we can get a grip on the theory that describes the world as it is. Both the argument from relativism and the argument from verificationism thus promise to show that we cannot identify a theory which, beyond mere adaquacy, is also the one which describes the world as it independently is.[19]

But even if the metaphysical realist cannot claim to know *which* theory describes the world as it is, or even *that* there is such a description, he can still claim that there is a way that the world is. The metaphysical realist then becomes a sceptic with regard to our epistemic access to the way the world is – this is what Putnam achieves – but still holds onto the ontological claim that there is a way of THE WORLD. We are thus faced with the fact that the metaphysical realist's position involves two distinct claims.

The first is an ontological claim to the effect that there is some ontologically independent world. This is what I called ontological realism in the last chapter. The second claim is epistemological. It in turn might involve either a weaker claim, that there might be a true description of that real world; or a stronger claim, that we can identify this true description. This is what I called epistemological realism in the last chapter.

---

[19] There is obviously room for critical discussion of the argument from relativism, but we need not go into this here. In later chapters I will raise some of these further points, pertaining to work on relativism by Williams and Davidson.

Putnam does not distinguish adequately between these different strands in the metaphysical realist position. This can be seen both from the description of the metaphysical realist view in 'Realism and Reason', and also from his definition of it in other places. For example, in *Reason, Truth and History* he introduces metaphysical realism in this way (p. 49):

> One of these perspectives is the perspective of metaphysical realism. On this perspective, the world consists of some fixed totality of mind-independent objects. There is exactly one true and complete description of 'the way the world is'.

The various claims made by the metaphysical realist are similarly run together in his description of this position elsewhere (e.g. in 'Why There isn't a Ready-Made World' – see 3.6 below). Consequently in the course of his discussion Putnam does not identify precisely which of the two claims – ontological or epistemological – his arguments are directed at.

The argument from verification applies to the stronger version of the epistemological claim. It shows why we could not identify which among our empirically adequate theories is also true in the sense of providing an accurate description of THE WORLD. The further constraints that could single out the one true description cannot be provided. This is one point at which metaphysical realism collapses. But Putnam says that there are other points (p. 130). It is here that he introduces the argument from relativism.

This argument is directed at what I have called the metaphysical realist's weaker epistemological claim; the claim that there is a true description of the world (even if we cannot identify it). The fact that so many consistent and adequate theories are incompatible with one another, so the argument runs, and yet can equally well be successfully mapped onto the world, suggests that individually none of them could constitute a full description of the way the world is. The more properties turn out to be theory-relative and mutually exclusive properties, the less it seems that any one theory could *be* a description of THE WORLD, quite apart from the fact that we could not identify it as such even if it were. Every theory still leaves some possible feature of the world undescribed, to await description by another, incompatible theory. Thus the world recedes beyond the grip of our theories, beyond the descriptive capacity of any one of them, to the status of a noumenal world.

This argument in 'Realism and Reason' against there even being a single true description of the world is given more force by way of the argument which turns on reference in chapter 2 of *Reason, Truth and History*. In the absence of a magical theory of reference we cannot make sense of reference to objects independently of their description. We can only refer to objects *internal* to a description, objects into which we have sliced the world within the context of our description. There can be no reference to objects as they are independently of all descriptive contexts. Putnam's argument leads to the conclusion that we have to give up the idea that words stand in some sort of one-one relation to things and sorts of things in the real world. Thus he ends up with his internal realism which is very much like Kant's empirical realism. None of our theories, apart from referring to objects-for-us (i.e. within the theory), can refer to objects as they are in themselves. And insofar as such reference emerges from Putnam's discussion as unattainable, our descriptions can only be of the world for us, not of the world as it independently is.

It should be noted that this argument from reference in *Reason, Truth and History* only reinforces the previous argument from relativism which stood on its own merit. Even if we could posit some 'magical' theory of reference which recognised reference to the world as an ultimate fact, the epistemological problems accompanying such a view would, Putnam reminds us, still be insuperable:

> For assuming a world of mind-independent, discourse-independent [he presumably means *ontologically* independent] entities (this is the presupposition of the view we are discussing), there are, as we have seen, many different 'correspondences' which represent possible or candidate reference relations (infinitely many, in fact, if there are infinitely many things in the universe). (*Reason, Truth and History*, p. 47)

However, the fact that we cannot – as the arguments from reference and from relativism show – have a theory which provides (possibly unknown to us) a description of objects and properties of the real world; and the further fact that we could not in any case identify such a theory even if there was one – as the argument from verification shows – does not in itself give us reason to assume that there is no real world, no way that the world independently is. In other words *all* Putnam's arguments only seem to address the metaphysical realist's weaker and stronger *epistemological* claims. They do not, however, count against the realist's *ontological* thesis which asserts merely that there is an ontologically independent reality, even if none of our descriptions can capture the way that reality is.

Putnam's arguments against the metaphysical realist do suffice to reduce that realist to scepticism – which is what remains once epistemological but not ontological realism is rejected. The realist has to admit that the real world might well not be as his ideal theory describes it. But Putnam is wrong to think that his arguments suffice to reject the very idea that there is a real world. The particular arguments against the epistemological claim do not undermine the ontological claim.

It might be thought that this is not the case: that Putnam's considerations from reference regarding the epistemological claim suffice to undermine the realist's ontological claim as well. The idea would be that the argument against the epistemological claim expands to show that our access to the real world is so impoverished as not to leave any room for the conviction that there is one. In fact this is not so. By extension these epistemological considerations can begin to shake our confidence in, but cannot establish the outright incoherence of, the ontological claim. Strictly speaking, all that follows is that we cannot refer to the real world as it is independent of our descriptions, since it is only by light of our descriptions that we can refer to it at all. But it would nevertheless seem that we can still refer to it from within our descriptive contexts, non-magically, by way of the minimal description present in any descriptive context, as that which is ontologically independent of all descriptive contexts and to which all descriptions ultimately apply. Consequently, despite the *epistemological* problem, viz. that it seems impossible to refer to the real world *as it is* independently of all descriptive theory, there is still room left for the ontological claim that there is a real world, just insofar as within any descriptive theory we can still make minimal reference to that real world. Indeed Putnam seems to admit as much in passages like the following:

> The problem – as Nelson Goodman has been emphasizing for many, many years – is that this story may retain THE WORLD but at the price of giving up any intelligible notion of *how* THE WORLD is. (p. 132)

> The fact is, *so many* properties of THE WORLD...turn out to be 'theory relative' that THE WORLD ends up as a Kantian 'noumenal' world, a mere 'thing in itself'. If one cannot say *how* THE WORLD is theory-independently, then talk of all these theories as descriptions of 'the world' is empty. (p. 133)

Putnam at most has shown that there cannot be a true description of the world, in the sense which the metaphysical realist wished. But the failure of this epistemological quest still leaves room for the assumption that there is an independent reality, indeed that there is a way this independent reality is. The intelligibility of such talk has not yet been impugned. It is merely that since that reality is flexible enough to accomodate all our various theories, we can get no descriptive grip on it within any one theory, and it recedes to the status of a Kantian noumenal world.

Nevertheless, in the introductions already mentioned as well as

2. Focussing a Philosophical Perspective

elsewhere, Putnam expresses hopes to have avoided the commitment to some such noumenal world. He presents his view as 'a demythologized Kantianism', without 'things in themselves'[20] and 'transcendental egos'.[21] We have now seen that, as he himself seems forced to admit in other places, his arguments do not go quite so far. The hope that they will might result from his not distinguishing clearly between the metaphysical realist's epistemological and ontological claims. Had he done so, Putnam would have realised that his arguments against there being a true description of THE WORLD did not undermine the metaphysical realist's other, ontological assertion to the effect that there is some such world. Consequently Putnam, just as much as Quine, is still in a position of leaving room for transcendental idealism. Whether or not Putnam actually accepts that there is some independent reality, the possiblity that there is something real which exists independently of all experience is left open in his account, without any argument having been presented to undermine it, indeed without its having been recognised as a separate strand in the metaphysical realist's position. And it should be noted that as long as the metaphysical realist's epistemological claim is attacked, but not his ontological claim, there is no escape from the lurking sceptical suggestion that the world may not be as we experience it to be. This will emerge quite clearly in the next chapter (3.6 below).

For Putnam, as for Quine, the question 'What does the world consist of?' makes sense only from within a description, a point of view. But in itself that does not show that there is reason to reject the idea of there being something independent of all points of view. Regarding that which inhabits the world independently of all points of view (i.e. that which is real), Putnam would thus indeed seem to fall in with Kant, however unwillingly. And on pp. 61-2 of *Reason, Truth and History* he says:

> Today the notion of a noumenal world is perceived to be an unnecessary metaphysical element in Kant's thought. (But perhaps Kant is right: perhaps we can't help thinking that there is *somehow* a mind independent 'ground' for our experience even if attempts to talk about it lead at once to nonsense.) At the same time, talk of ordinary 'empirical' objects is *not* talk of things in themselves but only talk of things for us.

It is only fitting that Putnam should make such parenthetic concessions. For as we have seen he has not aimed his argument at the

---

[20] The plural form of 'things in themselves' ignores the fact that properly speaking we cannot even apply cardinality to the noumenal world. Putnam raises this issue himself, but does not mention that the matter is a common problem in the interpretation of Kant, insofar as unity and plurality are among the categories, and so to impute them to things in *themselves* is more than we can rightly do. But of course, for the same reason it is misleading to talk about a thing in itself.

[21] *Meaning and the Moral Sciences*, pp. 5-6.

ontological thesis to the effect that there *is* something real – something which inhabits the world independently of all points of view. He has offered arguments only against the assumption that we can have knowledge of *what* is real in this sense.

The epistemology of internal realism still leaves us with the apparently coherent ontological notion of there being something real, something which just *is*, independent of all experience. This notion was not impugned by Kant's relegation of what is real in this sense to a mere thing in itself; and it is not undermined by Putnam's specific arguments from verification, reference and relativism which apply only to the metaphysical realist's epistemological thesis. I will attempt to argue later that there are in fact certain other considerations regarding reference which could be brought to bear directly on the metaphysical realist's ontological thesis. The point for now is to note that Putnam is interested in the epistemological inquiry into what we can know, and he shows that the metaphysical realist cannot claim to know the ontologically independent reality as it is. But the ontological issue of there *being* something real seems to have been side-stepped or fudged, more or less elegantly.

It should be recalled at this point that Kant's introduction of the thing in itself was not merely supposed to play a part within his epistemological account (which it might well fail to do, or which might not be necessary in the first place), but that it also takes care of the basic *ontological* conviction which Quine and Putnam are prepared to ignore. They do not address this ontological conviction.

Equally this ontological conviction is not addressed or challenged within the controversy between traditional realists and idealists. Although that controversy, unlike the one between internal and external realists considered above, is indeed an *ontological* rather than an epistemological debate, it remains a shared premiss of both parties that there *is* something real. Accepting that as common ground, the discussion gets underway when the parties beg to differ with regard to what they deem to be real and what to be mere appearance. There are various positions to be chosen. Traditional idealists say that only souls (or minds) are real. Materialists and physicalists of the realist camp say that only matter is real. Functionalists appear to agree with physicalists as to what is real, and provide an explanation of the emergence of mental states in those terms. The solipsist holds that only he is real. But, despite all these weighty differences in the proposed candidates, all agree that there is something *real*. The distinction between what is real and what is not, is accepted by all of them – they differ only in the way in which they demarcate the two.

Even extreme idealism which denies that there is anything independent of all experience does not challenge, but rather accepts,

2. Focussing a Philosophical Perspective 45

the legitimacy and the meaningfulness of the distinction between what is real and not-real. Such idealists work within this distinction, presenting the limiting case where nothing is real and everything is not-real. But the claim that nothing is real, without further argument and elucidation, must be taken as still accepting the real/not-real distinction as fundamental – merely failing to find anything to file in the rubric designated for real things. The assertion that nothing is real is itself parasitic on the notion of something being real. The nihilist simply answers 'nothing' where the others answer 'something' to the question which both regard as central: 'What is independent of all experience?' To use a notion negatively is still to use it.

As opposed to the epistemological issue of what we can know, there is this ontological issue regarding an independent reality. This issue pertains to the basic conviction, unscathed by Kantian relegation to a mere unknowable thing in itself, and untouched by epistemologically oriented internal realists, that there *is* something real; something, that is, which exists in the world independently of all (object-directed) experience. The concern here is not that of the internal realist. The internal realist is merely, albeit importantly, concerned to show that we cannot provide an account of knowledge which assumes truth to involve correspondence to a reality independent of experience; and that there is no need for this in any case. But he does not show what reason he has for challenging the very notion of there being something real. Our epistemic access to the real world might be shown to be impoverished, but it is not shown to be impoverished in a way that renders unintelligible the very notion we have of a real world.

To review our story so far: We have seen with regard to Quine that the emphasis is such that his epistemological arguments do not question, head on, but rather presuppose, or can at least most readily be interpreted on the backdrop of ontological talk. Lurking in the background there remains some kind of noumenal world which sustains the raw experience, which is then cut up into objects in different ways by different theories, with their different ontologies. And we have now seen that Putnam's discussion of internal realism turns on whether or not we can refer to, and have knowledge that is true of, external as opposed to merely internally individuated objects. But this still does not clearly attack the notion of there *being* something real. It only attacks the notion that *that* is what our knowledge is of, that *that* is what we refer to when we refer to cats and cars.

I conclude this section with a further note on Quine. Quine asks what objects are posited by a given theory. Perhaps, however, the more revealing question would relate not to the differences between different theories, but rather to a simple point of similarity between them all. Which objects a theory posits is a matter to be decided by considerations of explanatory force, simplicity, etc. A theory need not posit those objects which common sense recognises. But apart from the dissimilarities between theories with regard to the question which objects are posited, there is the underlying similarity that all theories do posit *some* object(s), *however* vague and rudimentary these may be, *however* much these may differ from one theory to the next. Quine notes, but is insufficiently attentive to, this underlying similarity between theories. He concentrates on the way in which we posit objects, on translation, inscrutability of reference and ontological relativity. That all theories posit *some* objects is an obvious and seemingly trivial fact.

But by focussing on this fact, it is possible to appreciate my reasons for concentrating on the object-directed feature of experience. 'We are,' Quine asserts in the opening sentence of 'Speaking of Objects', 'prone to talk and think of objects.' He goes on to mention the 'objectifying pattern' of our understanding, which we are bound to impose without warrant upon any alien pattern of understanding. He then goes off to focus on the concerns mentioned above, without revealing the significance of the simple fact that 'we talk so inveterately of objects'.[22] But the fact that every theory we can design to account for experience posits some objects reflects the quite different idea that we cannot make sense of experience which is not object-directed. Experience is structured by intentionality, which involves a distinction – however rudimentary – between the subject and the object-world of experience. (I flag this issue rather baldly here: its significance to the present project will be better understood in the light of the more detailed discussion of it in Chapter 4.)

2.4 Strawson's descriptive metaphysics

To the extent that experience necessarily involves a subject-object distinction, there must be subjects and objects for experience to be possible. However, there is multiple ambiguity in saying that there must *be* subjects and objects. This could be taken to mean that subjects and objects must be real entities, that they must exist independently of the form of all experience. This is not the line to be taken here.

A second reading of the claim that there must be subjects and objects for experience to be possible gives up the assertion that these must be *real*. Subjects and objects are conceived, to put it in Kantian terms, as empirically real, rather than as transcendentally real. The suggestion

---

[22] 'Speaking of Objects', p. 1.

is merely that, since all experience involves the bifurcation into subject and object, subjects and objects must be present in the context of experience.

However, this is still ambiguous. Saying that there must be empirically real subjects and objects could – on one interpretation – be taken to imply that the subject is an entity, an *object* after all, albeit a very *special* kind of object, like a thinking substance. But, notoriously, there are no such empirical entities to be found. Furthermore, where the subject is thought of in this way, as a very mysterious, elusive *object*, philosophical problems emerge. If there are two entirely different kinds of entities, subjects and objects, how can they be connected – how can they affect one another? We need to introduce some relation between them. And it is not clear what this relation might be. A causal relation is the obvious candidate; but it is notoriously difficult to explain how a causal relation can connect two such different kinds of entities. It is in this way that the traditional mind-body problem arises.

In view of this it now seems more rewarding to see the distinction between subjects and objects as one between *roles*, rather than between ontological categories of objects (or substances). Subject and object can be defined merely in terms of the relation of intentionality; the subject being at the experiencing end of the relation, the object being that which is at the experienced end.[23]

Perhaps the best example of a strictly empirical realist treatment of these matters is provided by Strawson.

Strawson's *Individuals*[24] is to be understood in the same light as his later essay on Kant's First Critique, *The Bounds of Sense*.[25] In the latter he attempts to disentangle and separate from the doctrines of transcendental idealism an answer to the question regarding the structure of any conception of experience such as we can make

---

[23] This could serve to explain why there can be no experience of the subject as such, why it is so elusive relative to our experiential net. The attempt to cast our experiential net over it forces the subject to shift into the role of an *object*, that which is experienced. Yet the subject is by definition at the knowing end of the relation, and so cannot be pinned down at the objective end. T. Nagel in his paper 'Objective and Subjective' (in *Mortal Questions*, CUP, 1978) is concerned with a similar point, cf. pp. 201ff. He develops this concern in his more recent book, *The View from Nowhere*, Oxford University Press, 1986.

This claim that the subject cannot be pinned down at the object side of the relation is, incidentally, not refuted by the Cartesian cogito act; the cogito act does not present us with the subject (in object form), but only with a proof (whether performative or inferential) of its existence.

[24] *Individuals – An Essay in Descriptive Metaphysics*, London, Methuen, 1959. Page references are to the University Paperback edition, 1964, reprinted in 1977.

[25] *The Bounds of Sense – An Essay on Kant's Critique of Pure Reason*, London, Methuen, 1966. Page references are to the University Paperback edition, 1975, reprinted in 1978.

intelligible to ourselves. This involves, in part, recognition of the object-directedness of any conceivable experience.[26] In *Individuals* Strawson engages in descriptive metaphysics – an attempt to describe in some detail the structure of *our* experience.

2.4.1 Two points for interpretation

Strawson argues that our conceptual scheme requires persons and material objects as the basic particulars. Clearly, if the question was what *any* conceivable form of experience must involve, the identification of persons and material objects as the basic particulars would be too specific. We can, as Strawson acknowledges, conceive of a form of experience in which material bodies would not be basic particulars; the distance between *subject* and *object* can be 'narrower'. Thus we can conceive of a form of experience that takes only raw feels as objects.[27] Nevertheless, perhaps it is indeed the case that persons and material objects are the basic particulars in our actual experience – which is all that Strawson is attempting to examine in *Individuals*.

Strawson argues from the impossibility of describing our conceptual scheme without persons and material bodies, to the conclusion that these are necessarily the primary particulars – which he in turn takes to mean that they must exist – while avoiding any commitment to saying that these particulars exist in a special, more basic sense of the word, or that they are *real*.[28] Nevertheless, while Strawson does hold such an empirical realist view, whereby there must be subjects and objects, two qualifications should be mentioned.

Strawson quite explicitly argues against taking subjects as a special kind of entity which resides in the human body. He takes the concept of an ego-substance to be one which cannot exist as a primary concept in terms of which the concept of a person can be explained or analysed. Rather, it can only exist, if at all, as a secondary, non-primitive concept which is to be explained in terms of the concept of a person. The latter is the basic concept of an entity to which both predicates ascribing states of consciousness and predicates ascribing corporeal characteristics equally apply.[29]

However, it remains to say in virtue of what these persons – essentially connected to a material body – can take on the role of

---

[26] This will be taken up in section 4.3 below.

[27] But it is assumed that these would then, at least in part, be taken as independent objects – for reasons that Strawson brings out in *The Bounds of Sense*, op. cit., pp. 98-102, and p. 109; see discussion in section 4.3 below.

[28] See, e.g., *Individuals*, pp. 59-60.

[29] ibid., pp. 101-3.

2. Focussing a Philosophical Perspective

subjects; in virtue of what predicates ascribing states of consciousness can be applied to them. Some explanation is needed. After all, if there were merely human bodies and other material bodies this would not meet the requirements for experience to be possible. (Strawson himself raises a similar question: How is the concept of a person possible? 'When we have acknowledged the primitiveness of the concept of a person, ...we may still want to ask what it is in the natural facts that makes it intelligible that we should have this concept....' Strawson concedes that he cannot properly answer the question.)[30]

Functionalists and physicalists attempt to provide some account of this matter, and are committed by their answer to saying that subjects could not function as such in the absence of their physical embodiment. In contrast, where the subject is taken to be a special kind of object which merely resides in the human body, there can be talk of disembodied experience.[31] Accordingly, unless Strawson is after all implicitly viewing persons as fulfilling the role of subjects in virtue of some special entity, we would expect him to say similarly that we could not conceive of disembodied experience.

Yet Strawson contends that this would in fact be possible, although he does not appeal to a primary concept of a pure individual consciousness, but only to a logically secondary concept of some such pure-ego, derived from the primitive primary concept of a person.[32] He seems to think it is both reasonable and sufficient for him to say in defence of this view that such disembodied existence is ultimately vicarious and could not occur if the subject had never been embodied in the first place, and that it could not last in this disembodied state for very long. This claim is rather strained, and adherence to it would threaten to collapse his view into an empirical realist strain of a Cartesian duality after all.

The second point that should be mentioned relates to the fact that, contrary to what the present exposition might have implied, Strawson does *not* argue to the conclusion that there must be subjects and objects, from the grounds that all experience involves a subject-object dichotomy. Rather he follows a different strategy, which seems to move from referential dependence within any account of conceivable experience to ontological dependence. Strawson approaches the issue by asking a question about what is referentially prior in any conceivable conceptual scheme, and argues from that to a conclusion about what must be ontologically prior.

---

[30] ibid., pp. 110-11.
[31] I should perhaps state here that I have tried to ensure that this book runs its course without either requiring, or taking a particular stand on, the nature of the self, or on related issues such as the possibility of disembodied experience.
[32] ibid., pp. 115-16.

In essence this approach to settling questions of ontology resembles Quine's. However, here some clarification is required of the specific connection that is being assumed between referential and ontological dependence. Strawson, in looking for basic particulars of our actual conceptual scheme, is looking for those particulars which are basic in relation to our identifying references to particulars. In other words, he is asking what particulars are required for us to make all the identifying references we do make. But, having identified material bodies and persons as basic with regard to questions of referential dependence, the question arises whether the particulars which are basic in this sense are *therefore* also to be awarded the status of being ontologically basic. The question as to the connection between referential and ontological dependence seems to be important. Strawson's prime concern is with the former, with referential dependence. However, in places he seems to assume that the results of his enquiry concerning referential dependence establish the latter, ontological, dependence as well. The question is, whether it is legitimate to move without further ado from conclusions regarding referential dependence to those regarding ontological dependence. Is the connection between the two kinds of dependence such that it is legitimate for Strawson to move from the one to the other in just the way that he does?

This point is raised and discussed by Bernard Williams.[33] Williams mentions that there is at least one sense in which referential priority does involve ontological priority. This is the sense in which ontological priority means, as Williams puts it, 'having priority for inclusion in our ontology', i.e. ' "x is ontologically prior to y" means "if y is included in our ontology, then x must be, but not conversely" ' (p. 113). But it is not clear that Strawson, who accepts that we may call his basic particulars 'ontologically prior', means no more than this. As Williams points out, it is difficult to resist the impression that the emphasis on being basic, beyond questions of referential priority, is in some way connected with questions of the ontological status that is to be ascribed to various types of thing – and there are several places, including the closing sentences of the book, where Strawson does seem to reveal that his manifest concern with referential dependence is indeed bound up with ontological dependence in such a way that his basic particulars are also what primarily exist. One connection between referential and ontological priority is that the former is in a sense a necessary condition of the latter. Williams says:

> However, the 'ontological connexions' of Strawson's enquiry can be put like this: that it is a necessary condition of our ascribing reality to a thing that we can identify it, and hence that the establishment of priorities of

[33] 'Strawson on Individuals' in *Problems of the Self*, CUP, 1973, pp. 108; 112-15.

identification does in a weak sense go to show why we should think of one sort of thing as 'more real' than another (p. 114).

It does clearly seem to be the case that it is a necessary condition of our ascribing reality to a thing that we can identify it. But I do not see why it follows from this ('hence') that the establishment of *priorities* of identification should correspond to *priorities* of being 'real'.

But at any rate Williams must be right in pointing out that beyond referential priority there must be other criteria which determine how, *within our actual conceptual scheme*, we establish ontological priorities. And, given that descriptive metaphysics is concerned with what goes on in our conceptual scheme, Strawson ought perhaps to have provided these criteria. (Beyond referential priority, the criteria for ontological priority would perhaps involve being fully determined in our experience.) In particular Strawson might have made clearer the specific connection between referential and ontological dependence. Neglecting to clarify the relation between referential and ontological dependence, Strawson seems at times to assume that what is basic with regard to referential dependence is also that which within our conceptual scheme primarily exists.

Of course quite apart from this is Strawson's disclaimer about these basic particulars being real. It is one thing, albeit objectionable, for him to assume that what is referentially basic is *therefore* also ontologically prior, without further explanation or qualification. It is quite another thing when, having thus moved to regard referentially basic particulars as what primarily exists, he disclaims that these ontologically prior particulars are *real*. Here, as I think Williams too is suggesting (p. 115), Strawson is concerned to make clear that he is not overstepping descriptive metaphysics – he is taking care to avoid claiming that what, within our conceptual scheme, he identifies as ontologically prior, is ontologically independent of that scheme.

Having identified persons and material bodies as ontologically prior, he is rightly concerned to make clear that he is not thereby overstepping empirical realism. He might not be careful enough in reaching the ontological basics of his empirical realism, but he is when it comes to maintaining their character as admissible within the confines of an empirical realist position.

2.5 Strawson and ontological talk

Following these general introductory comments on Strawson's empirical realism, I want now to rejoin the mainstream of the present discussion, by showing that on the specific issue of ontological talk

Strawson's empirical realism suffers from the same shortcomings pointed out above in the case of both Quine and Putnam. Yet, unlike Quine and Putnam, Strawson does not end up with an implicit assumption of transcendental idealism. Strawson explicitly rejects all talk of what is real (in the metaphysical sense), particularly the minimalist identification of what is real with a Kantian thing in itself. Consequently Strawson's empirical realism reveals even more clearly the need for further argument concerning ontological talk.

Transcendental idealism was suggested by Kant as part of an answer to a question regarding the possibility of knowledge. How can we know that the world is as we experience it to be? Kant's answer works, as we have seen, by granting that we cannot know the ontologically independent reality (transcendental idealism), while claiming that by paying this price we do attain certainty that we can know the world given in experience (empirical realism). Strawson, in keeping with his times, is bothered by the metaphysical excesses of transcendental idealism and the commitment to the thing in itself which is involved in it. In *The Bounds of Sense* he suggests rejecting as unintelligible this part of Kant's doctrine. He hopes, like other philosophers so inclined, to maintain empirical realism on its own. And it is, presumably, such empirical realism that he has in mind when, in *Individuals*, he says that he does not mean to say that the basic ontological particulars are (independently) *real*.

However, it is not clear *how* such empirical realism can be maintained after having explicitly rejected Kant's transcendental idealism. As we saw above,[34] the doctrine of transcendental idealism is a central part of Kant's attempted answer to the sceptical question as to how we can know that the world is as we experience it. By rejecting transcendental idealism as unintelligible it seems that the question remains, unanswered now and yet not undermined, waiting to confront Strawson's own empirical realist account.

The only way to maintain empirical realism as a stable position after rejecting Kant's transcendental idealism seems to be to show that the sceptical question which Kant was, in part, answering – how do we know that the world is the way we experience it to be? – is itself not legitimate. Without doing this we are in the position of having denied the only way of answering a still potent question: the very question that threatens empirical realism. Merely to *reject* Kant's doctrine, and the question, without showing what is wrong with the question, does not seem to leave empirical realism safely airborne. Left undefended against the pull of the original sceptical question, it must surely fall.

Admittedly, Strawson is interested in describing the structure of

[34] In section 2.1

2. Focussing a Philosophical Perspective   53

our thought about the world as it is; and this he has done. Wary of heady ontological issues, he has turned away to take up other remaining problems. From the perspective of the present enquiry a certain discontinuity then results, of a kind which reflects the change in intellectual climate, which in itself is most fortunate. However, it might be possible to turn back and provide arguments which transform discontinuity born of exasperation into philosophical continuity, by filling in missing links. In this way a future observer of the history of philosophy can be presented with philosophical continuity rather than with this apparent discontinuity left behind where the innovative winds of fashion have already had their say. It is possible to see the present concern in this light.

A gap opened up when Strawson and others turned away from certain metaphysical issues. Strawson rightly rejected Kant's transcendental idealism, as did others, leaving aside the question to which it helped to provide an answer. But the question will not go away if we merely turn our backs on it. And as long as the question is legitimate, it is difficult to hold a stable and unadorned empirical realism (as Kant saw). So, if we are to turn away from this question, we ought to *justify* ignoring it. This is the gap that remains to be filled. One obvious way to do this is to show that there is something wrong, incoherent, about the question.

In formulating the problem in this way I am indebted to Barry Stroud's paper 'The Significance of Scepticism'.[35] In part, the present work might be seen as an attempt to take up the challenge Stroud leaves us with at the end of his paper (pp. 292-4); hence the reference earlier to 'Stroud's Challenge'. I cannot claim with any certainty to be able to meet this challenge myself; but this makes it all the more important to impress upon others what the value of meeting it would be.

The question 'How do we know that the world is the way we experience it to be?' assumes that it is legitimate, within critical philosophy, to talk of there being a world which exists in some determinate way and with some determinate constitution, independently of all experience. But if the very notion of something which is – or is not – ontologically independent of all experience could be shown to be incoherent, the question based upon it would also be incoherent. And insofar as the question is incoherent, Strawson was surely justified in leaving it unanswered and turning away from it. Leaving this question unanswered, as Stroud says, 'would be satisfactory only if the incoherence, unintelligibility, or illegitimacy of those putative

---

[35] *In Transcendental Arguments and Science*, (ed.) P. Bieri et al., Dordrecht, Reidel, 1979, pp. 277-97. The same challenge is repeated, more forcefully, at the end of his more recent book, *The Significance of Philosophical Scepticism*, op. cit.

questions had been independently established'.³⁶ And it is by meeting this challenge that an argument against ontological talk of something which is or is not real would provide retrospective justification of Strawson's approach.

To put the matter in a broader perspective: The present concern is in the spirit of the philosophical views which have been discussed in this chapter. Quine, Putnam and Strawson all manifest an aversion to the metaphysical (external) realist point of view, preferring to avoid any reference to an independently existing reality, and rather to confine the discussion to an internal point of view.³⁷ But none of these philosophers meet the ontological questions head on; or rather, they reinterpret them more cautiously as questions about what exists in our experience or on a given theory, rather than in the traditional sense of what exists in the world independent of all experience. This leaves large sceptical questions lurking in the sidelines. That we may choose not to ask them is of little bearing on the fact that they are there to be asked.

Of course it might be said at this point that we simply have no *need* to assume that there is anything independent of all experience in order to account for the way our experience is. Indeed this point is made by Rorty in 'The World Well Lost'.³⁸ Rorty rejects the notion of a real, independently existing world beyond all conceptual schemes (pp. 661-5), asserting: 'I think that the realistic true believer's notion of the world is an obsession rather than an intuition' (p. 661). He does not offer any argument to support his rejection of such an independent world beyond saying: 'I have no arguments against the true believer's description of our so-called "intuitions". All that can be done with the claim that "only the *world* determines truth" is to point out the equivocation in the realist's own use of "world"' (p. 662). But the line between obsession and intuition is fine. The fact that we are obsessively concerned with the real world, or indeed that we do not need *it* in accounting for truth and other matters, does not provide sufficient ground for concluding that there is no fact of the matter. It is possible to be obsessive about rather important things which would not rightly be discarded simply because we tend to be obsessive about them. As long as nothing is done to show what is *wrong* with the notion of there being – or not being – a real world, i.e. as long as we do not know it to be a *mere* obsession, we cannot be justified in turning our philosophical eye away from the ontological issue, and from the sceptical questions regarding knowledge which would arise from there

---

³⁶ ibid., note 43, p. 297.

³⁷ Internal and external questions (Carnap, Putnam) correspond to Kant's empirical and transcendental realism.

³⁸ Richard Rorty, 'The World Well Lost', in *Journal of Philosophy*, vol. 69 (1972).

being something real. To meet the ontological issue head on it is necessary to argue not merely

(a) that an account of our experience is not dependent on the assumption of a reality independent of all experience;

but also

(b) that there is something incoherent and misguided about the very question of there being – or not being – something real, so that there is reason to reject it despite its seemingly intuitive nature;

and

(c) why this notion seems so intuitive all the same.

It is not enough to say that, because (a) has been argued, we can reject the concern with what is real. Without showing (b) and (c), this would be an unjustified leap to an admittedly desirable conclusion. It is only by making the complete case that we could adequately defuse the ontological issue. Only in this way could we move beyond merely ignoring the issues raised by an independently existing world to a justified rejection of the very notion of there being – or not being – a real world.

If this were accomplished, there would not be any reason why Kant's transcendental idealism should not be rejected, given that there is then no longer any legitimate question that would go unanswered in its absence. There would no longer be any sceptical pull towards empirical idealism. The sceptic's question 'How do we know that the world is as we experience it to be' would have been defused along with the notion of a real world upon which it rests. Stroud's challenge would have been met. Some sort of descriptive account of the structure of our experience (empirical realism) would then indeed be entirely sufficient, simply because an argument against the relevant ontological talk would have decisively cut the philosophical map down to size. It would have emerged that there just is no philosophical ground (and so no sceptical storm) beyond the door the internal realist has shut behind him.

While much of contemporary philosophy proceeds on the assumption that this is so, because the notion of there being something ontologically real has not been explicitly defused, we find that the philosophers discussed above are not always quite clear about it and do still tend to presuppose, perhaps when convenient, that there is something real.[39] This will emerge more clearly in the next chapter, where I take a closer look at Putnam's discussion in *Reason, Truth and History*.

---

[39] And it is for this same reason that we still find some other philosophers attempting to defend versions of full-blown metaphysical realism.

3. Brains, Vats and Putnam's Internalist Approach

Putnam sets out to attack the metaphysical realist. In the last chapter I discussed his argument briefly; in this chapter I wish to examine it in greater detail.[1] Insofar as the metaphysical realist is also one of the targets of this book, there is a certain amount in common between the present project and Putnam's.

But, relative to the present concern, Putnam's argument does not seem to go far enough. It does not directly confront the ontological notion of there being something independent of all experience, which is the bed-rock of the realist's position. Nor, in consequence, does this attack deal with the sceptical doubt that the metaphysical realist himself was troubled by: How can we know that the world is as we experience it? Indeed it threatens to reduce the metaphysical realist to precisely such scepticism.

To understand the difference in scope between Putnam's approach and the present one and to elucidate the way in which they relate to one another, it is worth examining the strength of Putnam's approach more closely, particularly its relation to the kind of scepticism mentioned above and in the last chapter.

3.1 The BIV-case: Puzzle about reference or anti-sceptical proof?

Putnam employs the case of Brains in a Vat (to be abbreviated here as 'BIVs') to launch his argument against the metaphysical realist. It is, however, not quite clear just how much Putnam means the BIV case to show. More significantly, it is not clear how much the BIV case *can* show. Is it supposed merely to highlight a puzzle about reference which faces the metaphysical realist, or is it supposed further to answer the sceptic who might have asked whether we were in a position to know that we are not in fact BIVs? Is the BIV case intended, moderately, as a

---

[1] I will concentrate on *Reason, Truth and History* op. cit. (henceforth abbreviated as *RT&H*). All page references in this chapter are to this publication unless indicated otherwise.

3. Brains, Vats and Putnam's Internalist Approach 57

puzzle about reference, or more boldly as some kind of anti-sceptical *proof*?

It is clear that Putnam at *least* means to employ the BIV case in the more moderate way, as highlighting a problem facing the metaphysical realist about reference. This aim emerges clearly in several places, in particular in chapter 3 of *RT&H*. Thus Putnam says, for example, that 'the question of 'Brains in a Vat' would not be of interest, except as a sort of logical paradox, if it were not for the sharp way in which it brings out the difference between these philosophical perspectives [metaphysical and internal realism]' (p. 49). Or on p. 51: 'It is because the modern realist wishes to have a correspondence theory of truth *without* believing in noetic rays...that the Brains in a Vat case is a puzzler for him.' That his concern is not primarily with scepticism regarding the external world, but rather to raise a question regarding reference, is indicated also by the statement on p. 6:

> When this sort of possibility is mentioned in a lecture on Theory of Knowledge, the purpose, of course, is to raise the classical problem of scepticism with respect to the external world in a modern way. (*How do you know that you aren't in this predicament?*). But this predicament is also a useful device for raising issues about the mind/world relationship.

This would seem to suggest that perhaps Putnam's answer to the question posed above straddles both options; he thinks that the BIV case *can* be used as a proof against the sceptic, but he (in *RT&H*) is primarily interested in it insofar as it poses a puzzle about reference. However, in other places in *RT&H* Putnam does seem to regard the BIV case rather as answering the sceptic by proving that we cannot be brains in a vat. Thus, for example, he says: 'I am claiming that there is an argument we can give that shows we are not brains in a vat' (p. 8).

To clarify the two possible uses to which the BIV case might be put, and to discover its adequacy to either, we should first turn to some further preliminary clarification of the BIV argument itself. Corresponding to the two philosophical uses mentioned above, puzzle and proof, there are two ways of drawing the conclusion from the BIV argument.

The first is as follows: If we are BIVs, our notional world is identical with the notional world of non-BIVs. But, the argument goes, for BIVs no reference is possible to objects external to the BIV situation. A causal theory of reference, Putnam claims, will not lead us from the brain to the external objects which correspond to the objects in that brain's notional world; 'it might refer to trees in the image, or to electronic impulses that cause tree experiences, or to the features of the programme that are responsible for those electronic impulses' (p. 14). These are not ruled out, because there *is* a close causal connection between the use of the word 'tree' in vat-English and the presence of trees in the image, of electronic impulses or of certain features in the machine's programme. But it is still the case that, when the brain in a vat, in a world where every sentient being is and always was a brain in a vat, thinks 'There is a tree in front of me', his thought does not refer to actual trees, simply because it has no causal connexion to those external trees. So Putnam holds that a causal theory of reference will not enable BIVs to refer to external objects.

At the same time Putnam rejects traditional theories of reference: theories which claim that the mental state by itself fixes the reference. Putnam argues that the notional world (the mental states) does not fix the intension and extension of terms (p. 29). There is no way that simply having a certain mental image can take us beyond the notional world to refer to an external object. 'Once we see that the qualitative similarity...between the thoughts of the brains in a vat and the thoughts of someone in the actual world by no means implies sameness of reference, it is not hard to see that there is no basis at all for regarding the brain in a vat as referring to external things' (pp. 13-14). (See also pp. 22-5.)

In view of this the BIV problem becomes clearer. The BIVs could have the same notional world that we (non-BIVs) have, down to the last detail – and still none of their terms would have any external world reference at all (pp. 28-9). The problem is not merely, as we might have thought, one of verification; that if we were BIVs we could not step outside ourselves, our notional world, to tell that we were, to establish what is real independently of us. The problem is rather more acute. If we were BIVs, we could not even think, or say that we were. It is not merely that we could not *verify* the hypothesis, we could not even *formulate it*. We could not, if it is indeed a true hypothesis, even consider whether it is true or false. For if we are BIVs, although we could have the thought 'we are brains in a vat', with all the appropriate mental states, our words 'brain' and 'vat' would refer to notional-brains and notional-vats – or perhaps to something related (e.g. electronic impulses), but certainly not to real vats and real brains. Since there is no specific causal connection between the BIV's term 'brain' and the brain it actually is, or between the word 'vat' and the vat it is actually in, and barring an implausible magical theory of reference,[2] there is no way for this reference to be established. So even when the BIV entertains the thought 'Perhaps I am a brain in a vat', the hypothesis

---

[2] By a magical theory of reference Putnam means 'a theory on which certain mental representations necessarily refer to certain external things and kinds of things' (p. 15), as if this reference were guaranteed by some special mechanism. 'For example, we might assume that some occult rays – call them "noetic rays" connect words and thought signs to their referents' (*RT&H*, p. 51). See also pp. 3ff.

3. Brains, Vats and Putnam's Internalist Approach

being entertained is *not* that of possibly being a brain in a vat, which is more than the BIV can think given the impossibility of its referring to external objects. It is rather a different hypothesis to the effect that perhaps it is a notional brain in a notional vat. And this is *not* something that the brain in a vat is. It is not the case that the BIV is merely hallucinating that it is a brain in a vat. Thus because of the breakdown of reference it seems correct to say that, if x is a BIV, it cannot even consider or formulate the hypothesis that it is, and that what it does consider by thinking 'Perhaps I am a brain in a vat' is, if it is anything, a rather different hypothesis, which is actually false.

So far the direct conclusion from the BIV argument is simply that, if we are BIVs, not only can we not verify that this is the case, but furthermore we cannot even formulate the hypothesis that suggests we might be – for our attempt to do so, given the limitations that there then are on the reference of our terms, expresses quite a different (and false) hypothesis. This is what Putnam indeed concludes, saying that

> although the people in that possible world can think and 'say' any words we can think and say, they cannot (I claim) *refer* to what we can refer to. In particular they cannot think or say that they are Brains in a vat (*even by* thinking 'we are brains in a vat'). (p. 8)

Or on p. 14:

> I have now given the argument promised to show that the brains in a vat cannot think or say that they are brains in a vat.

This is the basic, more moderate, way of describing the conclusion of the BIV argument, and it might, if valid, be sufficient to allow for the more moderate philosophical employment of the BIV case: as a puzzle about reference facing the metaphysical realist, rather than as an anti-sceptical proof. The BIV situation is admitted to be physically possible; yet the unfortunate brains in this situation find themselves in the uncomfortable predicament of not being able even to think that they are in this situation. And the explanation of why this is so brings to the surface certain general problems regarding reference which, although more acute in the BIV case (hence its philosophical value), are also relevant in general. Taken in this way, the BIV argument, if valid, is indeed, as Putnam intends, 'a useful device for raising issues about the mind/world relationship' (p. 6). It highlights a problem for the metaphysical realist with regard to the notion of 'reference'. I refer to this as the moderate approach.

However sometimes, particularly in the first chapter, Putnam seems to phrase the conclusions to be drawn from the BIV situation in bolder terms: in a way that suggests that its significance is not merely as a puzzle about reference, but as a definite reply to the sceptic's doubt as to whether we know the external world as it is. He seems to regard his argument about the BIVs as proof that we are not in this predicament. Thus he says:

> Suppose this whole story were actually true. Could we, if we were brains in a vat in this way, *say* or *think* that we were? I am going to argue that the answer is 'No, we couldn't'.

So far so good. But he then goes on to say:

> In fact, I am going to argue that the supposition that we are actually brains in a vat, although it violates no physical law, and is perfectly consistent with everything we have experienced, cannot possibly be true, because it is, in a certain way, self-refuting. (p. 7)

Now this indeed sounds as though the BIV case is supposed to result not merely in a puzzle regarding reference, but in a proof that it cannot be the case that we are BIVs. Thus Putnam asserts:

> What I shall show is that the supposition that we are brains in a vat has just this property. If we can consider whether it is true or false, then it is not true (I shall show). Hence it is not true. (p. 8)

And then:

> I am claiming that there is an argument we can give that shows we are not brains in a vat. (p. 8)

And after presenting the argument, which might indeed show that BIVs would not be able to refer to the brains that they are or to the vats that they are in, and so would not be able even to consider the BIV hypothesis, Putnam again indicates that he thinks that beyond showing a problem about reference, his argument proves that we are not brains in a vat, and thus perhaps answers the sceptic. Thus he says:

> The existence of a 'physically possible world' in which we are brains in a vat (and always were and will be) does not mean that we might really, actually, possibly *be* brains in a vat. What rules out this possibility is not physics but *philosophy*. (p. 15)

The moderate conclusion to the BIV case, that BIVs could not consider that they were BIVs, leads to the moderate employment of the BIV situation as posing a puzzle about reference in a highlighted way. But this other, more ambitious conclusion from the BIV case, that we

3. Brains, Vats and Putnam's Internalist Approach

cannot *be* brains in a vat, seems to involve, or at least allow the more ambitious employment of the BIV argument as also providing an answer to the sceptic. So we see that there is a moderate and bolder way of formulating the conclusion to be drawn from the BIV argument, appropriate to the two philosophical tasks for which we might wish to employ the BIV case. And we have seen that Putnam seems to be in sympathy with both employments; both puzzle and proof. But the question, apart from what Putnam is interested in, is what the BIV argument does actually sustain.

In view of this, it is clear that in order to assess Putnam's treatment of the BIV case, we must separate (more carefully than Putnam does) the different conclusions and the appropriate philosophical harvest each might be thought to yield. What exactly is it that the BIV case is supposed to show? In answering this the present chapter finds its overall structure.

In the next section I will ask whether it is in fact the case that BIVs could not consider/think that they were BIVs. Is it in fact the case that BIVs could not refer to external objects? (i.e. does the more moderate conclusion of the BIV argument follow, thus sufficing to set the BIV case up as a philosophical puzzle regarding reference?) The following section (3.3) will be concerned to establish whether – even if this is the case – it follows that we cannot *be* BIVs (i.e. does the more ambitious conclusion of the BIV argument follow?). Section 3.4 will then turn to examine whether, if this does follow, it suffices to set up a philosophically significant reply to the sceptic who wonders whether the world is as we experience it to be. Then (in 3.5) I will suggest that in fact, apart from not answering the sceptic, Putnam's internalism seems to commit him to just such scepticism. It will be argued (in 3.6) that the sceptic should be approached by concentrating on the ontological rather than the epistemological issue. The final section will then attempt to explain the nature of the difference between Putnam's approach and that of this book.

3.2 Is it in fact the case that BIVs could not think that they were BIVs?

In this section I turn to the first question listed above – to see whether the more moderate conclusion regarding the BIV case follows: not the conclusion that we cannot *be* BIVs, but the conclusion that BIVs could not formulate the hypothesis that they were BIVs.

The exact reason why this conclusion, that BIVs could not think or consider the hypothesis that they were brains in a vat, is supposed to set up a puzzle about *reference* emerges when we consider that Putnam sees his procedure as bearing *a close relation* to transcendental arguments. He argues that the preconditions of being able to consider that we might be brains in a vat are such that brains in a vat could not meet them. And these preconditions have to do with reference. So the moderate conclusion as to what the BIVs could not consider is seen as indicative of the underlying issues regarding reference.

The idea is to investigate the preconditions of thinking 'I am a brain in a vat'. A precondition of thinking this is that the reference to brains and vats is open to me. And the preconditions of reference are determined by two theoretical premisses which Putnam explicitly assumes[3] (pp. 16-17). The one premiss is that what he calls magical theories of reference are wrong.[4] The other is that we cannot refer to certain kinds of things, e.g. trees, if we have no causal interaction[5] with them, or with things in terms of which they can be described. Since these two premisses constitute the framework within which Putnam is arguing, he proceeds to examine them more closely. And indeed perhaps he is right with regard to these two premisses. But Putnam *also* assumes that BIVs could refer to external objects only in the way described by magical theories of reference. The idea behind this is that the causal route of reference to external objects such as trees would not be available to BIVs, since 'we are to imagine a case in which the Brains in a Vat *never* get out of the vat, and hence never get into causal connection with trees, etc'.[6] Given this, it seems to follow that BIVs do not meet the preconditions of reference as determined by the two general premisses, and insofar as this is so they cannot refer to brains and vats; which is in turn a precondition of being able to consider the hypothesis that they might be brains in a vat. So we see the connection between this conclusion and the use of the BIV case as highlighting a problem about reference, which the metaphysical realist must face. Unlike the internal realist the *metaphysical realist* claims that the BIV hypothesis should not be dismissed as a mere story. But, given that magical theories of reference are unacceptable, it would not seem possible to consider that we might be brains in a vat, if indeed we were. So the metaphysical realist would be faced with a problem of providing an account of reference which *would* allow for this hypothesis.

However, the crucial assumption here is that, of the two theories mentioned, the BIVs would indeed have only magical theories of reference available to them. That is, that the direct (causal) theory of

---

[3] It is because of these assumptions that Putnam claims only that his procedure has *a close relation* to transcendental arguments: it is not a wholly apriori investigation (p. 16).

[4] See n. 2 on p. 58 above.

[5] I am not sure that Putnam's 'causal interaction' is the correct notion, but insofar as this is a large and independent issue I leave it aside for now.

[6] p. 16, n. 3.

3. Brains, Vats and Putnam's Internalist Approach

reference would *not* be open to them when it came to referring to brains and vats. This is the assumption I wish to query. Is it in fact the case that BIVs could refer to brains and vats only by assuming some magical connections between their notional world and the real world?

In considering this question we should remember that if we were brains in a vat our experience would be exactly as it is now, except that all this would be internal to our notional world; we would never step into conscious (epistemic) contact with the external world (although of course we might be in physical contact with it). This, in effect, is Putnam's modern way of constructing a Kantian model. The BIVs are empirical realists, and transcendental idealists.[7]

The point is that brains in a vat would, although confined to their notional world, not have experience any different from ours. Now, we in our experience can, for example, see a dissected animal lying on the laboratory work-bench, can proceed to dissect it further and reveal its brain. There is no reason why, properly set up, the BIV could not have just such experiences. After all, the idea is that the BIV would experience everything we do, within its notional world. So it would experience itself engaging in the kind of 'objective' scientific experiments just alluded to, among which would be included the investigation of brain structure, chemistry etc. Or, at least, it would seem to the brain that it was so engaged.

It is also easy, and perfectly acceptable, to imagine further that in one corner of this vat, bobbing up and down in the nutrient fluid, we have a cluster of reflective brains – call them the Frege-brain and several acolyte student-brains. These philosopher-brains now ask themselves what determines the reference of any term they use. (Of course, if asked what the term 'they' refers to they would probably not immediately come up with the BIV hypothesis!) Their answer to their question, given slight alterations introduced by the Searle-brain or the Linsky-brain, is essentially that of descriptive reference. The referent is whatever satisfies the set (or some of the set) of properties associated with the sense of the expression. By contrast, there is another group of brains, the Kripke-brain being the most extrovert among them, but equally prominent is the Putnam-brain and the Donnellan-brain, who have been clustered (perhaps not physically) around the now aged (or 'aged') Mill-brain. These hold a direct non-descriptive theory of reference (although this does not commit them to denying that reference can be *fixed* by way of description; it often is).

Now if these philosopher-brains all turn to the question of how a natural-kind term (say 'horse') refers, the descriptional-theory brains

---

[7] It is important to remember that 'idealism' in this Kantian sense is epistemic and not ontological: the idea is not that there *is* nothing beyond experience, but that we cannot *know* what there is.

will probably come up with a list, or cluster, of properties that is supposed to determine the extension. The other philosopher-brains will say that natural kind terms such as 'horse' are non-descriptional labels for a certain kind of thing. This involves accepting that what determines a *kind* of thing depends on something shared by individuals in the extension, by virtue of which the term applies only to them. Now, as Putnam has pointed out, this direct reference theory, unlike the descriptional view, does not accept that meanings are in the head. It is not the case that understanding an expression is regarded as wholly internal and involves nothing in addition to the speakers' thoughts. Extension, and intension, are determined contextually – not solely by internal general properties. This is what Putnam means by saying that meanings just aren't in the head. The meaning of 'horse' is accounted for by the context surrounding the speakers, and not merely by their internal psychological state of mind. Meaning is determined not merely by linguistic, but also by extralinguistic settings in which the speakers function.

To return now to our question 'Could BIVs refer to brains and vats?', on the descriptional theory of reference BIVs would not have any particular problem, since they have thoughts and psychological states and so, just as well as non-BIVs, could entertain, in a wholly internal psychological state, a set of general properties which determine the intension which in turn determines the extension of the term, say, 'brain'. So the BIVs could say that anything that fits the description '............', where the blank is filled in with the salient features known about brains in the experience of the BIVs, is a brain.

But Putnam's response to this is that, although this is true, and BIVs could do this just as well as non-BIVs, this is not an adequate account of reference to begin with. The extension of a term is not fixed by a concept that the individual speaker has in his head/brain, and this is true both because extension is in general determined socially and because extension is, in part, determined indexically. 'Traditional semantic theory leaves out only two contributions to the determination of extension – the contribution of society and the contribution of the real world.'[8] And to allow for the latter some sort of direct reference is needed, such as causal connections. Thus he says that 'one cannot refer to certain kinds of things, e.g. trees, if one has no causal interaction at all with them, or with things in terms of which they can be described' (pp. 16-17). So Putnam rejects the possibility that BIVs could refer to brains, not because they could not provide the kind of descriptions which the *traditional* theory of reference requires (they could) but

---

[8] 'The Meaning of "Meaning"' (to be abbreviated as MOM), in *Philosophical Papers*, vol.2, CUP, 1975, p. 245. See also *Reason, Truth and History*, pp. 17-21.

3. Brains, Vats and Putnam's Internalist Approach

rather because that theory of reference is inadequate. Meaning does determine reference, but psychological state does not determine meaning.[9] Psychological state *under*determines meaning.

However, even if psychological states do not *determine* reference, we might accept that they can serve to fix a reference (it could even be argued that ultimately there is no other way of *fixing* the reference) – and so that BIVs could formulate the hypothesis 'Perhaps we are brains in a vat', where brains and vats are just whatever, if anything, does answer that description.

But let us accept Putnam's criticism and rejection of the traditional theories of reference. Granting Putnam this, it follows that the Frege-brain cannot, indeed, refer to the brain that it is, and so cannot consider the appropriate hypothesis. But what about our Kripke-brain? Once we see, Putnam says (p. 25), that mental states alone (in either the individualistic or the collective sense) do not fix the reference, we should not be suprised that the BIVs could not succeed in referring to external objects, even though they have the same mental states we have, and hence could not say or think that they are BIVs. But for this to be the case we have to assume that direct (e.g. causal) reference is not available to the BIV.

This is precisely what Putnam assumes. Recall Putnam's assumption (second premiss) that one cannot refer to certain kinds of things if one has no causal interaction at all with them, or with things in terms of which they can be described (pp. 16-17): Putnam assumes further that no such interaction, and therefore no such reference to external objects, is available to BIVs. But he does not go into a discussion of this. He does indeed say (p. 17) that he must examine his premisses more carefully, but in what follows he concentrates on the first premiss – that magical theories of reference are wrong; and on the distinct fact that mental states on their own do not fix reference (p. 25), that intension and extension are not fixed merely by notional worlds (p. 29). But the assumption that BIVs could not refer in any other way (i.e. in the way described by the second premiss) is not examined carefully. It is this assumption that I wish to query. Is it in fact the case, as Putnam assumes, that BIVs cannot refer in something like this way to external objects (brains and vats)? Is there something wrong with our idea of a Kripke-brain?

Now it might seem obvious that the direct theory of reference makes requirements which the BIV cannot meet – the direct theory of reference requires some sort of reference to external objects, whereas the BIV is by definition denied any such reference. *All* it has are mental states. However, this short answer to the effect that the direct

---

[9] See *MOM*, p. 270.

theory of reference is not available to the BIV is *too* short. It takes the idea that the BIVs are confined to their notional world too narrowly; narrowly enough for it to seem sufficient to point out that it is confined to its psychological states for this to seem like an end to the matter.

We should be more careful in rendering the notional world to which the BIVs are confined. We, having described the case, can say that the brains cannot refer to anything external to them. But we are also assuming, in setting up the case, that the 'nerve endings have been connected to a super-scientific computer which causes the person whose brain it is to have the illusion that everything is perfectly normal. There seem to be people, objects, the sky, etc.' (p. 6). If this were not so, it would not be a philosophically interesting case at all. And, given that it *is* so, it is not the case that we can simply say that BIVs have no more than their mental states to go on. This is the confinement they seem to be in from our point of view. But things are quite different from their point of view. From the point of view of the BIV there is a distinction between a psychological state of mind, and an experience of an 'external' object. This, for the empirical realist BIV, is as much a qualitative difference as it is for us (supposed non-BIVs). This is true by hypothesis; since the BIVs experience is just like ours. For the BIV the internal-external, or the inside-outside, distinction is as real as it is for us. So the BIV, just as much as we, will distinguish between a hallucination of a horse and a 'real' horse, in just the way we do. And, given this, from the empirical realist view in which it is confined the realist-brain, say the Kripke-brain, might say that 'horse' is a natural-kind term which directly refers to horses in just the way Kripke-Saul in our world says it does. Now suppose this brain, still holding to the direct theory of reference, turns to consider the term 'brain'. It has 'conducted' all sorts of experiments, involving behaviour studies of various organisms and machines, and the appropriate anatomical studies. Imagine that this vat-world is fairly advanced, and that the brains inhabiting it are quite accustomed to the possibility of constructing thought experiments regarding BIV-cases. For any such BIV there is a very intuitive difference between its objective studies and merely imaginative thought-experiments, just as there is for us. There is a very clear difference for this BIV between an actual brain and the mere thought of a brain. It would seem to the BIV that thoughts involve merely intentional objects, whereas the scientific experiments it carries out involve external (real) objects, which it can see, touch, etc. The difference would be no less acute or intuitive for the BIV than it is for us.

Thus there is an empirical realist perspective which structures the notional world in which the BIV is confined. Given this perspective, it is clear that it was an oversimplified view that took the fact that BIVs

3. Brains, Vats and Putnam's Internalist Approach

are confined to their notional world to mean, without qualification, that they are confined to psychological states. Although they cannot step beyond their notional world into a position which affords them epistemic contact with external objects, and in this broad sense are confined to their psychological states, the notional world that they are confined to is such that *within* it there is just as strong a distinction between merely internal psychological states and externally existing objects as there is for us between this entire notional world and what for us are the objects external to it. From our perspective they are confined to their notional world with its illusion. But from their perspective they can refer to external objects just as much as we can. If we are to avoid perspectival chauvinism in answering the question about what BIVs can refer to, we must not stop at the observation that they are confined to their notional world. We must rather avoid this rough characterisation of their predicament and see whether the problem of reference remains once we take into account the internal structure of the merely notional world in which these BIVs spend their lives.

It is perhaps valid to argue that reference is not determined by psychological states alone, but it might now seem that it is rather too simple to say that the BIVs are confined to psychological states and so cannot possibly determine the reference of their terms. The trouble with this is that it fails to take into account that, although from our point of view there might be a difficulty in BIV reference, there would not be one from the point of view of the BIV. And it is after all the BIV that has to establish the reference. To repeat the central point, it is too simple to say that the BIVs are confined to their psychological states without paying attention to the empirical realist structure of their notional world. Once we do pay attention to this structure, we will realise that although from our perspective it is true to say that they cannot get beyond their psychological states, from their internal perspective the referent of the term 'psychological state' is different[10] and is such that it can be surpassed, just as *we* in our experience can get beyond *our* psychological states. It is from this internal perspective that the reference to brains is supposed to be established. Yet it is from our perspective that such reference seemed impossible. And this was because, in saying that the BIV was restricted to its notional world, we did not emphasise the empirical realist structure of this world when viewed from within and the effect this might have on the possibility of BIV reference.

Given this empirical realist structure of its experience, we might imagine the philosopher-BIV stepping back to consider the collection of

---

[10] And so therefore is that of 'external object' as well.

dissected brains lined up on the laboratory work-bench. These, the BIV knows, have all been collected from various animals. But, this querying philosopher-brain asks, 'How does the term "brain" refer to these objects?' Well, given that it is not a Frege-brain, but a Kripke-brain, it suggests something like this. It is necessarily the case that: something is a brain if and only if it is a member of the same *actual* natural kind that *this* is *actually* an instance of. Here 'the same *actual* natural kind that *this* is *actually* an instance of' is a rigid counterpart of 'the same natural kind that *this* is an instance of'.[11] Another way, using Kaplan's *dthat* operator to rigidify the definite description would be: It is necessarily the case that: something is a brain if and only if it is a member of *dthat* (the same natural kind of which this is an instance).[12] (It remains to clarify what the hidden nature of the paradigm referred to is; and perhaps what being 'the same natural kind' consists in.) The point is that, just as this kind of definition, rigidly denoting a sample of, say, water in the actual world would be used by us to explain the meaning of the natural kind term 'water' in any possible world, so too could the BIV use it, since its experience of water and of water-samples is qualitatively identical with ours. And just as the BIV could use this definition to explain the meaning of 'water', in a way that did not determine the meaning solely by *its* psychological states, so too could it fix the meaning of 'brain'. In terms of possible worlds: For every possible world w, and every individual x in w, x is a brain in w if and only if x in w is the same organ as *this* (or those) in the actual world. (Where *'this'* refers to the brain that the scientist-BIV has just extracted from, say, a rabbit).

Of course, it might be queried whether 'brain', and more obviously 'vat' are indeed natural-kind terms. But even if not, the same kind of definition could be given for them. Something is a vat if and only if it is an artifact of *dthat* (the same type of artifact that *this* is an instance of).[13]

So the BIV, by referring directly to that which *in its* experience is an external instance of brainhood, or vathood, can explain the meaning of 'brain' and 'vat' and thereby rigidly fix its reference, in a way which does not – as far as the BIV is concerned – depend solely on the wholly internal 'psychological state' of the speaker. Rather the BIV goes beyond its psychological states and hooks on to what are (again, as far as the BIV is concerned) independent objects. And, given this possibility, which simply follows the direct theory of reference, why

---

[11] In thinking about these issues I have benefited from Nathan Salmon's discussion in *Reference & Essence* (Oxford, Blackwell, 1982) to eliminate use of possible worlds.

[12] D. Kaplan, 'Dthat' in P. Cole (ed.) *Syntax and Semantics 9: Pragmatics*, New York, Academic Press, 1978, pp. 221-43.

[13] Cf. Salmon, op. cit.

3. Brains, Vats and Putnam's Internalist Approach

could the BIV not consider the hypothesis that it is a brain in a vat? Why could the BIV not say, and *mean*: 'Perhaps I am a brain in a vat?' The meaning and reference of these terms is fixed in this hypothesis just as it would be in any possible world, on the basis of the actual brains (and vats) it takes as paradigms in its actual empirical world. Just as the meaning of 'water' is fixed, and thereby applies to samples of water we never have, and perhaps never could have, come across, so too in the case of these BIVs with regard to brains, etc.

But of course, we now remind ourselves, the BIV might think it is fixing the reference; but it isn't *really*. It is under the illusion that it distinguishes internal states of mind from external objects, but it does not really do so. So that in referring to *this* brain the BIV was referring not, as it thought it was, to a brain, but rather to a notional brain, to a brain in the image.[14] To put it differently, the reference of 'brain' in any possible world was indeed fixed by direct reference to an actual item in the actual world. But if the actual world is one in which the thinker is a BIV, then what it referred to directly was not in fact an actual *brain*, but rather the image (or thought) of a brain (an intentional object). It *thought* it was referring to an actual brain in the actual world, but it was not, given that in its actual world what seem like actual brains – external objects – are no more than notional brains. And so the very first step of the above attempt to fix the reference is, despite appearances to the thinker, not in fact reference to an actual brain, insofar as the thinker is a BIV. The reference could only be fixed as above if the thinker were not a BIV in the actual world. The BIV might think that it can fix the reference in this way, but if it *is* a BIV then, unknown to it, it is in error – because what it takes as direct reference to the external brain in front of it is merely internal reference to an image of a brain, not to a real brain. The BIV, illusions aside, is still trying to determine reference solely by what goes on in the head.

This is basically the objection Putnam would raise at this point. And so the conclusion would follow, that if x is a BIV, x cannot refer to brains, and so cannot formulate the hypothesis that it might be a brain in a vat. For, regardless of what the BIV might think, its terms refer to other entities (notional rather than actual brains), and so in considering the hypothesis the BIV is in fact considering something quite different. It is on these grounds that Putnam concludes that if we *are* BIVs, we cannot *think* that we are.

---

[14] Putnam prefers on the whole to talk of a 'brain in the image', or a 'vat in the image', rather than of notional brains and notional vats, although he does for example talk of 'notional water' (p. 28). I have preferred the latter locution throughout as makes it entirely clear that we are talking about the contents of a notional world. On the concept of a notional world and a notional object cf. Daniel Dennett's 'Beyond Belief' (particularly pp. 38-9) in *Thought and Object – Essays on Intentionality* (ed.) Andrew Woodfield. Oxford, Clarendon Press, 1982.

However, I believe that this is not right. In the first place, Putnam makes too much of the distinction between the merely notional (intentional) objects that the BIVs can refer to and the external objects. He assumes that there is no way of fixing the reference to the latter by way of referring directly to the former. However, in this he seems to be subject to just the kind of hard dichotomy between subjective and objective that on the whole he seems eager to weaken. Thus I do not think that it is very damaging to say that the BIV really only refers to notional brains. In its experience these *are* external and independently existing objects, which it can investigate as having a nature of their own. BIVs could refer to what they take to be paradigms of actual brains, and say that anything that shared the same essential nature (whatever that turned out to be) would be a brain. They might then even acknowledge the possibility that the paradigm they refer to might be no more than a notional brain – and go on to say that in that case anything which shared the same hidden nature as the paradigm, but was not merely a notional brain, would still be a brain. In other words, it is entirely coherent to assume that being notional is no more an essential feature of their paradigm than being yellow is an essential feature of being gold. Just as we could say that anything that was essentially of the same kind as this piece of yellow gold would be gold even if it were white, so the BIV could say that anything that was of the same structure and function etc. as the (possibly notional) brains they explore would still be a brain even if it were not merely notional.[15] And they might then proceed to suggest/think/consider the possibility that they might be just such brains. They could indeed never verify this to be the case; but they *could consider* the hypothesis.

The problem perhaps stems from the fact that Putnam seems to assume that the only way for BIVs to determine the reference to external brains is by showing a referential chain to those external brains that the BIVs are, and to those external vats that the BIVs are in. This is like saying that the only way we can think the proposition 'There was a first horse' is by showing that it is possible to refer via a referential chain to that horse. But surely if there was a first horse in some pre-historic world, say a world which was then totally destroyed, we can still consider that there was such a horse even though the horses we now use to determine the reference of the term 'horse' evolved separately and are not linked by any causal chain to that

---

[15] Alternatively, and somewhat less contentiously, they might simply concede that something is a brain *only* if it is not notional. They can then acknowledge that the paradigms available to them might all be merely notional, despite their empirical reality (to them). They would therefore say that anything that exhibited the same hidden structure and function, etc. as those paradigms *and was not merely notional*, would be a brain.

3. Brains, Vats and Putnam's Internalist Approach

horse? In just the same way the BIVs can determine the reference of 'brain' in the BIV-hypothesis even though they do not do so by referring to *those* external brains. They do so rather by referring directly to the brains they do encounter in their physiology lab, saying that *if* these are merely notional it is possible that being merely notional is not an essential feature of being a brain; and that if there are non-notional (i.e. external) brains and vats it is possible that they are just such brains. The BIV does not need to be able to say 'That is the brain that I am' in order to consider the possibility that he might be one, any more than we have to be able to say 'That is the first horse' in order to consider the possibility that there might be one.

The second reason why I do not think Putnam is right in saying that if we were BIVs we could not consider this hypothesis is this: We do not have any certainty that we occupy a position more privileged than that allowed to the BIVs with regard to formulating the problem. The way Putnam sets up the hypothesis cannot in fact be any different from the way we have seen to be open to BIVs. That is, we should examine the point of view Putnam himself has to take up in order to formulate the problem. Consider Putnam saying: 'If we are brains in vats, we cannot *think* that we are.' How has Putnam himself, in formulating and thinking the antecedent, established the meaning, and hence the reference of *his* terms 'brains' and 'vats'? He cannot have used a magical theory of reference, or one whereby his own psychological state determines meaning, for this is something he objects to, and denies the BIVs from using. So, if his statement is to have any meaning, the meaning of his terms must be determined in some other way; presumably by some sort of direct reference to paradigmatic cases. But of course Putnam is no more (or less) sure that he is in fact referring in this way to the external objects to which he thinks he is referring than are the BIVs. If *he* is a BIV after all, his terms 'brain' and 'vat' go no further than the BIV's terms – both then refer to exactly the same possibly 'notional' objects. And on this ground Putnam is hardly in a position to say what it is BIVs could not consider – or if he is (by the method described above) so are the BIVs. *What* is it that Putnam says BIVs could not consider or refer to? The terms 'brain' and 'vat' in the antecedent must be given meaning in such a way that would not be available to BIVs; in such a way that could not be captured by the thoughts of BIVs. For if it could we would have no grounds for thinking that we ourselves were not simply BIVs engaged in the same thoughts. I cannot see that Putnam is in any position to know that he is setting up the BIV predicament in a way that would not be open to BIVs as well. Yet this is what is presupposed by saying that if we were BIVs we could not think that we were.

The conclusion to be drawn from the BIV case is therefore not that if we were BIVs we could not consider this hypothesis, but rather that there is no reason to think that BIVs are in any different a situation with regard to the possibility of thinking that they might be BIVs than non-BIVs would be, given that the latter do not *know* that they aren't BIVs (how could they?). Putnam's conclusion only seems to follow because (a) the manner in which BIVs could directly refer from within their empirical realist world to brains and vats is not spelt out; and (b) it is not noticed that in the sentence 'If we were brains in vats we could not think it' the way in which we fix the meaning (and reference) of 'brains' and 'vats' is *precisely* the way BIVs could fix it – from *within* our experience. We cannot claim any more privileged epistemic position. And yet, from within, our experience is to us *exactly* as the BIV's is to it.

Now if this is right, the more moderate conclusion that Putnam draws from the BIV case does not follow. It is *not* the case that if we were BIVs we could not think that we were, or refer to just these objects (brains,vats) and consider just this hypothesis.

Nor, incidently, will it do to attack the theory of direct reference, say, by arguing that the idea of 'being of the same kind as *this*' makes no sense. (This is what Putnam says on p. 53.) This would not be to fault the BIVs' reference to brains on grounds that have anything to do with their being BIVs. It would simply be to criticise that theory of reference in general, whether it is being employed by BIVs or by non-BIVs. The entire theory of reference employed by the realist will have been attacked. This will not show that the BIV, *by virtue of being a BIV*, cannot consider this hypothesis. The BIV could not consider this hypothesis, but then neither could the non-BIV consider the hypothesis that the first piece of gold was yellow. In saying that this theory of reference does not work we are not raising a special problem for BIVs, any more than we were in pointing out how the traditional theory of reference broke down. And indeed, in raising this difficulty Putnam has already turned to his more general attack on external realism via the notion of reference.

If what we have argued in this section is accepted, then in reply to our initial question we must say that it is *not* in fact the case that BIVs could not consider that they might be brains in a vat. And insofar as this, the moderate conclusion of the BIV argument, does not follow, the BIV case itself does not constitute a paradox which can be employed to highlight a philosophical problem about reference.

3.3 *If we grant the moderate conclusion – does it follow that we cannot actually be BIVs?*

Apart from the moderate conclusion that BIVs could not consider the

3. Brains, Vats and Putnam's Internalist Approach

hypothesis that perhaps they might be brains in vats, Putnam also draws the conclusion that we cannot *be* brains in a vat. This sounds like a stronger conclusion, which seems to go some way towards answering the sceptic.[16] The argument for this is of the following general outline: (1) If we are brains in a vat, we cannot think that we are, except in the bracketed sense. (2) This bracketed thought does not have reference conditions that could make it true. Therefore (3) it is not possible after all that we are brains in a vat. (See Putnam pp. 50-51)

If we are brains in a vat, we cannot refer to brains and vats, because our terms 'brains' and 'vats' refer to something else, say notional brains and notional vats. So, if we are brains in a vat, the sentence 'We are brains in a vat' expresses a quite different and *false* proposition, namely, that we are notional brains in notional vats. In short, if we are brains in a vat, then 'We are brains in a vat' is false. Hence it is necessarily false (see p. 15).

Now in the previous section I tried to argue against the first stage of the argument. I argued that it is in fact not the case that BIVs could not refer to brains and vats, and so that they could in fact consider the BIV hypothesis. However, let us now assume that I was wrong. Assume that BIVs could *not* refer as required, and so could not consider the hypothesis that they are brains in vats. Let us rather question whether, even if this is the case, it follows from this predicament that (3) we cannot *be* brains in vats.

It might seem possible to argue that this does not follow. All that follows from the referential predicament of BIVs is that the sentence 'We are brains in vats' does not express a true proposition *by the lights of those BIVs*. But this is not to say that the proposition expressed by the sentence cannot in fact be true – it might be the case even if it cannot be recognised as true from any point of view.

The assumption is indeed being made that the BIV situation is one in which every sentient being is, and always was and will be, a brain in a vat. So there is no 'evil scientist's' external point of view. But the statement that we cannot *be* BIVs is presumably meant to answer the sceptical worries to the effect that the world might be very different from the way we experience it to be. And such worries typically take a no-eye view of truth. They rely on truth as altogether independent of observers. (For them truth, unlike justice, does not have to be seen to be done.) So such a sceptic would accept that, owing to the breakdown in reference involved, the sentence 'We are brains in a vat' cannot possibly be true, but claim that this only accounts for what can be known to be true *by our lights*, and that it might still be the case that

---

[16] Whether it in fact does so is the question we will turn to in the next section.

we are brains in a vat. That is, independently of what we can consider, this might be the way the world is.

The idea is that Putnam's argument from the breakdown of reference only shows what can be known to be true by our lights; not what might be true independently of all lights. The argument from the breakdown of reference only suffices to prove that we are not BIVs for someone who has adopted the internalist point of view. For the externalist, however, the argument that turns on the impossibility of reference does not suffice to show that we cannot be BIVs, since truth on this view does not depend on the possibility of reference.

Premises (1) and (2) turn on a breakdown in reference. The externalist might query why it follows from this that (3) it is not possible that we *are* brains in a vat. Truth of our *descriptions* depends on reference. But presumably what is the case does not. So the impossibility of referring to brains and vats if we are BIVs only means that if we are BIVs we cannot even *say* that we are. But this would not involve it being the case that we are not brains in a vat. It might rather be the case that we *are* brains in a vat, and that this simply leaves us trapped in the uncomfortable position of not being able to give a true description of what is the case, even by saying 'We are Brains in a Vat'. The breakdown in reference which occurs if we are BIVs does not, in other words, suffice to show that it is not the case that we are BIVs; rather it shows that, if we are, we cannot formulate true descriptions of this fact, insofar as the conditions of reference are not met. All we will be able to have is the bracketed thought ('Perhaps we are BIVs'). And indeed we cannot tell that we have any more than this.

This is the kind of argument that might be thought to show that the BIV case cannot sustain the stronger conclusion that it is not possible that we *are* BIVs; even if it does involve the more moderate claim that, if we are BIVs, we cannot even say or consider that we are. In other words, even if the BIV case did constitute a puzzle about reference, it would not go so far as to yield the stronger conclusion, which seemed like an approach to an anti-sceptical proof, that it is not possible that we are in fact BIVs.

However, this seems to be a careless line of argument. The following objection points out why. Putnam would at this point rightly comment that if it is granted that we could not, as BIVs, even consider that we were BIVs, what is the content of saying that it might still be the case that we are *BIVs*? 'BIVs' could not then be a description of what we in fact were, in view of the impossibility of such a description, brought about by the breakdown in reference. To put it differently, if the moderate conclusion regarding the referential breakdown is granted, when the sceptic says that we might *be* brains in a vat even though as such we could not formulate the hypothesis he is in a muddle.

3. Brains, Vats and Putnam's Internalist Approach

Assuming that as BIVs we cannot formulate the hypothesis (due to the supposed impossiblity of reference) the sceptic cannot in fact be saying that we might nevertheless *be* brains in a vat, since as such he could not refer to them. The very attempt to say that he is presupposes that he isn't a brain in a vat after all. If the hypothesis can be formulated, it is false.

So it is not possible to argue that, even if it is the case that due to referential breakdown BIVs could not consider that they were BIVs, they might nevertheless *be* BIVs. This would only make sense from the point of view of someone who could consider the hypothesis, who could say what it was that the BIV might be, i.e. someone who was not a BIV. But we are assuming the philosophically interesting situation in which all sentient beings are in the same BIV predicament. Given this, it would seem that we must accept that the stronger conclusion that we cannot be BIVs does indeed follow from the more moderate claim that if we were BIVs we could not formulate or think the hypothesis that we were. (In the next section we will question whether this is in fact the *stronger* conclusion.)

To recapitulate: In the previous section I argued that it is in fact not the case that BIVs could not refer to brains and vats etc. – and so that it is not the case that they cannot, just because they are BIVs, consider the hypothesis that they are. And if that argument is valid, it is not the case that we cannot be BIVs. However, this only stops the stronger conclusion by showing that the weaker claim is not true of BIVs either. It blocks the conclusion (3) by arguing against the steps (1) and (2). And I do think that this argument against the weaker claim *is* in fact valid. BIVs *could*, by their own lights, formulate the hypothesis that they were BIVs, and from their point of view would be considering this hypothesis just as much as from our point of view we are considering it. And given this, it remains possible that we are BIVs. It is not the case that either we consider it and aren't or we cannot consider it at all. It might well be that we are BIVs, *and* we consider the hypothesis. There is no way of telling whether we are non-BIVs considering the hypothesis, or BIVs doing the same. This argument against Putnam's stronger claim that we cannot *be* BIVs rests on our argument against his weaker contention regarding the BIV case.

But the question we asked ourselves in this section was whether, even if we granted the weaker contention (referential breakdown), the stronger conclusion that we could not *be* BIVs followed from it. I attempted to show that even if we accepted (1) and (2) the conclusion (3), that it is therefore not possible that we *are* brains in vats, did not follow. We have, however, now seen reason to regard this attempt as mistaken. So, if we were to grant the more moderate claim regarding the referential predicament of BIVs, the stronger claim that it is not possible that we are BIVs would follow. The question is whether this conclusion is indeed, as it seems to be, of philosophical significance as an answer to the sceptic. Is this the 'stronger' conclusion it seems to be? This is the issue we must now proceed to consider.

3.4 Does this constitute a significant reply to the sceptic who asks whether the world is as we experience it to be?

Let us assume that the moderate conclusion does follow: that if we were brains in a vat we could not refer to the brains we are or to the vat we are in, and so could not even consider the hypothesis that we are brains in a vat, even by saying 'We are brains in a vat'. In the previous section we saw further that given this moderate conclusion it seems to follow that it is not possible that we are brains in vat. We cannot be *BIVs*. Well, if this were the case, where would this leave us with regard to scepticism?

This 'stronger' conclusion that we cannot be BIVs nevertheless amounts to a very specific claim, and one which turns entirely on the argument regarding referential breakdown. Even given this specific claim, does it not remain possible for the BIV to think, not specifically that it might be a *brain* in a *vat*, but that it might be an unknown *x*, which it perhaps cannot refer to, and so cannot identify, but which is utterly different from what seems to be the case within its experience? In other words, assuming that there is a problem about the BIV being able to refer, it might be the case that if we were BIVs we could not think that this is *what* we were, but we *could* still think, consider, formulate the more general hypothesis that we might be something quite different from what we seem to be. We could consider that despite the way in which we experience the world to be, it might be some *x*, some we-know-not-what; where this *x* is defined negatively, and solely, as being that which is the case independently of our experience and to which we cannot refer in any other, less impoverished, way.

This can be put differently. I mentioned that in effect the BIV case merely presents a scientific model of the Kantian view. The BIV, in its experience, is an empirical realist. But insofar as it is unable to refer to brains and vats, and so is unable to consider the transcendent truth about the world, it is a transcendental idealist. But here, as in Kant, 'idealist' expresses an epistemological position rather than an ontological claim. The BIV is a transcendental idealist because it cannot *know* what is the case beyond the way the world seems in its experience; but this does not involve saying that there is nothing beyond its experience (which would be ontological idealism).

The point is simply that the claim 'BIVs could consider that they were *BIVs*' is considerably more specific than the general claim that 'BIVs could consider that the world is not as they experience it to be'. The former turns on the possibility of reference to BIVs – whereas the latter does not. Consequently, Putnam's argument, which (if successful) would show the impossibility of such reference, only counts against the former more specific claim. It remains the case that BIVs could consider that the way they experience the world to be may not be the way the world (thing in itself) is independently of all experience. To remove *this* sceptical doubt we would need an argument aimed not at the possibility of referring to what the content of the real world is, but rather one aimed at the very legitimacy of ontological talk of there being something independent of all experience, whatever its nature is.

This should clarify the relation between the conclusion that we cannot be BIVs, reached at the end of the last section, and the sceptic's worry that the way of the world might not be as we experience it. The conclusion that we cannot be BIVs was derived from the moderate argument from reference. We can now see that although it was legitimate to conclude that we cannot be BIVs from the breakdown in reference, this route to the conclusion weakens its standing in such a way that it is of no general relevance to the philosophically interesting sceptic.

In the last section I started out by trying to argue that it is one thing to conclude that if we were BIVs we could not think that we were, and quite another to conclude that it is not possible after all that we are BIVs. But at the end of that section we were left with the fact that Putnam could reply that if it is conceded that as BIVs we could not even consider that we might be BIVs, then what is the meaning of saying that it might still be the case that we are BIVs? What would it mean to say that we might be *BIVs*, since 'BIV' could not then mean what we were supposing we might be – i.e. *brains* in *vats*? We are now in a position to say that although this does show that Putnam is right to conclude from the presumed referential breakdown that it is not possible for us to be BIVs, the significance of this claim, on the basis of this argument, is not as great as it seems.

If, in saying that it is not possible after all that we are brains in a vat, Putnam is merely saying again that we could not formulate the hypothesis describing *what* we were, this is not an anti-sceptical proof, but merely a restatement of the more moderate conclusion about what we could not say, given referential breakdown.[17]

If, on the other hand, Putnam does mean the statement that we

---

[17] We have in fact seen that there is reason to think that even this moderate conclusion does not follow – since BIVs could in fact refer to brains and vats, and so could formulate the BIV hypothesis.

cannot be brains in a vat as a proof that answers the sceptic, his claim clearly is too weak. Turning, as it does, on his argument from reference to BIVs, it can sustain the specific conclusion that we cannot be *BIVs*, but this base is too weak for it to be of general significance as an anti-sceptical proof. The sceptic suggests that it is possible that, despite what seems to us to be the case, we are (really) brains in a vat. Putnam replies to this that no, we cannot possibly be brains in a vat, because saying that we are assumes that we aren't. If we were brains in a vat, we could not say that we were, because 'brains' and 'vats' would then express something quite different. At this point, slightly puzzled, the sceptic must reply that Putnam has not quite understood his worry. He was not concerned to say that we might specifically be *brains in a vat*. He meant to put in a vivid way that we might be something quite different to what we think we are. The thrust of his statement was that the real world might not be as we experience it to be. His interest was not primarily to say *what* we might be, but to say *that* the world might be very different from our empirical realist view of it. And so in response to Putnam's argument he would say that he is quite prepared to grant that in saying that we might be brains in a vat he was ignoring certain problems about reference, which if considered would have prevented him from suggesting specifically that we might be *brains* in a *vat*. But this specific description of what we might be was not important to him. And the important *sceptical* suggestion that things might not be as we experience them to be is left untouched by Putnam's arguments for the conclusion that we cannot be *BIVs*.

We can of course urge that for the sceptic's suggestion to be genuine, he would have to give it content by saying in what way things might be other than they seem. But the sceptic could reply by saying that he can always do this, simply by saying that the real world might *not* be A, B, and C, where A, B and C are features of the world as we experience it to be. The sceptic might accept that his question would be made more *pointed* if he could also give it positive content, by saying how things could in fact be, where this is other than they seem to be. But he need not accept that he is under an obligation to give it such content for the issue to be genuine. (Of course, if the argument in section 3.2 above is accepted, the sceptic could in fact also continue to hold the specific claim that we might be *BIVs*, without being troubled by the suggestion that as a brain in a vat he could not be considering this hypothesis.)

In this way it should be clear that, even if successful, Putnam's argument that we cannot be brains in vats does not amount to a satisfactory anti-*sceptical* proof. At most, what is shown to be impossible is not the deeper sceptical worry *that* things might not be as we experience them to be, but the specific and more pointed description of *what* it is that we might be. But this does not seem to be central to

3. Brains, Vats and Putnam's Internalist Approach 79

the sceptic's worry, and may be regarded as no more than a fancy dress intended to make the question more pointed. Schematically, the sceptic says (loosely) – for all we know the world might be like *this*. Putnam's argument, based on reference, at most shows that it could not be like *this*, insofar as 'this' would then have a different meaning and reference. But the basic point, that the world might not be as we experience it to be, still stands. This is why even if the argument in the previous section as to why it is not possible that we are *BIVs* is valid, it still does not amount to any serious anti-sceptical proof. Putnam's argument from reference simply does not carry us far enough.

3.5 *That Putnam, apart from not answering the sceptic, is in fact committed to such scepticism.*

The world may not be as we experience it to be. Putnam's argument does not suffice to defuse this possibility, insofar as his argument turns on reference to BIVs, whereas the sceptic's doubt does not presuppose the possibility of describing in any detail the content of *what* is real. It rather turns on the assumption *that* there is or might be something real, to which reference is made simply as that which is independent of all experience. And, as long as this ontological assumption remains uncontested, the kind of reference breakdown for which Putnam is arguing, far from answering the sceptic's doubt, would only seem to strengthen it.

In this section I will attempt to show how Putnam's general internalist approach indeed seems to encourage the sceptic's claim that the world may not be as we experience it to be. That Putnam is open to this sceptical doubt is implicit in his attack on the external realist's account of reference, and emerges quite clearly in his account of his own internalist approach.

Thus he says:

> Internalism does not deny that there are experiential inputs to knowledge; knowledge is not a story with no constraints except *internal* coherence; but it does deny that there are any inputs *which are not themselves to some extent shaped by our concepts*, by the vocabulary we use to report and describe them, or any inputs which admit of only one description, independent of all *conceptual choices*. ... The very inputs upon which our knowledge is based are conceptually contaminated; but contaminated inputs are better than none. If contaminated inputs are all we have, still all we have has proved to be quite a bit. (p. 54)

This talk of inputs is reminiscent of Quine's sensory inputs and raw experience. And the same point ought to be made with regard to such talk here as was made in discussing it above in the context of Quine's philosophy. Putnam, in talking of conceptually contaminated inputs, seems to be suggesting that there is something real which is the source of these inputs, but which we, conceptually contaminating creatures that we are, cannot know as such. If the 'very inputs upon which our knowledge is based are conceptually contaminated', we can say that there are presumed uncontaminated pre-inputs (this would be precisely the Kantian thing-in-itself) which we cannot directly refer to, since our referring to them would thereby contaminate them.

Putnam here follows Kant in giving up a theory of truth as correspondence to some real objects which are utterly independent of all experience. Truth is no longer correspondence, of the metaphysical realist kind, to independent objects. Truth is correspondence to objects-for-us. Objectivity is the objectivity of appearance. What we know are not things in themselves.[18]

Putnam's account is thus very similar to Kant's empirical realism and transcendental idealism. His internalist view is like Kant's empirical realism; what we know are objects for us. But like Kant he bases this internal realism on experiential *inputs*. This implies that he does not doubt that there is some independent reality, only like Kant claims that this is not what we have knowledge of, since we cannot refer to this as it is in itself, but only in the conceptually contaminated way in which things appear to us. And knowledge is of these contaminated appearances. In fact we have already seen (section 2.3) that in discussing Kant (on pp. 60-4) Putnam concedes that 'perhaps Kant is right: perhaps we can't help thinking that there is *somehow* a mind-independent "ground" for our experience even if attempts to talk about it lead at once to non-sense' (pp. 61-2). Indeed it would be odd if Putnam did *not* concede this, since his internalist account as it stands simply seems to presuppose some such mind-independent reality.

That some mind-independent (noumenal) reality is presupposed is apparent not merely in the above statement regarding experiential

---

[18] But just as BIVs could, we claimed, *consider* that they might be BIVs, so we seem able to consider that perhaps the mind-independent reality, uncontaminated, is as we experience it to be. For all that we have seen so far, we *can* think that it just might be that the independent world is like *this* ... If Putnam means to deny this possibility when he says 'Nothing at all we say about any object describes the object as it is "in itself"'(p. 61), he is again going further than his argument will allow (for the reasons outlined in section 3.2). As long as the notion of a world in itself is accepted, it would seem possible that we might suggest that that world is so-and-so..., and that in so saying we are describing it as it is in itself, even though we do not know it. Of course the fact that we might accidentally be getting it right about what the world is like would hardly suffice to meet the sceptic, who denies that we can *know* that we are getting it right.

3. Brains, Vats and Putnam's Internalist Approach

inputs, but also at various places throughout the book.[19] An example would be the treatment of the issue of survival and evolution, on pp. 38-41. There again the general thrust reveals Putnam acccepting that there is some external reality – only saying that there is no *'unique* correspondence (or even a reasonably narrow range of correspondence) between referring expressions and external objects' (p. 41). He appears to assume a reality 'out there', which controls evolution and produces representation systems whose sentences are mainly true. It is just that the truth of whole sentences does not determine the reference of the sentence parts. Putnam seems to be saying that for survival all theories must have in common that they are to some extent determined by the world, by reality; only he also thinks that they are essentially underdetermined by the world – so that they all agree with the world so far as to allow for survival, yet there is no one true theory that corresponds to the way of the world.[20] The requirements of survival could all be met, and still large differences between theories be allowed. The world, although it partly moulds our theories by trial and error, still leaves room for variance. As he puts it in 'Realism and Reason', 'It is a property of the world itself, I claimed – i.e. a property of THE WORLD itself – that it "admits of these different mappings"' (p. 132). Thus reality, although there is one (and this is the point to be made here), cannot go so far as to determine reference of any single term – or even to narrow significantly the range of possible correspondences.

We have seen that the Brains in the Vat argument, even if its various stages were acceptable, would not substantiate an anti-sceptical proof. The sceptic's doubt – that the world may not be as it is experienced to be – does not depend on reference to *what* the independent way of the world is, and so is immune to argument based solely on the failure of such reference. In view of what has been said in this section so far, it is now possible to go further by saying that, apart from the fact that the BIV case does not substantiate an anti-sceptical proof, Putnam's general internalist position actually strongly suggests this doubt. To get off the ground such doubt requires only the assumption that there is something independently real, along with the absence of any *accepted guarantee* that we must succeed in matching our beliefs to it. And we have just seen that Putnam's internalism amounts to just this by committing him to there being some

---

[19] In correspondence based on this chapter Putnam has assured me that in fact he does not believe that the notion of a 'mind-independent' or 'noumenal' world makes sense. I should therefore emphasise that I am referring to his published position, which does seem to *accept* the Kantian noumenal backdrop, and which at any rate, as we have seen, offers no argument against the notion of some such noumenal world.

[20] A point which emerges even more clearly in 'Realism and Reason', op. cit.

independent reality (thing in itself), which he holds is not what our knowledge is of (transcendental idealism). To encourage this doubt we do not need to assume that we can refer to the way this independent reality is.[21] On the contrary, this doubt is strongly suggested by the argument for the impossibility of reference to the independent way of the world.

It might be thought that *this* is enough to show that Putnam is in fact not merely open to the doubt, but is actually committed to the claim that the world is not as we know it. But from the fact that there is said to be something real and that this is not what we know, it does not follow that the independent world is not as we know it. It follows only that we cannot remove the doubt that it might not be. We have no reason to think that it *is* as we know it, but it nevertheless *might* be. This is why I say only that Putnam's internalism strongly suggests the sceptic's *doubt*, rather than that it entails the validity of the claim that the world is not as we experience it to be.

Far from refuting the sceptic who suggests that the world might not be as we experience it, Putnam's internalist account, following Kant's, suggests that the sceptic's doubt is entirely appropriate: that the world is perhaps not what we experience it to be. The redeeming feature of this Kantian account is that it does at least push this doubt 'out', so that it applies only to the noumenal world, thereby securing empirical realism from empirical idealism, at the cost of transcendental idealism. Although more palatable, this does still involve conceding to the sceptic that ultimately the world is perhaps not as we experience it to be. Thus whereas Putnam initially seemed to be proposing an answer to this sceptic, he turns out to have fallen rather closely in line with him.

But this might not seem to be quite right. At this point an objection which has been held off must be introduced. I have said that Putnam seems to acknowledge that the world may not be as we know it. That perhaps the world is not the way we experience it to be. But this seems to assume that there is a way that the world is, apart from the way we experience it, apart from our point of view. However, on Putnam's internalist account 'there are only the various points of view of actual persons' – there is no God's eye point of view that we can know or usefully imagine. For the internalist there is no talk of the way the world independently is. According to Putnam's internalist, there *is* something independent, real, as we have seen, but it apparently makes no sense to talk about *the way* that real something really is, apart from all points of view. And insofar as this is the position, it does not seem to

---

[21] Which is why Putnam's argument on the BIV case, turning as it does on the reliability of reference, did not defuse this doubt but only, at most, the more specific doubt which tries to suggest *what* this independent reality might be.

be quite right to accuse this internalist of leaving room for the doubt that perhaps the world is not the way we experience it to be. This would attribute to the internalist a view which he rejects. He *has*, it seems, accepted *that* there is something real, but is attempting to drive a wedge between that claim and the assertion that there is a *way* that real something really is, which he rejects.

Now perhaps Putnam's internalist would, if faced with this analysis, baulk and say that this is not what he meant to hold, and that either he was guilty of careless argument, or I was guilty of careless analysis. If however he would choose to maintain that this analysis is indeed acceptable to him, he faces the task of showing that this wedge can be made to hold fast. It is not at all clear to me that this can be done. It is one thing to say that all we have is knowledge of appearances (empirical realism) not of what is independently real, the thing in itself. This leaves it open to say that there is a real world, to which we can make impoverished reference, and that although this is not what our knowledge is of, there is presumably also a way that that independent world is. On this view, the Kantian accepts the sceptic's point that perhaps the way of the world is not as we experience it to be, merely making this doubt less worrying insofar as it applies only to the noumenal world, while the empirical world is now exempted, protected, from this doubt. But on the more radical view, which seems to be the one Putnam's internalist has opted for, or at any rate ended up with, it is not merely that our knowledge is of appearances and not of the way of the independent world; but furthermore that although there is some independent reality, it only makes sense to talk of the way the world is from some point of view, so that there *is* no *way* that the world itself is. It is not merely that we cannot know what is real – but that it is not even the case that what is real *is* one way rather than another, independently of us.

The difference between the two views can be brought out using the notions of secondary and primary qualities. Putnam says, on p. 61, in interpreting Kant, that all properties are secondary. Now this can mean, unproblematically, that we only ever have knowledge (experience) of secondary properties – the way things are for us. It then remains to say either that there are no other properties, or that there are primary qualities, which constitute the way the real world is independently, but that we cannot have experience of them. On the latter view we have the Kantian view as assumed above, which does allow the sceptic's doubt. But the statement that all properties are secondary might be taken to mean that all properties are properties for us – that it is not merely that we cannot experience primary properties, properties of the independent world, but that there are none, even though there *is* an independent world. It is simply not the case that the world independent of us has, as such, any properties. There just is no *way* the world independently is, although there is an independent world.[22]

In places, however, Putnam does say things that suggest that perhaps he is, after all, not holding this extreme view. Thus he says, p. 61, 'Nothing at all we say about any object describes the object as it is 'in itself', independently of its effect on *us*...'. This seems to presuppose that there *is* a way the object (world) is 'in itself' – it is merely that nothing we say describes it. To the extent that Putnam is not merely giving Kant's view at this point, which he very well might be doing since it appears in a section on Kant, our conclusion that Putnam's account strongly suggests the sceptic's worry was correct, and the objection we are at present considering comes to nothing.

But if Putnam is indeed saying that, apart from the fact that all properties in experience are secondary, it is further the case that there are no properties of the real world which are not secondary, this objection must be considered. Putnam, as we have seen, does still seem to hold that there is an independent ground to our experience, so if all properties are secondary, not merely in the weak sense that we can only know secondary properties, but in the stronger sense that there just are no other (primary) properties, i.e. there just are no properties independent of what we can know, Putnam is indeed asserting not merely that what we know is not the way of the independent noumenal world, but furthermore that there just is no way the independent, noumenal world is. And if this is the case, it cannot be right to accuse Putnam of accepting the sceptic's doubt that perhaps the way the world is is not the way we experience it to be. There *is* no way the world independently is.

In view of this objection it is necessary to pause before proceeding

---

[22] This more radical view, of a world which exists independently of all experience and yet is wholly indeterminate, might seem reminiscent of some things Dummett has suggested. Dummett talks, e.g. in the Preface to *Truth and Other Enigmas* (London, Duckworth, 1978) p. xxix, of an external reality which is not fully determinate. In the same volume, in 'Wittgenstein's Philosophy of Mathematics', he also talks of a world becoming determinate in the course of our experience. But he does not commit himself to it being an independently pre-existing world which is wholly indeterminate until we experience it. All he says is that we could 'interpose between the platonist and the constructivist picture an indeterminate picture, say of objects springing into being in response to our probing' (p. 185). Again, in 'Truth' (same volume) he says, 'We could have instead a picture of a mathematical reality not already in existence but as it were coming into being as we probe. Our investigations bring into existence what was not there before, but what they bring into existence is not of our own making' (p. 18). This idea remains obscure, but it does not seem to involve a world which exists independently of our experience in some indeterminate state, and which then becomes determinate upon our experiencing it. The idea is not of objects that were already there, existing in a wholly indeterminate way. Yet it is this more extreme idea that Putnam's view would seem to involve.

3. Brains, Vats and Putnam's Internalist Approach

with an answer to it, in order to correct something that was said before. I said that to accept that there is something real (without providing acceptable guarantees that this is what we know) is sufficient to allow the sceptic's doubt that perhaps the world is not the way we experience it to be. But I was there simply assuming that to say that there *is* something entails that it is of some nature, whether or not we can know it. That to say that x exists, just is to say that, known or unknown, x has some property. Or, loosely, the assumption was that to assert *that*, presupposes the meaningfulness of asking *what*. This was the hidden assumption, which seemed so unassailable as not to warrant discussion. It seemed reasonable that if something is said to be independently real, it is legitimate to ask whether it is as we experience it to be; and that in the absence of accepted guarantees the question gains force. Thus we argued that:

if

(1) x is real, and
(3) We experience x in a certain way (i.e. as having certain properties),

then

(4) It is legitimate to ask whether, independently of our experience of it, x is the way we experience it to be.

But we now see that in addition to this, there was a concealed premiss:

(2) If it is the case that x is real, it is the case that independently of our experience of it, x has some property.

On the more radical interpretation now being considered, the internalist is trying to drive a wedge in between the assertion 'that' and the question 'what?'. He is denying premiss (2). He is, as we have seen, accepting *that* there is some reality independent of experience, some noumenal thing-in-itself (the uncontaminated source of experiential input); but is then denying that this has any independent properties – that there is some way in which it is, quite apart from the way we experience it to be. It is said both *that* it is real *and* that it is not real in *any determinate way*, i.e. it has no independent properties.

To return now to the objection: It is in fact doubtful whether this wedge between the 'that' and the 'what' can be made to hold fast. For one thing, to say that there is a noumenal world but that it has no independent properties seems very much like ascribing a property to it – namely, that of not having any. Secondly, it is not clear that it really is coherent to assert that there is some*thing*, and to deny that it is some*how* (as opposed to denying merely that we can know what it is). But to the extent that the internalist *is* making this more radical claim, does this mean that he is not prone to the sceptic's doubt that perhaps the world is not as we experience it to be?

I think not. The sceptic can come back with one of two replies. In the first he can simply concede this, and phrase his point differently, thus: that what we know is not what is ultimately real. *This* is a point that even our more radical internalist will not merely have to allow, but in fact endorse. For *this* point, unlike the previous one, makes no assumptions that there is a way that that independent reality is. It does indeed turn on no more than the assumption that there is something real, independently of experience. Given that, we can legitimately *ask* whether that is what we know. And the Putnam internalist, even of the more radical kind, having allowed that there is some reality independent of all experience, and further that this is not what we have knowledge of, is thus trivially committed to agreeing with the sceptic who suggests that perhaps what we know is not what is independently real. This is, as we said above, made philosophically palatable by still leaving room for empirical realism. The concession to the sceptic that the internalist is forced to make, merely in virtue of saying that there is some mind-independent reality, might be captured by this formulation of it: However perfect our knowledge, we can in principle never have knowledge of that which is real. There will always be something real (i.e. that independent world) of which we have no knowledge. This formulation of the sceptical worry makes no mention of the *way of* the independent world, and in this form even the more radical internalist is committed to it.

The second reply the sceptic can make to the more radical internalist who denies that there is a way that the real world independently is, while accepting that there is some real world, would be simply this. As we experience it, there *is* a way the world is (in general terms). So if it is then said that there is *no* way the independent world independently is, it follows trivially that our doubt whether the world is really the way we experience it to be was justified. This reply does not necessarily trade on the fact mentioned above, that to say that there is no way the independent world is is itself to ascribe a property to it and hence to describe the way it is.

So, to conclude this section, we have seen that not only does the BIV case not provide an anti-sceptical proof (section 3.4), but Putnam's general internalist account, however interpreted, in fact seems to fall in with just this kind of doubt.

3.6 How could the metaphysical realist be attacked without this inviting the sceptic?

We see that so far the internalist, however radical, cannot quite avoid allowing, if not endorsing, some form of this scepticism. The sceptic's general question – 'How do we know that the world is as we experience it to be?' (or, 'Can we know that which is real?') – has remained potent throughout the discussion. I would now like to emphasise why this is so, and what the significance of this is.

Remember, that in the last chapter I noted the gap that was left after Strawson had rejected Kant's response to the sceptic's question without first defusing that question. It should, in view of the present discussion, be still clearer that Kant's transcendental idealism is not so much an answer, but rather part of a sophisticated ploy for tranferring the *unanswered* problem to the noumenal world where it can rage unanswered without bothering us in our empirical realism. Given that Kant could not answer the sceptic's question, he did the next best thing. He exiled it. And the *reason* why Kant could not answer the sceptic is that in his transcendental idealism Kant still accepted that there is some real world. It is not possible to refute the sceptic finally while still asserting that something is real; or indeed while still asserting merely that there either is or is not something real. For this is precisely what fuels the sceptic's question.

The very importance of the sceptic is, in fact, that he will continue to voice his opinion loudly – like a patient in symptomatic pain – forcing philosophers to consider issues further, until they identify the cause of the sceptic's problem. Nothing short of this will assuage the sceptic, and hence his importance as a philosopher's unwitting compass. The only final answer to the sceptic's question, as opposed to the Kantian ploy for locking it up, is to *undercut* it by identifying the error upon which it thrives. Only then will the sceptic, including the one in Kantian exile, be defused. This is why it is significant that even after the attack on the metaphysical realist, the sceptic is not satisfied, and still goes on asking the same questions as before; and this is why I have concentrated on the relation between Putnam's internalism and scepticism in this chapter. Although I obviously agree with Putnam's attack on metaphysical realism, by concentrating on the more sensitive issue of the sceptic we shall be able to make satisfactory headway towards identifying the central problematic issue that underlies his and other ontological positions. The attack on the metaphysical realist, even once it is completed, still leaves us only half way. That this cannot adequately be seen as an end of the matter is evident from the survival of the sceptic. By concentrating on the sceptic's problem we will direct ourselves further down the same path.

Putnam is, as should by now be quite clear, primarily interested in attacking the metaphysical realist. His argument is directed at the kind of reference involved in such an account. As we have seen, such an argument can at most show that we cannot even consider (let alone know) *what* is independently real. This argument, while perhaps strong enough to cripple the metaphysical realist, is too weak to meet the sceptical question. This question rests primarily on the premiss that there is – or might be – some reality independent of all experience. The obvious way then effectively to attack this sceptic is by focussing on the notion of there being something which is or is not independent of all experience. In fact we should concentrate on this notion since it is of independent interest, quite apart from the sceptic's problem, which merely points the way.

To make clearer the difference between this approach and Putnam's, we might turn to a statement of his approach as it appears in a paper published after *Reason, Truth and History*. Towards the end of 'Why There Isn't a Ready-Made World'[23] Putnam writes of the view he is criticising:

> The approach to which I have devoted this lecture is an approach which claims [1] that there *is* a 'transcendental' reality in Kant's sense, one absolutely independent of our minds, [2] that the regulative ideal of knowledge *is* to copy it or put our thoughts in correspondence with it, ...

Now although there is a distinction here between the ontological and epistemological claims which I have numbered [1] and [2], Putnam does not take heed of this distinction either here or in the argument and structure of the paper. As in *RT&H*, he focusses his attack on this metaphysical realist view by arguing solely against [2] – against the kind of reference involved in our knowledge *copying* a ready-made reality. This, as we have seen, might be enough to make life uncomfortable for the metaphysical realist, but it is not strong enough to answer the sceptic.

And when it comes to considering the claim made in [1], that there is a 'transcendental' reality in Kant's sense, Putnam says very little, and omits a critical discussion of the issue. He seems, in fact, to be unsure of what to say. He says:

> I am not inclined to scoff at the idea of a noumenal ground behind the dualities of experience, even if all attempts to talk about it lead to antinomies. Analytic philosophers have always tried to dismiss the transcendental as nonsense, but it does have an eerie way of reappearing. (For one thing, almost every philosopher makes statements

---

[23] *Synthese*, May 1982, pp. 162-3. Reprinted in *Realism and Reason, Collected Papers*, vol. 3, CUP, 1983.

3. Brains, Vats and Putnam's Internalist Approach 89

which contradict his own explicit account of what can be justified or known ... For another, almost everyone regards the statement that there is *no* mind-independent reality, that there are *just* the 'versions', or there is just 'discourse', or whatever, as itself intensely paradoxical.) Because one cannot talk about the transcendent or even deny its existence without paradox, one's attitude to it must, perhaps, be the concern of religion rather than of rational philosophy. (p. 163)

While this latter might be an approximately sound sentiment, this way to it is much too quick. Putnam is evidently unsure of what he should do about the claim that there is something real, some transcendental reality, and this is why he concentrates his attack on the metaphysical realist on the notion of reference [2] and, when it comes to talk of there being something real [1], he rather vaguely mentions that although many have tried to dismiss it, it reappears obstinately. While it is clear that he tends to accept rather than reject the notion of a noumenal world, he does so rather hesitantly, divorcing the issue from the bulk of his argument by relegating it into parentheses, and then on into the remote domain of religion.

Similarly, as we have seen, in *RT&H* Putnam says (p. 61):

Today the notion of a noumenal world is perceived to be an unnecessary metaphysical element in Kant's thought. (But perhaps Kant is right: perhaps we can't help thinking that there is...)

Again we find parenthetic acceptance of the realist's notion *that* there is a noumenal reality, a reality independent of our minds; leaving the rest of the book, free of any discussion of this point, to concentrate the attack on metaphysical realism entirely via the idea of knowledge as correspondence to this reality (claim [2]). But this at most shows, to repeat what we have said, that the metaphysical realist is in trouble, that we cannot have the kind of knowledge he desires, that we cannot know what the world independently is – *not* that it cannot be the case that the sceptic is right in saying that perhaps the world is not as we experience it to be.

For *this* Putnam would have to engage in critical discussion of the notion (above [1]) that there is a real (noumenal) world, something independently real. He would have to meet this ontological claim head on within the context of his 'rational philosophy', rather than accepting it in parenthetic asides and then, after exiling further discussion of it to a monastery, proceeding to focus exclusively on the issue of reference. Had he done this he would have realised that while *denying* that there is an ontologically independent reality indeed involves paradox, it is not the case that the philosopher either asserts or denies that there is some such reality, or else in desperation becomes religious. There is room to examine whether these two are indeed coherent as philosophical contradictories. (If not, then the issue would not be whether to affirm, deny or mystify some noumenal world, but rather to *show* that it is necessary to avoid the very introduction of the question.)

Why is it that Putnam does not turn to discuss more seriously (i.e. in more than parenthetic asides) his tacit acceptance of the realist notion *that* there is something real? Well, obviously, part of the reason is precisely that Putnam is primarily concerned to argue against the metaphysical realist position he once held, and for that the argument from reference seems to be strong enough, and there is no reason for philosophical overkill. Had he been more concerned to answer the sceptic, he might have seen reason to proceed further to discuss the notion of there being something real in a less parenthetic manner. As his interests stand, however, the argument from reference might seem able enough to take him as far as he wants to go. This is probably the main reason why Putnam does not discuss, but merely accepts parenthetically, the notion of there being an independent reality. He has not got his eye trained on the same philosophical compass. He is not attempting to go any further than he does.

But underlying his reluctance to discuss this issue there is a serious philosophical tension, which itself can explain the cautious and parenthetic nature of his commitment to there being something real, some thing-in-itself. On the one hand, Putnam wants to avoid the 'quicksands of relativism' ('Why There Isn't a Ready-Made World', p. 162) which might seem to follow from saying that there is no mind-independent reality, only different versions, only discourse. It is to avoid this 'anything goes' view that Putnam wants to hold on to the notion of there being some independent world.[24] Or, as we found him saying in *RT&H* (quoted in full in previous section):

> Internalism is not a facile relativism that says, 'Anything goes'. Denying that it makes sense to ask whether our concepts 'match' something totally uncontaminated by conceptualisation is one thing; but to hold that every conceptual system is therefore just as good as every other would be something else... Internalism does not deny that there are experiential *inputs* to knowledge; knowledge is not a story with no constraints except *internal* coherence; ... The very inputs upon which our knowledge is based are conceptually contaminated; but contaminated inputs are better than none.

Again, Putnam here does not *explicitly* commit himself to accepting

---

[24] The idea is that some such world could, at least in part, determine our theories; in this connection see the discussion of survival and evolution, *RT&H*, pp. 38-41.

that there is an independent reality, but this is surely a presupposition of his talking about experiental inputs in this context (i.e. as constituting constraints on relativism).[25] So, one reason for his tendency to accept that there is an independent reality is the hope that it would stop him from falling into 'anything goes' relativism. Another is that it seems impossible to *deny* that there is something real without paradox. These are perhaps reasons why Putnam is 'not inclined to scoff at the idea of a noumenal ground'. On the other hand, however, is the fact that all attempts to talk about the independent reality lead to antinomies – one cannot even talk about it without paradox. This constitutes a pull in the opposite direction, against accepting that there is a noumenal reality. These conflicting reasons reveal some of the philosophical tension that underlies Putnam's relegation of his commitment to a noumenal reality to parenthetic remarks.

But there is more than this tension behind Putnam's unclear position on the issue of noumenal reality. There is reason why Putnam in particular cannot simply accept that there is an independent reality, even if he settled the above tension. Putnam wants to deny that there is a ready-made world. (The *title* of the above-mentioned paper is 'Why There Isn't a Ready-Made World'). But he does not want to deny that there is a noumenal world – to avoid 'anything goes' relativism he wants to hold on to some mind-independent reality from which we have inputs, however contaminated. This means accepting that there is an independent world, while denying that there is a ready-made world. There is an independent reality, but there is no way that this independent reality independently is. And we have already seen that it is difficult to explain how a wedge can be driven in between being x, and x's being a certain way. If anything, it would then seem that not-being-ready-made is the way this independent reality is ready-made. So, given the difficulty of keeping this wedge in place, it becomes very difficult for Putnam to hold both that there isn't a ready-made world *and* that there is an independent world. Insofar as he wants to hold the former, he seems compelled to give up the latter. And yet, giving up the noumenal world, Putnam's internal realist suspects, would plunge his internalist account into extreme relativism, which he wants to avoid. Putnam seems to be in the unfortunate position of wanting both to keep the cake whole and to eat it.

Putnam fails to make explicit the tension between these two strands

[25] It could, of course, be argued that it was the common source of *contamination*, rather than of the *inputs*, that blocked 'anything goes' relativism. That is, something to do with the nature of our experience, rather than of the world beyond. This is a reasonable line of argument. However, it seems evident that this is not what Putnam has in mind. It is not the contamination that is doing the work – it is the inputs that can do it *despite* contamination: contaminated inputs are better than none, but uncontaminated inputs, the implication is, would be better yet.

of his internalist position: on the one hand, that there is no ready-made world, on the other, that to avoid extreme relativism we assume that there is a noumenal reality (the source of these contaminated inputs). He could not have entertained both without the question of their compatibility emerging, if it were not for the fact that he avoids explicitly discussing the notion of there being an independent reality. And he could not have avoided this discussion if, instead of concentrating on arguing against the metaphysical realist, he had given more thought to the sceptic. (Again, the importance of the sceptic as a philosophical compass emerges.) It would then have emerged quite clearly that, even if his specific argument from reference is sufficient to cripple the metaphysical realist, Putnam cannot regard that as a satisfactory end of the issue, insofar as his own alternative internalist account stumbles on the issue of whether there is some real world, however noumenal.

Thus, underlying the innocent-looking relegation of the noumenal issue to parentheses, or out of 'rational' philosophy altogether, there lies a real philosophical impasse in which Putnam's internalist finds himself. There is good reason why Putnam should be unsure what to do with the claim that there is a noumenal world. To imply that there is a noumenal reality and then skirt around a *discussion* of this issue – enclosing it in brackets or exiling it beyond the philosophical domain – will not do. It would seem that even for his purposes the argument from reference must be supplemented by further consideration of the notion of there being some independently real world.

At any rate the fact is that Putnam does not engage in a critical discussion of the notion that there is some noumenal real world. He rather concentrates on the issues of reference and correspondence. This might enable him to argue against the metaphysical realist account of knowledge, but leaves him open to the sceptical doubt that the world may not be as we know it. To argue against this sceptic (although – as we have seen – not only, or primarily, for this reason) we would have to discuss the premiss shared by both this sceptic and the metaphysical realist (and Putnam's internalist): *that there is – or might be – an independently real x (world)*. This is precisely the ontological notion that lets in the sceptic.

3.7 From Putnam to the present enquiry

Putnam's attack takes the form of arguing – against the metaphysical realist's *epistemological* thesis – that we could not have knowledge of an ontologically independent ready-made world. The present inquiry focusses rather on whether we should accept talk of there *being*

3. Brains, Vats and Putnam's Internalist Approach

something real. Apart from whether we could *know what* is real, apart from whether truth can be defined as correspondence to what is real, there is the issue of whether we are even in a position to consider *that* there is, or even might be, something real in the first place.[26] It should be clear that these two approaches are not incompatible. It should also be clear now that the present approach is, in a sense already indicated in the first chapter, the more basic of the two, insofar as its results determine the possibility of getting the other project underway, and not vice versa. If it were to emerge as incoherent to consider that there is something real, it would not be necessary to show that we cannot *know* it. But, given only that it is not possible to know that which is real, it still remains reasonable to assume that there *is* something real, only *that* is not what we have knowledge of. And it is clear that in this latter situation we are still prone to the sceptical doubt that perhaps the world is not as we experience it to be. Only by making the more basic claim against the metaphysical realist's *ontological* thesis could we possibly hope to defuse this sceptic's question as well.

---

[26] The idea would not be to combat realism with idealism: Putnam might be right in saying that it is intensely paradoxical to say that there is *nothing* independent of experience. The attempt would rather be to show that there is no room for *any* use of such ontological talk.

4. Goodman: Final Focus of the Philosophical Perspective

I turn now to Nelson Goodman's relativist approach in *Ways of Worldmaking*.[1] An examination of Goodman's position, and of certain problems pertaining to it, will occupy the first half of this chapter. This will lead on to a more adequate conception of the framework of the present enquiry in the second part of the chapter.

4.1 The 'irrealist' direction in ways of worldmaking

Goodman would have us accept unequivocally that all we have are descriptions; that it is wrong to regard them as descriptions of an independent underlying reality. It could seem, from this, that he might be rejecting the idea of some underlying substance for just the reasons which made Locke suspicious of that notion, and which led Hume to reject it finally. However, this is not the case. Goodman is not merely pointing out that all we have is the complication of many simple ideas joined together, or bundles of perceptions. He is not rejecting the notion of an underlying ontological reality on the basis of an argument from empiricist epistemology, to the effect that the given bundle of discrete perceptions does not sustain a belief in some underlying substance. He adds an element of relativism; and can be seen as making the point that we do not even have a single fixed set or bundle of perceptions to begin with.

Rather than any one correct set of secondary properties, there are infinite possible ascriptions of properties, endless possible descriptions. These descriptions vary according to the conceptual framework or 'version' (the term Goodman uses) at hand. Different versions identify objects differently, or perhaps simply identify different objects. Such versions might individuate the world so differently as to make it

---

[1] Nelson Goodman, *Ways of Worldmaking*, Hassocks, Harvester Press, 1978. Further page references in this chapter will be to this text.

4. Goodman: Final Focus of the Philosophical Perspective

difficult to render them compatible.[2] We can strip away one particular description, to reveal another. We can exchange that for yet another. We can go on indefinitely.

Goodman thus proposes to sell us radical relativism. This effort is in obvious continuity with his earlier work, both in *The Structure of Appearance* and in *Fact, Fiction and Forecast*.[3] The problem of distinguishing between lawlike and accidental hypotheses, between projectible and non-projectible descriptions is at the root of *Ways of Worldmaking*. Goodman seems to be suggesting that we ought to embrace boldly the conclusion that a grue version just is every bit as acceptable as a green one. He insists, in several places, that this is not an irresponsible 'anything goes' relativism:

> What I have said so far plainly points to a radical relativism; but severe restraints are imposed. Willingness to accept countless true or right world-versions does not mean that everything goes, that tall stories are as good as short ones... but only that truth must be otherwise conceived than as correspondence with a ready-made world. (p. 94)

Nevertheless we have little more than his insistence to go on. He does not really explain what these severe restraints are, or how they work.

Putnam, in his attack on the metaphysical realist, goes some way down this same path. Following Goodman, he seems willing to go so far as to give up a ready-made world – but, as we have seen, he stops there, subject to some degree of hesitation.[4] Goodman, on the other hand, is considerably less apprehensive. He is prepared to give up altogether the idea of a reality independent of all versions which we might have in our experience. The point is that once we have allowed for all the different descriptions, each right by their own lights, the real world to which they might all be directed is forced back to a mere noumenal status. We cannot say anything more of it than that it is the world of which all those theories are true. This Kantian thing in itself, at which Putnam is still loath to scoff, is one which Goodman is quite willing to reject. Goodman thus accepts that all we have are versions – that there is no reality which all these versions might have been of:

---

[2] See, for some problematic cases, Putnam's 'stories' in 'Realism and Reason', op. cit., pp. 130-3.

[3] *The Structure of Appearance*, Dordrecht, Reidel, 1977 (3rd edition). *Fact, Fiction and Forecast*, Hassocks, Harvester Press, 1979 (3rd edition).

[4] We saw in the last chapter what the reasons for his hesitation might be: namely, the concern to avoid an 'anything goes' relativism, and the fact that the noumenal has a strange way of reappearing. Clearly, the danger of an 'anything goes' relativism cannot be ignored. Goodman claims not to ignore it but still leaves it unclear what distinguishes tall from short versions. I will attempt to indicate a way in which, even without the hard-rock of the real world, we can still avoid such philosophical relativism (see below, Chapter 8, on perspectival ascent).

> When we strip off as layers of convention all differences among ways of describing *it*, what is left? The onion is peeled down to its empty core. (p. 118)

> ...if we abstract from all features responsible for disagreements between truths we have nothing left but versions without things or facts or worlds. (p. 119)

For Goodman, reality is always *only* the reality within a version:

> This world, indeed, is the one most often taken as real; for reality in a world, like realism in a picture, is largely a matter of habit... Not only motion, derivation, weighting, order but even reality is relative. (p. 20, §1.6, 'Relative Reality')

This suggests a point of similarity with Quine's ontological relativity: For Quine an ontological commitment is always internal to a theory. Just as Goodman believes that we are essentially confined to one *version* or another, so Quine would have us confined to *theories*.[5]

However, there are certain differences between Quine and Goodman; Quine exhibits a bias for the physicist's description or version of the world, while Goodman, more consistently, holds that there is nothing particularly prior or basic about any one version. He does not share Quine's view that ultimately only physics can offer a true description of the world.[6] This difference perhaps reflects the deeper difference between Quine and Goodman. As I have pointed out above (and see also Putnam, ibid., Introduction, p. xiii) Quine allows the confinement to theories to rest on a background of transcendental idealism – on the assumption that beyond all theories lies some noumenal reality. It is possibly because of *this* commitment that Quine can assume that the world does have a single true physical description. Goodman goes further than Quine, insofar as he boldly rejects this idea, leaving us with *nothing* beyond the different versions. Thus on the same page he poses the question and his answer to it:

> Shouldn't we stop speaking of right versions as if each were, or had, its own world, and recognise all as versions of one and the same neutral and underlying world? The world thus regained, as remarked earlier, is a

---

[5] In conversation and, I believe, in a forthcoming book, George Secada has aptly suggested calling this 'Quine's theoricity'.

[6] This point is emphasised by Putnam in 'Reflections on Goodman's *Ways of Worldmaking*', in *Realism and Reason – Philosophical Papers*, vol. 3, pp. 164-5. In this paper, as in the introduction to the entire volume, Putnam perhaps seems to be closer to Goodman's position than the exposition of his views in *Reason, Truth and History*, and in 'Why there Isn't a Ready-Made World' op. cit., or 'Realism and Reason', op. cit. would

4. Goodman: Final Focus of the Philosophical Perspective

world without kinds or order or motion or rest or pattern – a world not worth fighting for or against.

This world which is not worth fighting for or against is supposedly that rudimentary trace of reality which Kant called the thing-in-itself. It should be noted, however, that in fact what is being said to be *rudimentary* here is not, as Goodman assumes, an independent reality, but rather our possible *knowledge* of one. This might explain why Goodman will not manage to convince the realist that this kind of reality is not worth fighting for or against. This is a point to which I will come back shortly.

The point for now is that Goodman is prepared to give up quite unequivocally the Kantian thing-in-itself, and it is precisely here that Goodman moves still further than Putnam or Quine. Quine still seems at least to allow a backdrop of transcendental idealism; Putnam's internal realist strongly invites it. Goodman, however, is quite prepared to take the plunge: to reject even the element of ontological realism which is involved in transcendental idealism.

> The message, I take it, is simply this: never mind mind, essence is not essential, and matter doesn't matter. We do better to focus on versions rather than worlds. (p. 96)

> This does not mean, I must repeat, that right versions can be arrived at casually, or that worlds are built from scratch. We start, on any occasion, with some old version or world that we have on hand and that we are stuck with until we have the determination and skill to remake it into a new one. Some of the felt stubbornness of fact is the grip of habit: our firm foundation is indeed stolid. Worldmaking begins with one version and ends with another. (p. 97)

4.2 The difference between Goodman's position and the present concern

I would now like to single out three features central to this programmatic attack that Goodman launches against realism. Contrast with these features will further reveal the nature of, and the need for, a somewhat different project.

---

allow. There, as we have seen, he seems to *presuppose* or at least *allow*, however unwillingly, that there is some noumenal world (see 2.3 and 3.5-6 above). See also Quine's review of *Ways of Worldmaking* in the *New York Review of Books*, 25 November 1978.

4.2.1 The force of the argument for irrealism

In the first place, although the position of 'irrealism' which Goodman promotes is rather extreme, and the rhetoric of its exposition is colourful, the actual argument to the effect that we should give up the commitment to a reality which is ontologically independent of all experience, is rather weak.

The rejection of the idea of an underlying independent reality rests on the hope that once we have whittled away at it – so that it is not the ready-made world of the metaphysical realist, but merely a vague noumenal reality, a totally neutral world, without kinds or order or motion or rest or pattern – what we are left with will be a world not worth fighting for or against. Given Goodman's Ockhamism, this would be sufficient reason to reject it. But his rejection rests on no more that this. Indeed Goodman does not think that there is anything *wrong* with the ontological notion of an independent reality, as such. Thus, on p. 4:

> while the underlying world, bereft of these [right versions], need not be denied to those who love it, it is perhaps on the whole a world well lost.

The phrase 'a world well lost' here alludes to Rorty's paper which bears this phrase as its title.[7]

The allusion is appropriate. Goodman merely repeats Rorty's sentiment that the belief in an ontologically independent world is an obsession which could just as well be discarded. He does not attempt to argue directly against the assertion that there is some ontologically independent reality; and he definitely does not go further to question whether the very notion of an ontologically independent reality is in fact coherent. He would only have the reader concede that, in the watered-down form to which he has reduced it, it is totally ineffectual.

Consequently he is prepared, albeit disdainfully, to allow it to those who love it. He merely hopes to have persuaded the reader that it is not worth arguing for or against it.

But, despite the force of Ockhamism, the fact that something is not *worth* fighting for does not actually entail, either in logical or in practical terms, that it is not nevertheless fought for. Furthermore, it might be claimed that Goodman has not even shown that a reality whittled down to a mere thing-in-itself is indeed not worth fighting for. After all, what has been whittled away are merely our claims to *knowledge* of an independent reality. It might be thought, quite plausibly, that such reality, however impoverished our epistemic

---

[7] 'The World Well Lost', op. cit.

access to it might be, could still in fact exert a massive structuring effect on our experience – of the kind which could serve to contain relativism. If the watering down of the independent reality is seen in this light, as restricted to the epistemological level, that independent reality might still seem to be very much the kind of thing worth fighting for.

Besides, the inclination to recognise some independent reality, even as a mere thing-in-itself, rests not so much on the argued conviction that it is *worth* fighting *for*, but rather on the fact that it is so intuitive. Goodman's reply to any such appeal to intuition is that the notion of there being an independent reality is only intuitive as a result of our entrenched habit of taking it that there is some such reality. But this will not do, for it remains to explain why the habit became so well entrenched in the first place. And it would seem feasible to say that one obvious explanation for its becoming so well entrenched is simply that it gets things *right* – which would render the intuition reliable, regardless of whether it is taken to sustain, or to be sustained by, the force of habit. Consequently the onus is on Goodman to show why such an apparently intuitive notion is not worth fighting for or against, just as the onus lies with Rorty to prove that it is in fact an *obsession* rather than an *intuition*. Merely to say that such a reality is not worth fighting for or against not only does not, in itself, put an end to such fighting, but in fact should incline us to accept the apparently more intuitive of the two opposed views.

It is for this reason that I think a stronger argument is needed for rejecting the concern with an independent reality. Such an argument would show that there is something wrong with this concern, so that quite apart from whether it is worth fighting for or against the realist's ontological conviction, it simply *cannot* be fought for, at least not within the context of critical philosophy. Until this is shown, any philosopher still enchanted with the notion of an independent reality (for good, bad or no reasons) will see no need to discard it and follow Goodman into his position of irrealism. Rather, such a realist philosopher would stick to his intuitions and try to meet Goodman's arguments in the hope of reestablishing that 'independent reality' in a less rudimentary way, or at least in one that made it more obviously worth defending.

4.2.2 The ambiguity of 'irrealism'

Secondly, and more significantly, Goodman's position leaves a crucial ambiguity unflagged. It is not clear whether Goodman's 'irrealism' is meant to involve a move beyond ontological realism *and* idealism, or whether he is perhaps merely taking the side of the ontological idealist within the debate between such realists and idealists. It is not clear whether he is rejecting both the claim that there is an independent reality and the contradictory of it to the effect that there is not one; or whether he is rejecting only the former, while accepting the latter. In the Foreword, Goodman suggests that few labels fit the book, since it 'is at odds with rationalism and empiricism alike, with materialism and idealism and dualism, with essentialism and existentialism ... and with most other ardent doctrines'. Given the juxtaposition in context, Goodman seems to mean by 'idealism' not ontological idealism, but merely that doctrine which asserts that mind rather than matter (or both) is the stuff of the world. Such idealism, as we have seen, is still a form of ontological realism.

Perhaps Goodman does wish his position of irrealism to go beyond both idealism and realism in the sense in which they are relevant here. Yet while his irrealism is compatible with a position which goes further, rejecting the entire controversy between ontological realism and idealism, there is nothing in his arguments – even if we accept them all – that could take us that far. The grounds upon which Goodman urges us to accept his irrealist position leave it entirely plausible to see this position as rejecting ontological realism while leaning towards the endorsement of ontological idealism, rather than as a rejection of the ontological talk common to both realism and idealism. He does not question the very coherence of such ontological talk; merely the force of the realist's convictions set in terms of it. This leaves open the possibility of an ontological idealist position which employs the notion of an ontologically independent reality to the purpose of denying that there is one.

Moving to an unequivocal position beyond the ontological talk of both realism and idealism requires taking up the task left undone by both Rorty and Goodman. It is necessary to argue against ontological talk more solidly, not by whittling away at the realist's claims, but rather by showing that any such ontological talk – either of the realist or of the idealist – cannot be defended within critical philosophy.

4.2.3 The relativist basis for Goodman's irrealism

That Goodman is not led to pursue this more rigorous line of argument himself might be explained by pointing out the different emphasis of his entire approach.

He is interested in *versions*; in the different ways of worldmaking, which begin with one version and end with another. It is upon the plurality of versions, and the relations between them, that Goodman

4. Goodman: Final Focus of the Philosophical Perspective

concentrates, and he clearly regards this as having a delightfully liberating effect. This attitude of his is reflected in various places, both in the content and in the tone of the text.[8]

I have already suggested that, before Goodman can expect others to join him in the delights of an exclusive investigation into the relationships between versions, it is necessary to do more than merely suggest pursuasively that what is left of the realist's ontologically independent world is not worth fighting for or against. It should be argued not merely that the realist's ontological talk might as well be rejected, but that it *ought* to be. *Then*, with nothing left to stay behind for, there would be sufficient reason to join Goodman in rejecting such ontological talk.

However, it is, in fact, not altogether appropriate to object that Goodman does not do enough to argue against the realist's assumption of an independent reality before moving on to his irrealist position, and that he thereby leaves us in the rear to argue his unpaved paths into highways for all to travel on. In fact this shortcoming is indicative of a difference regarding Goodman's entire strategy. His overall strategy is not to start from an attack on realism, or indeed on the coherence of ontological talk involved in both realism and idealism, and move from that on to irrealism and the concentration upon mere versions. On the contrary, he begins by making the case for a variety of right versions, and sees *that* as providing the grounds for confronting the realist's notion of a reality independent of all experience (versions). His rejection of the realist's commitment to a real world is intended to be subsequent to his own commitment to relativism.

This strategy is nicely captured by the metaphor of the onion to which he appeals – by peeling away all the different right versions we eventually conclude that we are not left with anything else. Indeed when he describes the book in the preface he says:

> What emerges can perhaps be described as a radical relativism under rigorous restraints, that *eventuates* in something akin to irrealism.[9]

A consequence of this strategy is, however, that Goodman's resulting irrealism hinges upon his commitment to, and the acceptability of, radical relativism. And it is not clear that this hinge is at all reliable.

Even if radical relativism – radically different versions – were possible, this would still leave room for the introduction of a neutral world beyond all those versions; indeed, as Davidson has pointed out,

---

[8] Note, as an example, the tone on p. 119: 'As for me, I find these views equally delightful and equally deplorable – for after all, the difference between them is purely conventional!'

[9] p. x; my italics.

such radical relativism would actually require something external to all versions, either reality or raw experience.[10] However, the very possibility of radical relativism is doubtful, as Davidson has shown.[11] And indeed it is not clear that Goodman's radical relativism even purports to be anything more than a radical form of empirical (Whorfian) relativism; the kind of cultural variation that anthropologists study. It seems reasonable to argue, following Davidson and Williams,[12] that variations between versions remain empirical, local, insofar as they are made sense of only within a common matrix which encompasses them all, a matrix which allows Goodman to state in his version what other versions are and how they differ. This is itself proof of some common ground; of the fact that he is not describing radical relativism. Davidson makes this point with regard to other philosophers, such as Whorf, Kuhn, Quine and Bergson. Thus he says:

> Different points of view make sense, but only if there is a common coordinate system on which to plot them; yet the existence of a common system belies the claim of dramatic incomparability.[13]

Any suggested example of a radically different version, just insofar as it can be stated, reveals itself as translatable and hence as sharing a common ground, and consequently as not being radically different after all.

And with radical relativism undermined it might seem that empirical relativism alone – even if it were in fact as radical as Goodman would have us believe – is still sufficiently restricted, by the very requirement of translatability, as to provide inadequate grounds for concluding that the realist's world is not worth fighting for. It might simply mean that the attempt to describe the real world would involve stepping back from local, empirical differences between versions, regional variations, to a broader perspective – akin to what Williams has called the 'absolute conception' of the world[14] – which views the world through a grid itself as free as possible from any local perspective and yet flexible enough to allow for the cultural variation exhibited in the most exotic of travel books.

---

[10] Davidson, 'On the Very Idea of a Conceptual Scheme', op. cit., pp. 190-2.
[11] ibid.
[12] B. Williams, 'The Truth in Relativism', in *Moral Luck*, CUP, 1981.
[13] ibid., p. 184.
[14] See B. Williams, 'The Scientific and the Ethical', in *Objectivity and Cultural Divergence*, (ed.) S.C. Brown, CUP, 1984, p. 214; Williams first introduced the notion in *Descartes: The Project of Pure Enquiry*, Harmondsworth, Penguin, 1978.

4. Goodman: Final Focus of the Philosophical Perspective

4.2.4 Outline of an alternative

A Goodman-like project can serve to loosen our grip on the realist picture; and can thereby serve as a promotion device in the attempt to sell a different, irrealist or idealist picture. But it cannot force us out of the former realist view, any more than it can force us into the latter, somewhat ambiguous position. Goodman's project simply seems to require too much (by way of relativism) for which price it delivers too little (by way of what he calls 'irrealism').

Thus we see yet again, as in previous chapters, that there is room, and need, for a somewhat more rigorous approach: an argument which would be directed at the central ontological relation common to both realism and idealism. To the extent that some such argument were successful, it would become imperative to discard the ontological talk of both realism and idealism. Such an argument against ontological talk of a world being either dependent on or independent of all experience would be stronger than Goodman's in all three respects mentioned above: it would not hinge on the acceptance of philosophical relativism; it would show why the relevant kind of ontological talk is *unacceptable*, rather than the weaker contention that the issue is merely not worth fighting over; and it would make clear that the target is not only the realist's conviction, but equally that of the idealist and the sceptic. (Rather than leaving unanswered the question as to whether there is anything independent of all experience, which opens the door to the sceptic, it would attempt to show what is wrong with this entire question.)

I do not mean to suggest that such an argument is readily to be provided. But even so, or perhaps precisely because this is so, there is some value in setting up a philosophical perspective which reveals a project which is suggested by, but remains unexecuted in the work of, Kant, Quine, Putnam, Strawson and Goodman. Regardless of our success in providing the required argument in later chapters, it is possible to reserve philosophical space for it; and indeed to outline the kind of position it would serve. Having eliminated the ontological talk involved in realism, idealism and scepticism we would be left with the task of providing a merely internalist account of experience. It is significant that the desired argument against such ontological talk, and for stepping beyond it, would avoid being unnecessarily tied up with the acceptance, or indeed the acceptability, of relativism. To the extent that it was not the idea of a plurality of right versions that enticed us to dispense with such ontological talk, there would be no immediate need for that idea to structure the resulting position of internalism.

It is however now necessary to say more by way of distinguishing the relevant ontological talk of realists and idealists from the merely internalist talk which would remain on the philosophical map after the elimination of the former. This will return us to the ground covered in an anticipatory way in the first chapter.

4.3 Isolating the local ontological talk of an internalist position from global ontological talk

Satisfied to deal with the *differences* between various versions, Goodman does not stop to consider what anything must be like to count as a conceivable version in the first place. The emphasis shifts from the former to the latter, however, when the strategy is no longer to move from relativism to irrealism, but rather is to confront directly the ontological talk relevant to realism and idealism.

Interesting as the dissimilarities between experienced worlds might be, the less obviously fascinating fact – that there is something which all versions share in common – requires prior attention. This echoes the similar brief discussion of the difference between the present approach and Quine's (2.3 above).

Quine is interested in the question as to *which* objects a given theory posits; Goodman is concerned with the different objects recognised in different versions. These manifest epistemological concerns. They do not directly confront the issue of whether there is any object which exists independently of all theories or versions. It is for this reason that both Quine and Goodman leave open, in effect, the *possibility* that there is some ontologically independent reality. Whether or not they *choose* to reject it, the backdrop of some real world is not excluded by the merely epistemological enquiry in which both are involved.

However, when we turn to concentrate on the fact that any theory, any version, involves objects, we are forced to move beyond the shelter of merely epistemological arguments and towards the underlying issues. The fact that all versions, like all theories, assume some objects, underlines the different fact that any form of experience is essentially object-directed.

Some immediate terminological clarification is needed here to avoid confusion. Recall that in section 1.2.3 above I mentioned that by a form of experience we might mean that form which is unique to members of one group, or indeed species – say human beings – and sets them apart from others, whose experience is of a different form. Distinguished from this was the idea of the form of all experience, by which was meant that general structure which any of those particular forms, however different, share in common just insofar as they are all forms of experience. To avoid confusion it is important to note at this point the

4. Goodman: Final Focus of the Philosophical Perspective   105

use of an indefinite article ('a form of experience') in talking of one group among others, or of the plural ('forms of experience') in talking of more than one such group, whereas the phrase 'the form of all experience' will be reserved for talking of that which all those groups share in common.

I do not mean by this to suggest that I assume that there are or could be radically different forms of experience. Nothing of what follows turns on such an assumption. The idea, on the contrary, is to take into account the widest conceivable range of empirical and entirely translatable divergences between different forms of experience. Casting our net as wide as we can, we nevertheless cannot, it seems, conceive of a form of experience which does not involve object-directedness.

All experience necessarily involves directedness towards objects, conceived as being distinct from particular subjective states of awareness of them. The Kantian argument for this is well-known. Kant argues in the Transcendental Deduction that experience requires uniting the diversity of perceptions into a single consciousness; and that this unity of consciousness requires a like unity of an objective empirical world, so that it follows that all experience must be object-directed. Such object-directedness involves, as Strawson puts it, a weighty reading of the term 'object', carrying connotations of an objectivity which holds independently of the occurrence of the experience of it.[15]

For the purposes of the present essay we could readily accept this weighty Kantian reading of the sense in which object-directedness is involved in the form of all experience. But it is sufficient to take on a less weighty reading of the object-directedness which is necessarily involved in any form of experience. That is, perhaps the object-directedness could be prised apart from the connotations of a temporally extended experience of a single objective world. It might for example be thought that we can conceive of experience which is directed towards objects whose objectual (accusative) status is displayed at the time of the experience, for the duration of that experience, but without there being over and above that unity any thought of them having an objective unity in the weighty sense. Such items would be distinct from subjective states of awareness of them at the time of experience, and would have the unity of objects, but would not be thought to be a part of a unified objective world which exists independently of the experience of it. Whether this wedge can be held in place, and at what cost, is not at all clear. But for the present purposes it is not necessary to determine whether a narrow reading of

---

[15] Strawson, *The Bounds of Sense*, op. cit., p. 73.

object-directedness can be prised apart from the weighty Kantian reading, which carries connotations of an objectivity which holds irrespective of the occurrence of any particular experience of awareness. The point here is not to defend the claim that there can be a less weighty reading of the object-directedness involved in any conceivable form of experience. The point is simply that the present essay does not for its purposes require the weighty reading, and will make do with the least contentious sense in which all conceivable experience involves object-directedness.

The fundamental requirement for any particular experience, as Strawson puts it, is that it must be possible to distinguish a component of recognition or judgment which is not identical with – totally absorbed by, or collapsed into – the particular item which is recognised, which forms the topic of judgment.[16] All experience must be object-directed at least in the minimal sense that still allows for this logical distance between the recognition, and that which is recognised. It is to allow for this distance that I have throughout insisted that the form of all experience is characterised by object-directedness.

Of course this is not meant to deny that we can describe particular psychological *states* which are not object-directed; but experiencing those states requires that they be embedded in some form of object-directed experience, however rudimentary, sufficient at least to make sense of a distinction between the logical role of an experiencing subject[17] and the contents of his experience: otherwise all we would have are *states*, rather than *experiential* states. This point is well made by Strawson.[18] He grants that we can of course conceive of the most fleeting and subjective experiences, like a tickle, in which the accusatives are not distinct from the experience of them. In these cases there is some need to save the recognitional aspect from collapse into the item recognised, since given the collapse of that distinction there would be no sense in which it was an experience at all. Since there is nothing in the experience itself to sustain the distinction, it can be saved only insofar as the recognitional component is acknowledged to be present because of the possibility of being aware that this experience belongs to oneself, as Strawson puts it.[19] I must be able to acknowledge that this experience is mine. And for this acknowledgement to be possible it is necessary that at least some of my other experiences are such as to involve the distinction between an order of recognitional experiences and an object-domain of items recognised.

[16] ibid., p. 100.
[17] No commitment being made to there being any *entity* corresponding to this logical role – see section 2.4 above.
[18] ibid., pp. 101-2.
[19] ibid.

4. Goodman: Final Focus of the Philosophical Perspective 107

Once this much is allowed by some experiences, there is room to allow that some other experiences, such as tickles, might in themselves lack the grounds for this distinction altogether. That is, although individual experiences might not be object-directed, this is possible only insofar as they belong to a form of experience which is object-directed – at least in the narrow sense of leaving room for a distinction between the recognition or judgment of the subject, and the particular item that is recognised or judged. Accordingly, we can say that the form of all experience, that structure which all conceivable forms of experience share in common, must accommodate at least such object-directedness as will suffice to sustain a distinction between a given subject's recognition or judgment on the one hand and the item recognised or judged on the other.

While all experience is necessarily object-directed at least in this narrow sense, it is of course possible to conceive *that* somewhere there might be a group of experiencers who manifest a form of experience which does not involve object-directedness at all. But the point is that we cannot do more than this. We cannot conceive *of* (make intelligible to ourselves) anything other than a form of experience which does involve directedness towards an object-world of some sort which is set apart – however minimally – from the experiencing subject. All conceivable forms of experience would seem to require *some* sort of object-world.

To clarify further the framework of the present enquiry it is important both to set out more clearly the nature of this requirement and to see what distance there is between it and the relevant talk of an object-world which either is or is not real. Starting with the most rudimentary conceivable forms of experience, we ought to allow for the possibility that the narrow sense of object-directedness could be met without carrying with it a commitment to a more weighty reading of the objectivity involved. There would seem to be a conceivable form of experience which allows for the distinction between recognition and item recognised, between subjective state of awareness and the object of that awareness, and yet does not involve all the connotations of an objectivity which holds irrespective of the occurrence of any particular experience of awareness. As was indicated above, whether or not this possibility is ultimately acceptable does not matter for the present purposes. The aim is to proceed on the broadest basis, to cast the net wide, without relying on any weightier reading of the object-directedness that might be argued for. It seems plausible that what is inconceivable is only a form of experience which does not involve an object domain which is presented to the experiencing subject as distinct, set apart from it, at least at the time of the experience. There need be no added constraints regarding the ontological status of that object-world.

The object-world presented in the context of our human experience contains a wealth of detail, involving individuation into a wide variety of objects, including among others physical objects. But there does not seem to be anything inconceivable about there being other beings whose experience does not.[20] It might be speculated that other animals experience an object-world of a very different sort from the one we experience. And their object-world might seem to be significantly more rudimentary or impoverished than our human world is. It is of course impossible to describe what the experience of some other animal is like for it, what it is like to be that animal. We inevitably see things through our eyes.[21] And it is because we cannot think ourselves totally out of ourselves that we cannot make sense of radically different forms of experience. However, we can try, to the best of our ability, to reduce the infusion of colouring from our own (human) point of view to the minimum that is needed in order still to make sense of those other animals having experience. This is the closest we can get to isolating what is necessary for all conceivable forms of experience; i.e. what is involved in the form of all experience.[22]

Accordingly, let us try to conceive of a form of experience which does not involve more than raw sensations. Such sensations comprise precisely the sort of experiences in which *we* for the most part have no distinction between the recognitional components and their sensible accusatives, the items recognised. Consequently, as Strawson points out,[23] although we can each envisage a stretch of such experiences in our own case, it does not follow that there could be a form of experience which had throughout the whole of its extent the character of such a stretch. Any such stretch would not meet the basic condition of experience; it would not leave room for the emergence of a unified subjective component as distinct from the object domain it experiences. And, as Strawson says,

> if the basis of this idea were lacking, it would be impossible to distinguish the recognitional components in such 'experiences' as components not wholly absorbed by their sensible accusatives; and if this were impossible, they would not rate as experiences at all.[24]

However, we can overcome this difficulty by imagining further that our conjectured experiencer does not experience raw sensations only in this way; that in some cases sensations are presented to it as items distinct from the awareness of them,[25] such that there is room at least

---

[20] See, for example, Strawson's discussion in ch. 2 ('Sounds') of *Individuals*, op. cit.
[21] See T. Nagel, 'What is it Like to be a Bat?', in *Mortal Questions*, CUP, 1979.
[22] See 1.2.3 above.
[23] ibid. pp. 109-10.
[24] ibid. p. 102.
[25] Although not necessarily as existing independently of that awareness.

4. Goodman: Final Focus of the Philosophical Perspective

for the distinction between the recognitional component and the item recognised. There is then, for example, nothing inconceivable about a form of experience exemplified by a suitably wired BIV, such that all it ever experiences are feelings of pleasure and pain in its object-domain. Such a BIV might never experience (that is, come into epistemic, as opposed to physical contact with) any physical objects. Its experience will comprise only pleasures and pains. These will, however, constitute an object world, if only in the minimal sense that they must, if we are to conceive of this being a form of experience at all, be objects set apart from (in the sense of being non-identical with) the BIV as experiencing subject, in a way that pleasures and pains need not be set apart as objects in our own experience.

Imagine, to take a more vivid case, an animal walking over a gravel path towards the river. Imagine that this creature has no concept-using capacity; and more contentiously, that it has *no reflexive consciousness* either. Imagine that this creature does not experience physical or otherwise abiding objects. Making certain assumptions about these feathered bipeds, we can stipulate that what is thus described is the experience of a duck engaged in waddling its way down the path towards the river. Now, do such ducks have experience at all, or are they merely the kind of mechanisms Descartes would decree them to be? It seems that the answer would hinge entirely on whether there was any distinction for the duck, which we would describe as a distinction between subjective states and some object-world presented to it. That object-world might consist of no more than a subjective unity that is imposed on its own subjective states, converting them into an object-domain. Its object-world might consist of no more than flashes and twinges, or perhaps of no more than the momentary resistance of a uniform background at the time of experience. If the duck is intentionally related to some such object world, sufficient to maintain a distinction between an item experienced and the recognition of it, then being a duck involves having experience. If there is not, then such feathered bipeds will indeed be mere mechanisms. Obviously this does not provide us with a criterion for the empirical identification of a form of experience. It is not intended as such.

The point of these examples is to demonstrate the formal condition: that object-directedness, narrowly construed, constitutes a necessary and perhaps sufficient condition of experience – a sufficient condition for the most rudimentary forms of experience, a necessary condition of all conceivable experience. Object-directedness is one feature that we cannot think away in conceiving of a different form of experience. And its being necessarily common to all forms of experience reveals our grounds for saying (in 1.2.3 above) that object-directedness pertains to the form of all experience. Yet these cases also show that it seems to be possible to conceive of a form of experience which is directed towards an object-world which is experienced as *distinct*, without having to raise the issue of the ontological status of that world as either real or not real. The inconceivability of experience without some object-world does not in itself seem to necessitate the introduction of *any* kind of ontological talk.[26]

But of course, unlike the miserably wired BIV and the hypothetical feathered biped or any other hypothetical forms of experience we might attempt to conceive of, the actual object-world as it confronts us in our – human – form of experience is not so rudimentary, and is not presented as merely distinct from us. It accommodates the weightier reading of objectivity. It manifests ontological independence relations. The actual world consists of various objects, some of which could exist in the absence of others, some of which could not. And since the world includes persons which have experience, it is not suprising to find that they too enter into ontological relations. Even someone who wishes to reject arguments for the *a priori* necessity of this would grant that some objects are ontologically independent of such persons, while others are ontologically dependent on them. Some items are ontologically independent of, or dependent upon, a single person; some are ontologically independent of, or dependent upon, all persons.

However, such ontological independence or dependence relations between an object-domain and those who have experience of it hold between certain local items and other local items within the experienced object-world. We might call any such ontological talk *local*. Local ontological talk is indeed, as will become clear in the next chapter, of some importance in explaining the different status exhibited by the various kinds of objects. But this local ontological talk constitutes the perfectly uncontentious application of ontological relations anticipated in section 1.4.1 above.

If we were to formulate realism and idealism in terms of local ontological talk, the result would constitute a version of empirical realism and idealism. An empirical realist claim regarding x would assert that it is independent of all experiencers; an empirical idealist claim would assert that it is dependent upon some, or perhaps all, experiencers. But the latter will not do to capture a general idealist thesis to the effect that 'everything is ontologically dependent upon experience'. Interpreted in terms of local ontological talk that thesis would amount to the claim that all objects were locally dependent upon us (taken more or less widely). Yet that is patently not the case. Given the untenability of this position it would hardly be of much interest to

---

[26] Although, of course, once such ontological talk has been introduced, we can attempt to apply it back to these object-worlds.

4. Goodman: Final Focus of the Philosophical Perspective

engage in an appraisal of the debate between idealists and realists of this sort.

This suggests that the divergence between realists and idealists could perhaps take place when we leave the local (empirical, internal) ontological talk, upon which the idealist and the realist might be in total agreement, as in the case of Carnap's two geographers. The interesting divergence might emerge only when the ontological independence and dependence of all experience relevant to realism and idealism are formulated more generally.

Indeed it is precisely to avoid the absurdity of empirical idealism and to allow for the obvious fact that there are things which exist independently of human beings that an idealist like Berkeley had to introduce the idea of God. He argues from the premiss that 'sensible things cannot exist otherwise than in a mind or spirit', that since they do not depend on the thought of human beings and exist independently of them, 'there must be some other mind wherein they exist'.[27] Berkeley regards this as a proof of the existence of God. His 'proof' can be seen to result from the need to modify his commitment to idealism in the face of the obvious untenability of empirical idealism. Rather than regarding the need for modification as a proof of the existence of God, we today might be more inclined simply to modify the idealist position by reformulating its initial conception.

Thus, finally, we come back to the special application of ontological talk outlined in the first chapter, which involves not the independence or dependence of one item relative to another within the experienced object world, but rather the ontological independence or dependence of some items (or indeed perhaps all items) relative to the form of all experience. The foregoing discussion has perhaps helped to clarify what is involved in the form of all experience. Abstracting from the particularities of all conceivable specific forms of experience, we are interested in the most general form which all such forms exhibit (conform to). At this level of generality the form of all experience involves only the most skeletal relational structure which still provides for the relation of object-directedness, since that, as we have seen, has emerged as a necessary condition for any conceivable form of experience.

Independence or dependence relative to this, the form of all experience, requires not a relation between x and particular concrete experiencing animals but – over and above that – between it and the logical form of object-directedness displayed by those animals. I will call such ontological talk *global*. Global ontological *independence*

---

[27] Berkeley, *Three Dialogues Between Hylas and Philonous*, in *The Principles of Human Knowledge – With Other Writings*, (ed.) G.J. Warnock, London, Fontana, 1962. *Second Dialogue*, pp. 197-8.

asserts of a certain object that it exists independently of the form of all experience.[28] In contrast, global ontological *dependence* asserts of a given object not that it is dependent upon the existence of experiencers, but that, even if it is ontologically independent of all experiencers, it is still globally dependent on the form of all experience, so that in the absence of that form those objects would not exist.

It is now possible to understand fully why I set out, in the first chapter, by analysing the terms 'real' and 'not real', and the positions of realism and idealism, in terms of such global ontological talk. Berkeley's introduction of the notion of God served to mitigate the absurdity of the empirical idealism which results from a view which appeals to no more than local ontological talk. It is possible, however, to capture something of this appeal to a higher-level dependence without introducing the notion of God. This involves reformulating Berkeley's idealist position in terms of global ontological talk, as involving global ontological dependence. That is, Berkeley's God might be reinterpreted as a metaphorical embodiment of the form of all experience. His idealism then consists of the assertion that even those parts of the world that are locally independent of us are nevertheless dependent upon the form of all experience. The realist who wishes to oppose this must then assert more than local ontological independence, with which the idealist can agree; he must assert that that object-domain is ontologically independent of the form of all experience.

This then is the form of the realist-idealist dispute which must be confronted here. It is only reasonable that in confronting the debate between realism and idealism we ought to take on the more interesting and the most plausible formulation of these positions. And in view of the above it seems evident that this requires formulating those positions in terms of global rather than of local ontological talk.

Now it is important to note that local ontological talk remains internal. It is concerned solely with independence and dependence between objects in the experienced object-world. It could be suggested that these objects, or indeed all objects in this object world are *merely* intentional, i.e. no more than a manifestation of the intentionality feature which characterises the form of all experience; that they might be globally dependent upon experience. If so, it would be only insofar as the form of all experience is given that the items of this distinct object world exist. It is then merely a world *taken* in experience. Any such position would be a position of extreme ontological idealism.

---

[28] Remember that this is not to say that that object would also have to be independent of all experiencing creatures; it might be ontologically dependent on one or more such creatures, and yet all these objects together might be said to be independent of the form of all experience, i.e. real.

4. Goodman: Final Focus of the Philosophical Perspective

Alternatively, it might be thought that although the presented object-world does satisfy a structural requirement of experience, there is more to it than that. It – or some part of it – might in fact be ontologically independent of all experience, in which case, even in the total absence of the form of all experience, those items would still exist. If so, it is not merely a world *taken* in experience, but is indeed a world *given* to experience. This global ontological independence with regard to a given *x* amounts to ontological realism. It is not merely an intentional object, it is not dependent for its existence upon the intentional structure of experience. Depending on the identification of *x*, as physical or mental, such ontological realism will cover either traditional realism or idealism.

However, just as the inconceivability of experience without directedness towards some object-world did not in itself appear to impose any constraints on whether that object-world need be real or not, so too local ontological talk would appear to leave open the question as to whether any of the objects which stand in either local ontological dependence or independence to one another are either dependent upon or independent of the form of all experience. The possibility that they are one or the other is not as yet denied, it is simply left undecided.[29] Local ontological independence and dependence appear simply to be *logically neutral* with regard to the introduction of global ontological talk.[30]

It is important to note also that the logical neutrality attributed here to local ontological talk with regard to global ontological talk is intended to be twofold: on the one hand, the introduction of local ontological talk does not require one particular position within global ontological talk over the other;[31] nor, on the other hand, does it seem to require the introduction of *some* position of global ontological talk – without determining which – rather than none. It would thus be legitimate to employ local ontological dependence and independence relations within the object-world, even after having discarded all global ontological talk. Consequently, if an argument were provided for the necessity of rejecting both ontological idealism and realism, both

---

[29] However, if the matter were to be decided, it would – in all but one type of case – have to be decided in the same way for all the locally dependent objects concerned: they would either all be globally dependent or all be globally independent. This uniformity would not be required in the case of locally *independent* objects. (The exception to this uniformity in the case of *n*-sided local dependence would be, for example, where *a* is locally dependent upon *b*, *b* is presumed to be globally independent of experience, but *a* is not, because it is also locally dependent upon *c*, which is itself globally dependent upon experience. This issue is different from, and should not obscure, the fact that local ontological dependence is a transitive relation.)

[30] Allowing for the constraints mentioned in the previous footnote.

[31] Although, as has been pointed out, in some cases it might require *uniformity* within whatever position was introduced.

global ontological dependence and independence, we would be left with nothing more than the neutral account in terms of local ontological talk. Such neutral internalism starts from the mere recognition (a) that any form of experience requires an object-world which is set apart from the subject, possibly in such a way as to involve (b) objects which stand in local ontological dependence or independence to one another, or even to us in experience.

The purported *neutrality* of such an internalist account should not, incidentally, be confused with that of neutral monism. Neutral monism attempted to commence philosophical explanation from posited elements which were themselves neutral in terms of the distinction between knower and known, subject and object, thought and thing. In this sense it was supposed to be neutral between idealism and materialism. The proposed position of internalism is neutral in terms of the distinction between ontological idealism and realism. At first this neutrality might not sound so different from that of neutral monism. But this is only because 'idealism' has many uses. It can be taken, and was by neutral monism, to refer to theories which attempt a reduction to the mental, to thoughts; as opposed to materialism which refers to attempted reductions to material things, to physical objects. However, it should by now be clear that I take idealism rather differently, as an ontological position which asserts of something – be it mental, material or neutral to the two – that it is not independent of the form of all experience; as opposed to a position of ontological realism which asserts of that same entity that it is independent of that form.

Once this is appreciated it will be realised, on the one hand, that internalism would be neutral with regard to global ontological talk in a way that neutral monism may not be. After all, neutral monism asserts that there are elements, which are neither mental nor material, and that these are what reality consists of. These elements might be of pure experience (James,[32] Russell[33]), or might be simples (Holt[34]). Either way, since within neutral monism the subject-object distinction which is required for object-directed experience is constructed in terms of these neutral items, it seems most reasonable to assume that these elements – even those which are *called* elements of pure experience – would be ontologically independent of the form (object-directedness) of all experience which they must serve to construct; i.e. that they would

---

[32] William James, *Essays in Radical Empiricism*, Harvard University Press, 1976. Cf. pp. 268-71 and passim.
[33] Bertrand Russell, *Our Knowledge of the External World*, London, Allen and Unwin, 1914; *The Analysis of Mind*, London, Allen and Unwin, 1921; and *The Analysis of Matter*, London, Routledge and Kegan Paul, 1927.
[34] E.B. Holt, *The Concept of Consciousness*, London, 1914.

4. Goodman: Final Focus of the Philosophical Perspective   115

be identified as that which is, ultimately, real.[35] In any event, there is nothing to suggest that those elements are neutral with regard to such global ontological talk, as the suggested internalist position would have it. And, on the other hand, the position of internalism need *not* necessarily construct the mental and the material from elements which are neutral with regard to the subject-object distinction, as neutral monism does; indeed it need not *construct* them at all.

Having said all this, it should be clear that the discussion in this chapter is not intended as itself an argument for internalism, and against the introduction of global ontological talk. It most certainly does not constitute an argument against the coherence of the very notion of there being something which is ontologically independent of, or dependent upon, the form of all experience. Nothing of what has been said here suffices to deny that we might talk coherently of some such reality. It has merely been pointed out that this is a separate matter. Our daily experience indeed gives ample grounds for asserting that some objects (say, physical objects) stand in local ontological independence to us, whereas others are locally dependent upon us. But that is not the application of ontological relations which is in question. What is in question is the issue of ontological independence of, or dependence upon, the form of all experience.

It is of some significance that local ontological talk appears to be logically neutral, that from dependence or independence of us nothing follows logically about global ontological talk. If such global ontological talk is to gain support, this will have to rest on some other grounds. And should it ultimately emerge that there is in fact no need for, and indeed that there is no possibility of making global ontological judgments, and further that in fact we cannot even make sense of the notion of an ontologically independent or dependent reality, then with such *global* ontological talk undermined there will be nothing problematic in being left to fall back onto the present outline of a neutral account which is merely internal to experience. We would be left with an internalist concern to describe the object world and the local ontological dependence and independence relations within it.[36]

It is important to appreciate that an argument which undermined all global ontological talk would not be arguing against ontological realism in a way that might suggest, as indeed Goodman's irrealism does, the endorsement of ontological idealism as its coherent

---

[35] Although in the case of elements of pure experience they would not be *transcendent* to the web of experience. See James, op. cit., p. 271 (4).

[36] Whether or not this will entail a commitment to relativism is a distinct matter. It would, in fact, appear to restrict relativism to the plain empirical domain of cultural variation, which is not of sufficient metaphysical import to fuel the sceptic's question. Cf. Williams' 'The Truth in Relativism', Clarke's 'The Legacy of Skepticism' and Davidson's 'On the Very Idea of a Conceptual Scheme', cited in the bibliography.

contradictory. Rather, it would be rejecting both ontological realism and idealism as incoherent, in such a way as to reject also the possibility of scepticism regarding the global ontological status of the distinct object-world.

But before turning to examine some such arguments, I will turn in the next chapter to consider what grounds there might be for introducing such global ontological talk in the first place. This will also involve reconsidering the alleged neutrality of an internalist account.

5. The Need for Global Ontological Talk: The Ontological Fallacy

Now that we have seen that all the philosophers discussed so far still leave room for *global* ontological talk, the aim of this chapter is to examine the possible grounds for introducing global ontological talk in the first place (either of idealism or of realism). I wish to examine whether, quite apart from local ontological dependence or independence relations between objects in experience, there is any reason to speak about such relations holding between certain objects and the form of all experience.

To answer this question adequately it might be useful to distinguish two different lines of investigation, which will be taken up separately in the first two sections of this chapter. The first line of investigation is concerned to see whether further reflection might not reveal a general proof of the need to introduce global ontological talk. Such proof would take the form of a transcendental argument, attempting to move from internalism, or more specifically from local ontological talk, back to the necessity of introducing global ontological talk after all. This would undermine the logical neutrality of internalism with regard to the introduction of global ontological talk, alleged in the last chapter.

The second line of investigation addresses the question of the empirical adequacy of an internalist account. This line suggests an empirical argument for the introduction of global ontological talk.[1] Even if local ontological talk is logically neutral with regard to global ontological talk, there remains the question as to whether local ontological talk is sufficiently comprehensive on its own to provide a satisfactory account of the ontological status of the world. If it is not, there might after all be need to supplement it with the introduction of global ontological talk in order to allow for an adequate account of our common sense beliefs.

Should it emerge that local ontological talk is both logically neutral and empirically adequate, so that there is in fact no need to introduce

---

[1] cf. Kant's distinction between empirical and transcendental deductions, in the *Critique of Pure Reason*, B117.

the global ontological talk of either realism or idealism, it will be necessary to provide some explanation of how it nevertheless so commonly comes to be introduced.

5.1 Transcendental argument: Is an internalist account logically neutral regarding global ontological talk?

The aim of this section is to see whether a general argument can be provided to show the need to introduce global ontological talk. I will begin by attempting to show that starting from an internalist account there is no more need to introduce one position within global ontological talk than another. Since I believe that the prevailing predisposition today is in favour of realism, I will begin by considering a possible argument to the effect that an internalist account requires the introduction of global ontological *independence*. I will attempt to show that the internalist account is in fact equally compatible with the introduction of global ontological *dependence*, so that it is after all neutral between the two.

The following argument might be suggested. Although, as the discussion in the last chapter revealed, the object-world with which we must be confronted if experience is to be possible (where 'we' is taken as broadly as possible, in the Wittgensteinian sense)[2] is not one which *displays* global independence of all experience, it might be suggested that it is nevertheless *evidence* that there is some reality which is independent of all experience. That is, it might be suggested that there is no possible explanation of the fact that we are confronted with an object-world, regardless of whether it displays local ontological independence between objects within it, other than on the assumption that it is somehow supported ('grounded') by some noumenal reality. In fully Kantian terms: The idea is that we could not have a distinct empirical reality, if there was not something transcendent, which acted as the grounds for our experience of an empirical reality.

The form of the argument would be:

(a) If experience is to be possible there must be some distinct object-world in experience.
(b) For there to be some distinct object-world in experience it would have to be sustained by a world independent of all experience (i.e. of the form of all experience).
(c) Experience is possible.

[2] See section 1.2.3 above.

Therefore:

(d)   There must be a world independent of all experience.

Premiss (b) contains the central idea. However, in the absence of some further argument it is not at all clear why we should accept it. In the first place it is not clear how the fact of there being a globally independent reality *could* have any bearing on the structure of our experience. This is similar to the problem Kant encounters when he says that the noumenal reality is, in some sense, the ground of experience. This point loses much of its force, however, once we distinguish ontological from causal relations, and recognise that the assertion of ontological independence does not necessarily imply the absence of causal relations between the objects involved. But it still remains the case that, far from establishing that for there to be an object-world in experience there must be a world which is ontologically independent of all experience, it seems to be at least questionable whether it is in fact possible that such an independent reality could ground, or sustain, an object-world in experience.

More seriously, however, there is reason to question whether, to begin with, some ontological reality is *needed* to ground the fact that in our experience a distinct object-world is always given. It is far from clear what grounds there could possibly be for accepting that for there to be a distinct object-world *in* experience, there must be one independent *of all* experience. Why should the object-world presented in the context of object-directed experience be thought to stand in need of the kind of ontological underpinning provided by premiss (b)? In fact we do often have dichotomised experiences, in which something is set up as an object distinct from us, in which there is no inclination to say that there is an ontologically independent reality which in some way serves as the ground of this experience. Such, for example, is the case with phantom limbs, hallucinations, mirages and the like. If in such cases it is possible that we have some distinct object of experience without there being any independent reality to sustain it, it is difficult to see why the same should not be possible in other cases.

There thus seems to be no clear reason why we should accept the second premiss of the suggested argument. It is difficult to see why the object-world given as distinct from us in experience – again, in the widest reading of 'us' – should be evidence of the global ontological independence of some, or indeed *that*, world, rather than of its global ontological dependence. Thus the fact of a distinct object-world would seem to be neutral between realist and idealist accounts of it.

However, here we come to the further point, which queries the neutrality of local ontological talk directly: The mere fact that we are confronted with a distinct object-world perhaps does not in itself constitute evidence of there being something which is globally independent of all experience. But this distinct object-world also displays local ontological independence between objects within it. It might be that the further fact of such local ontological talk itself suggests, perhaps even presupposes, that there must be a world which stands in global ontological independence to experience.

Reflection tends, however, to weaken the force of this point. For one thing, notice that objects are presented as ontologically independent of one another even within the context of a dream, and yet dreams would not for this reason alone be thought to represent, or indeed be evidence of, the existence of a world which is globally independent of that context. Indeed the same is true in the case of the BIVs introduced in Chapter 3. There is no reason why the various objects presented to those BIVs within the context of their experience should not stand in relations of local ontological independence to one another, and yet that very fact would not in itself be evidence for there being a world which stood in global ontological independence of the context of their experience, any more than the fact of some distinct object-world without local ontological independence would be. And if such local ontological independence between objects is not evidence of some global ontological independence in these cases, it is difficult to see why it should become so in the context of ordinary human experience. Again, local ontological independence between items could be no more than a manifestation of the *programme* for experience (idealism), rather than evidence for some world which is ontologically independent of all experience (realism).

Yet even if all this is true of the distinct object-world required for any experience, and indeed of the local ontological independence which might be manifest within it, there is still room for a further objection. Local ontological independence does not hold merely between birds, branches, boulders and the like, but also between those objects and their perceiver, between certain objects and ourselves as the experiencing human subjects. Consequently it can be suggested that it is this particular form of local ontological independence that suggests, or indeed presupposes, a world which stands in global ontological independence of all experience.

However, there is little reason to accept this. For one thing, the same can happen in dreams; a fantasy object in a dream can be presented as ontologically independent of myself. But more importantly, if we ignore our special intimate relation to experiencing persons, that is, if we view the matter sideways – as we do birds and branches – it becomes clear that it is no different if an object stands in local ontological independence to some other objects of its kind, of some

5. The Need for Global Ontological Talk 121

other kind, or indeed to one of our kind. If the fact that chairs are ontologically independent of stones within the framework of experience does not require the introduction of a world which is globally independent of that framework, it is not clear why the matter should be any different when it is said that stones are ontologically independent of us (human beings). It is just the same relation of *local* independence between given items, and there is no reason why the fact that we identify with the one type of object, or even the quite different fact that that type of object is epistemically related to the object of which it is (locally) ontologically independent, should make any difference.

Self-centred bias aside, local ontological independence of us merely asserts of some x that that x would exist even if certain animals (ourselves) did not. It would seem that just as the very fact of an object-world in experience and of local ontological independence between objects is neutral with regard to the introduction of global ontological independence or dependence, so too the particular local ontological independence of some x from *us* will not force the introduction of a world which stands in global ontological independence of, rather than global ontological dependence upon, the form of all experience.

It thus seems that the internalist account, even taking into consideration the various forms of local ontological independence, does not provide reason to introduce one position within global ontological talk (realism) over another (idealism). But of course this does not yet show that there can be no general argument from internalism to the need for some position within global ontological talk, even if it does not matter which. To put it in other terms, we are trying to see whether internalism and local ontological talk are indeed neutral with regard to global ontological talk. However, in trying to establish such neutrality it must be asked not merely whether the ontological talk of an internalist account involves a commitment to global ontological independence (realism) over global ontological dependence (idealism) or vice versa; it is also necessary to establish that it is neutral between the introduction of some global ontological position (no matter which) rather than none.

It is, however, difficult to argue that local ontological talk of an internalist position logically entails the introduction of some global ontological talk rather than none. The fact of ontological independence or dependence between objects within the experienced world no more seems to commit us to entering into global talk of objects being or not being independent of the form of all experience, which is quite a different matter, than it commits us to not entering into such talk. It would be a mistake to deny that local ontological talk is logically neutral in this way, as a simple result of confusing that *logical* neutrality with the different issue, that *we* are not *intellectually* neutral with regard to the introduction of global ontological talk. There is no doubt that we are led by reflection on matters pertaining to local ontological relations to employ such global ontological talk (indeed we shall see how this might come about, in section 5.3 below). But it is not logical entailment that leads us from one to the other. In this sense then, internalism would seem to be logically neutral not only regarding the choice between realism and idealism, but also regarding the choice between introducing some position within global ontological talk, or none.

This brings us to the question of what, in the face of this logical neutrality, does lead us from local to global ontological talk.

5.2 *Empirical arguments: Is local ontological talk empirically adequate?*

Here we come to the second, and more empirically oriented, line of investigation. It might be that the local ontological talk of an internalist position is simply not sufficiently comprehensive to provide an ontological account of the world which we-humans actually encounter, so that, despite the logical neutrality of local ontological talk regarding the introduction of global ontological talk, its empirical inadequacy will nevertheless lead us to supplement it with global ontological talk.

Now again, on the assumption that the prevailing predilection is for realism, the following investigation will be slanted towards the idea that local ontological talk is not sufficient to account for the *independence* of the world around us, so that there is some need to supplement it by introducing global ontological independence (realism). It should however be clear that at the same time this investigation also shows the extent to which local ontological talk, unsupplemented by global dependence (idealism), is empirically adequate.

By proceeding gradually from the simplest to the more difficult cases, I will attempt to establish how much of the work that has to be done can be done solely in terms of the object-world given to us as merely distinct – or as involving local ontological independence and dependence.[3] By going as far as possible merely in terms of an object-world which is not asserted to be either ontologically

---

[3] Overlooking the omission of logical empiricism and of programmatic verificationism, the internalist spirit of this clarification resembles that of Carnap's attempt at a neutral constructional account.

5. The Need for Global Ontological Talk

independent of, or dependent upon, the form of all experience, it will be possible to locate quite precisely the point at which it appears necessary to introduce the notion of global ontological independence (realism) or dependence (idealism). The idea is to work our way around within the experienced object-world, edging gradually towards the point at which we seem to have exhausted the capacities of the neutral internalist account, and the apparent need for moving on to global ontological talk emerges. The general aim is to examine in some detail the possible empirical grounds for the move from local to global ontological talk, thereby investigating the adequacy of (no more than) local ontological talk to account for the ontological status of the world around us.

The briefest look at the history of philosophy shows that most philosophers would, given their use of it, agree that there is some reason to introduce global ontological talk of what is or is not real. But given that the precise content of global ontological talk is rarely given due consideration,[4] it is not likely that the *need* that global ontological relations are usually thought to fulfil will be very precisely conceived. Often global ontological talk is introduced as a way of unintended philosophical overkill. It is introduced heavy-handedly to handle issues which could in fact be satisfactorily handled without introducing what Carnap calls metaphysical reality. It will be useful to attempt to clarify this matter; to show precisely what role (if any) is left over for global ontological talk, by showing how much can be done without it.

From local to global use of ontological talk

5.2.1 Starting with the obvious, then, local ontological talk clearly allows for the merely intentional existence of private mental objects. These objects – which include sensations, fictional characters in dreams, or the image of the red pencil which I am currently visualising although the original pencil has long since been sharpened out of physical existence – are not thought to be ontologically independent of my experience. They are, rather, assumed to be locally dependent upon my experience of them. As such they are readily accounted for in terms of local ontological talk.

5.2.2 Next, consider public objects such as Hamlet, unicorns, folk music, political parties, national patriotism and the like. These, like the previous objects, are not physical objects. Yet they are not merely one individual's mental object(s) either.

---

[4] See 6.2 below on Carnap's lack of clarity about the precise content of the concept of ontological independence: this unclarity is symptomatic of a widespread unclarity of a similar sort.

If I had not been thinking yesterday about the red pencil which I had previously reduced to shavings, *that* mental object (the image of the pencil) could not have existed yesterday. There is thus an asymmetrical dependence relation between that object and myself (asymmetrical because I am not dependent upon that specific mental object, and would exist even without *it*).

The case is different with regard to unicorns and Hamlet. To account for these it is necessary to introduce the notion of ontological independence. But it is merely *local* ontological independence that is required; and rather a limited use of it at that. Such objects are not locally independent of *us*. If not only I, but also everyone else, were never to have had experience, it would follow that unicorns, Hamlet and all other such entities would not exist either. Such objects, although public rather than private, might still be seen as merely intentional cultural objects. Hamlet and unicorns, etc., are ontologically independent of any *one person's* experience, but they are nevertheless *dependent* upon the community of experiencing subjects. Since such public objects are thus ontologically *dependent* upon us in experience, they manifest local ontological independence only of any given particular subject. They do not involve local ontological independence of the entire community of experiencing subjects.

5.2.3 The matter becomes more complicated when physical spatio-temporal objects are considered. The public (cultural) non-physical objects just considered merely required ontological independence of a given individual. Physical objects require more than this. They, unlike public non-physical objects, seem to require ontological independence of all experiencing agents.

Let us consider the case of physical objects step by step. If we begin with the simplest cases, the extent of the similarity between physical objects and public non-physical objects will emerge.

Consider, first, the case of a physical object that confronts me at this very moment, here and now. There is, on the terrace in front of me, a stone. This stone features as part of the distinct object-world given in experience. Indeed, considered in the confinement of my own present experience of it, there might not seem to be any essential difference between the stone and the private non-physical objects considered so far. It is simply that it is given in a multiplicity of ways; it is what Leibniz would call fully determined. It can be seen, touched, smelt ...

At the very moment of present experience it is only this difference of complexity that makes the stone in front of me more forcefully distinct than the object which confronted me earlier, when I merely thought about the red pencil before coming out onto this terrace. The physical stone with which I am now confronted seems – as long as I confine my attention to this confrontation – to be a part of a distinct object-world in experience which has just the same ontological status as the private mental object had while I was considering it, the difference being merely quantitative. Only the *web* of ways in which it is now being presented to me as distinct sets it apart as a physical object from the object given in the mere imagination of such a stone. Insofar as this is so, the physical object with which I am currently confronted, just as much as the private mental object, can be accounted for in terms of the distinct object-world given in experience without the introduction of any ontological independence, global or local.

But, obviously, this does not do justice to the distinction between the physical object and the merely mental object.

5.2.4 Unlike merely private intentional objects, physical objects are not such that they exist only when and where I am experiencing them. The merely private intentional object, or the imaginary object presented in a dream or hallucination, is apparently only a distinct object *while* it is being experienced. Physical objects, however, are apparently also independent of my experience of them. This stone is not only a distinct object in my current experience of it. If I stop experiencing this stone, or indeed the mountain on the horizon beyond it, it will – surely – still exist as a distinct object. To deny this would be to fly in the face of common sense and to adopt the most extreme form of empirical idealism. This physical stone, for example, was certainly here before I came onto the terrace, and will be here long after I have left it.

Let us return, by way of analogy, to the case of a physical object which I am *currently* experiencing.

Having left the stone and the terrace, I have just sat down at a large desk. This desk is given, in my present experience of it, as an object which is distinct from me. Nothing in my experience of it *at this very moment* gives me grounds to think that it is in any way ontologically independent of my experience of it.

Now, as such, the desk is the object of my experience even though at the moment, and indeed at any given moment, I am only able to see some parts of it. I never have seen, and never intend to see, the part of it that lies two centimetres into the heavy desk top. More simply, at the moment I can see only the uppermost part of the desk, the desk *top* (and in fact only small parts of that are visible). Nevertheless other parts of the desk are indirectly given to me at this moment of experience despite not being currently perceived. I infer that they exist because of my (current) knowledge of how the desk hangs together as a whole.

The matter can be described in essentially the same way, merely the scale different, when I now consider an object such as the stone outside being ontologically independent of my experience of it.

In experience, there is an object-world that is distinct from me. The distant or remote parts of this entire object-world can be accounted for in a manner similar to that employed regarding the desk. The entire object-world, we might say by way of explanation, is given in my experience – just as we might say that the entire iceberg is presented to the experienced seafarer; but that is not to say that I can, at every moment, view all of it. At this moment, indeed at any moment, I can experience only some parts of it – the tip of the iceberg. At this particular moment I am confronted with this desk, as a distinct physical object; but out on the terrace there is another physical object, the stone, which I am not currently perceiving as a distinct object. Yet I do say that it is still there – it is indirectly given although not currently perceived. I infer that it is there because the various physical objects are part of the one object-world of experience which displays a familiar kind of constancy in the way it hangs together as I wander through it. There is a distinct object-world in my experience, and the fact that I am confronted only with a part of it at a given time, does not mean that the other parts are not given as distinct at that same time. They are given indirectly as parts of the same object-world with which I am currently confronted.

I should perhaps emphasise that I am not, for the moment, arguing or even asserting that the fact of unexperienced objects could not be explained as a simple consequence of their reality. I am currently attempting to show only that there is no *need* to introduce such global ontological independence to account for the existence of objects which I am not currently perceiving. The existence of a table or of the stone or of the mountain beyond it can be said to be locally independent of my experience of *it*, without this even appearing to require the introduction of a reality which is ontologically independent of all experience.

5.2.5 But the independence which has been accounted for here is only the independence of the physical object from my experience of it, insofar as it is part of the one object-world of which I *do* have experience.

This, however, still does not do justice to the kind of independence we believe the stone to exhibit. It makes the existence of the stone independent of my experience of it, but only by making it appear to be dependent upon my experience in general; that is, upon my experience of other parts of the object-world. Yet this is not the way we tend to think of physical objects. Just as the furniture in the next room is a distinct physical body which is not dependent upon my experiencing *it*,

5. The Need for Global Ontological Talk

so it is not dependent upon my experiencing any *other* part of the object-world in which it exists. It is, in other words, independent of all my experience. It would be there even if I was not, and never had been. This, of course, is true not only of physical objects. The same applies to the non-physical public objects, such as nations and novels, considered above. It is true of all public objects that they are not merely independent of my experience of *them*, but indeed of all *my* experience.

5.2.6 Public objects are given in experience in such a way that they are not dependent upon any one person's experience of them. This indeed constitutes a distinguishing mark of the public from the private object. The private object is dependent upon one person's experience of it. In contrast, the public object (physical or non-physical) is not ontologically dependent on any single person's experience of it. Even in my total absence as an experiencing subject, the public world – including the physical world – would still exist as a distinct object-world in the experience of those who remain to have it.

But this seems to assume that, while the public object is indeed ontologically independent of any one person's experience, it remains ontologically dependent upon there being *some experience of it*. Yet this does not hold true of all public objects. While independence of a given individual's entire experience is sufficient to do justice to the independence of the *public non-physical object* such as Hamlet and nations, it still does not quite capture the independence manifested by the physical world. It is here that the extent of similarity between physical objects and public non-physical objects is exhausted, and the point of difference emerges.[5]

5.2.7 It will most commonly be said of physical as opposed to non-physical public objects that they are not merely independent of any one individual's experience, but independent of their ever being experienced by *any* individual – that is, they would exist even if there was no experience of them at all. Surely remote objects, either in time or in space, do nevertheless exist? Surely a stone in some faraway galaxy, that never was or will be experienced by anyone, nevertheless exists? Surely there were rocks and mountains before life evolved? The appeal here is to the notion of an object which is never experienced at all. It is not merely that it is never experienced by *me*, or by some other

---

[5] It should be noted that I am merely drawing on our current common-sense distinctions between the physical and the non-physical; there is no necessity involved – some would count God or souls or Platonic Forms as public non-physical objects which manifest as much ontological independence of us as physical objects. The philosophical identification of *what* is real is, again, not the issue here. The point is merely to establish where, on our common view of what is most independent of us, it becomes necessary to introduce the idea of it being real, of its global ontological independence.

specific individual; it is never experienced by *anyone*. It is simply there, independently of anyone ever experiencing it. It is in this respect that physical objects seem to differ from public non-physical objects.

However, this kind of independence can still be accounted for solely in terms of local ontological independence, internal to the experienced object-world. It is important to distinguish between an object being independent of any experience of *it*, and its being independent of there being any experience of anything else.

To emphasise this I might repeat on the intersubjective level what was said above on the level of the single individual with regard to an object being independent of the experience of it. We can account for those unexperienced objects by saying that they are the far side of that which is present in experience. We know that they are there by way of inference from those parts of the object-world with which we *are* confronted directly – in exactly the way in which, on a different scale, we infer that this desk-top has wood inside it, without ever having seen its insides directly. We are simply familiar at any given time with the way our object-world seems to hang together.

We learn to tell what parts of the puzzle are missing, on the basis of the parts that we do have. Given two mountains, I can predict that a valley lies between them. Similarly, looking at our object-world astronomers infer that it contains, in its more remote regions, rocks and stones that never were nor will be experienced. Similarly geologists confronted with parts of our object-world in experience infer that in remote parts of this object-world, in the distant past, there were certain rocks, stones and other such things on this planet. Although these remote elements were never directly experienced themselves, they are said to exist, and we can see them as parts of a single object-world of our experience. They are simply the concealed parts of *this* world. We can account for the distant in terms of the near.[6] Indeed to say that they are *remote* is already to relate them as parts to the experienced object-world, which is not as yet being asserted to be globally independent of (or dependent upon) experience.

Thus to say that there are objects which never were experienced by anyone, and which never will be – and perhaps never could be – experienced by anyone at any time, does not yet require saying that they are ontologically independent of there being experience of other objects; let alone that they are independent of the form of all experience. It is sufficient to say that they are only ontologically

---

[6] The idea of reading the far in the near resembles Leibniz's saying that 'every body is sensitive to everything which is happening in the universe, so much so that one who saw everything could read in each body what is happening everywhere, and even what has happened or what will happen, by observing in the present the things that are distant in time as well as in space' (*Monadology*, section 61. Everyman edition, Dent 1973, p. 189.)

5. The Need for Global Ontological Talk 129

independent of being experienced *themselves*. We can say that they are internal to the object-world given in experience, and within it they exhibit local ontological independence of *all* experience of *them*. And it is this kind of independence which suffices to distinguish the physical as opposed to the public non-physical object (at least with regard to the common-sense distinction between them).

5.2.8 It should, incidentally, be pointed out here that it is not entirely accurate to say of all physical objects that they exist independently of whether or not they are experienced. Among physical objects there is room for the distinction between natural and artifactual objects. (Which is not to say that *all* artifacts are physical objects – clearly some are not.) It is true of *natural* physical objects that they are ontologically independent of being *experienced* (although, again, this is not to say that they are ontologically independent of all experience.) *Artifactual* physical objects, however, are not independent of being experienced in the same way.

It is not quite right, however, to say simply that such physical artifacts have to have been experienced by at least one person, namely the person who made them. We can imagine that a man in, say, Manhattan, has built an automatic machine for the production of, say, subway tokens. Imagine that he sets the machine running and then leaves the room – which is never again entered by anyone. Clearly the machine which he set running manufactures artifacts, subway tokens which accumulate and yet are never experienced. However, the point is that, although the individual tokens are never experienced, they are all tokens of a type which is experienced, indeed designed. This sets artifacts apart from natural physical objects, of which we would want to say that not only a given token, but indeed an entire type (say, some undiscovered metal), could exist without ever being experienced.

(Note, incidentally, that this places artifactual physical objects, appropriately, somewhere between cultural non-physical objects and natural physical objects. In respect of their *type* they are like cultural non-physical objects; in respect of their tokens they are like natural physical objects.)

It is of course possible that a person might produce something unintentionally, and so never experience the product, or rather the by-product – either token or type – of his endeavours. And if this by-product, despite being unintentional, is considered to be an artifact, what I have said here must be taken to distinguish a narrower category within that of artifactual objects.

5.2.9 Now so far we have seen that without using global ontological talk it still seems to be possible to allow for and distinguish between

(a) merely private mental objects, such as those in dreams, (b) public non-physical (cultural) objects such as philosophical schools, (c) artifactual physical objects, such as this terrace, and (d) natural physical objects, such as the stone on the terrace or in a faraway region of the universe.[7] All have been accounted for internally, within the parameters of the experienced object-world. The need to introduce ontological independence or dependence between the object-world and all experience has not yet emerged. Nothing so far has suggested that there is any need for global ontological talk.

5.2.10 However, a further step might be suggested. The above still does not seem to capture adequately the kind of independence manifested by the world with which we are confronted. Ancient rocks and distant dust, I have allowed, might not be experienced by anyone at any time – they exist independently of being experienced, as the hidden recesses of a complex whole which is experienced. But on this account it would seem that ancient rocks and the like can be said to have existed despite the fact that they were never experienced, only insofar as they belong to an object-world other parts of which *are* experienced.

Is it not, however, reasonable to say that the existence of stardust and the like is independent of the fact that we here, today, are experiencing other parts of that same object-world? The following certainly seems right: The rocks which the geologist searches for would have been there even if there had not been any geologists, or indeed any other form of conscious life later on. Even if experience, conscious life, had never emerged, it is surely the case that those ancient stones and mountains, indeed *these* ancient stones and mountains which I see from my window, would nevertheless have existed.

We thus need to allow for one further belief concerning the independence of the world. We have not yet accounted for the objects which would exist even if there were no such experience of anything at all. It is assumed that, say, those mountains – or whatever other such real items the world around us seems to contain – would exist regardless of there being any object-directed experience. Yet *this* belief, it might appear, is not one that can be captured by an account which appeals merely to local ontological independence.

It is at *this* point, to capture this further belief and to allow philosophical discussion of it, that the philosopher might think it necessary to formulate global ontological independence. The idea – that the dust on ancient planets would have existed even if there had never been any experience of anything – is certainly difficult to reject.

---

[7] For the more general relevance of this sketchy account, see section 1.2 above.

And to accommodate this common sense belief it is tempting to introduce — as a supplement to local ontological talk internal to the experienced object-world — the notion of an object-world, perhaps this very one with which we are in causal contact, which is ontologically independent of the form of all experience. Thus — introducing ontological realism at this point — we might say that there is something, the physical world for most but perhaps the world of spirit for some, depending on whether they are traditional realists or idealists, which exists not merely as distinct or as locally independent of us (as items within the experienced object-world) but as ontologically independent of the form of all experience.[8] It might be thought that only by introducing the global ontological talk of a world independent of all experience, as a supplement to the talk of local ontological independence within the object-world of experience, is it possible to do full justice to these further common beliefs about the independence of sticks and stones.

Purporting to support our common-sense beliefs, the ontological realist will thus assert that there is indeed some such ontologically independent domain, while the extreme ontological idealist (or transcendental nihilist), apparently opposing this common-sense belief, asserts that there is not. Both alike, however, would then be accepting the introduction of global ontological talk in confronting (positively or negatively) our common beliefs.

The task set for this section was to determine the point at which it might be thought necessary to introduce global ontological talk. This task has now been completed. I hope that it has, at the same time, become clear at least that to introduce global ontological independence *before* this point would indeed have been heavy-handed. I have tried to indicate just how much can be accounted for *without* introducing this notion, merely in terms of the local ontological talk which a thoroughly internalist account allows us.

The question now is whether the introduction of global ontological talk is in fact required at this point.

5.3 The ontological fallacy

I believe that it is not in fact the case that there is any common-sense belief about the ontological status of the world which requires the introduction of global ontological talk; that these common sense beliefs can after all be accounted for merely in terms of *local* ontological talk.

---

[8] The sense in which minds can be thought to be independent of object-directed experience has already been explained in section 1.4 above.

The specific common-sense belief in question is one to the effect that mountains and other physical objects display a stronger form of independence over and above what has so far been allowed for. They are such that, even if there were absolutely no experience of any objects at all, of them or of anything else, they would still exist. The idea is that they would exist regardless even of the emergence of conscious life. It is this belief which seems to require for its support the introduction of global ontological independence, or the introduction of global ontological dependence for its denial.

I am not interested for the moment in the coherence of such global ontological talk (that will be the concern of the next two chapters). I wish to concentrate at this point on the apparent grounds for its introduction in the first place. That is to say, the issue in this section is not whether global ontological independence *could* be introduced in support of our common-sense beliefs, but whether there is any *need* for it.

In terms of local ontological talk we can in fact go still further than we have, and so can capture the further belief regarding the independence of mountains. We can interpret the absence of experience more moderately, in a way that still falls short of global ontological independence, and yet at the same time eliminates experience sufficiently to capture the extent to which common sense tells us that mountains are independent of it. The further belief is only that even in the total absence of all conscious life, mountains would still exist. The introduction of global ontological talk to confront this common-sense belief is still, at least, premature. To appreciate this it will help to recall the main point, anticipated earlier, at which ontological realism and idealism must diverge.

Global ontological independence asserts more than mere independence of the totality of experiencing beings. It asserts independence of the form of all experience, which those beings manifest. The central significance of this assertion, regarding the form of all experience, resides in the fact that it is this abstract form of all experience that offers the non-empirical idealist his less metaphorical counterpart to Berkeley's God, on which he can rest his case. Given this form of all experience, the idealist can assert that mountains, ancient rocks and the like, although locally independent of us and of any other experiencing beings, are nevertheless dependent upon experience, upon the form of all experience which those experiencing beings contingently embody. The world, the idealist might say, is at most a feature which emerges from the structure (programme) of experience. To counter *this* the realist must appeal to global ontological independence and assert that mountains, quite apart from their obvious local independence of us, are independent even of the form of

5. The Need for Global Ontological Talk

all experience. The realist's global ontological independence is thus designed to meet the idealist's formal counterpart to Berkeley's God.

But from this it should be clear that there is no need to introduce the realist's talk of global ontological independence (independence of the form of all experience) merely in order to account for our common-sense beliefs to the effect that mountains are independent of the totality of experiencing beings. The idealist too, while asserting the negation of such global ontological independence, can still allow for our common-sense beliefs to the effect that mountains are ontologically independent of the totality of experiencing beings. The reason the non-empirical idealist and realist can agree on this is that our beliefs concerning the independence of mountains can after all be explained merely in terms of local ontological independence, that is, independence of all experiencing beings as items in the experienced world. Such independence falls short of asserting independence of all experience in the sense relevant to global ontological talk, since it says nothing about whether mountains are furthermore independent of, or merely dependent upon, the form of all experience. The important difference is between something being independent of *all forms of experience* (of *us* in the widest possible sense) and it being independent of *the form of all experience* (i.e. of the general structure which all different empirical forms of experience alike exhibit). Our common-sense beliefs about mountains involve only the idea of their independence of us (taken broadly), independence of the emergence of all forms of conscious life, and do not require any stand on the further issue of independence of the general form of all experience which that emergent life displays.

So it would seem that what was intuitive was, after all, merely the internalist notion of ontological independence, of the kind described above; which involves only local independence of us, as items within the experienced object-world, but not of the form of all experience which those items exhibit. To account for our common-sense beliefs we must, so to speak, be able to remove the actors and all of their acts, but the stage can still remain set with the form thereof. We do not have to take a stand on whether mountains are ontologically dependent or independent of the form of all experience (of the stage-setting in which any particular form of experience is played out) in order to understand how a mountain can be said to exist regardless of whether any creatures ever manifested those object-directed relations.

It is difficult to see that there now remain any further common-sense beliefs about the ontological independence of the world which have not been allowed for in terms of local ontological talk. Our common beliefs about the empirical world have been cashed out, and yet the result falls short of requiring the introduction of global ontological talk; of this mountain existing independently of the form of all experience.

The introduction of global ontological independence to account for the ontological independence manifest in the world around us thus seems, upon examination, at least to involve philosophical overkill. Indeed it would appear that such talk of global ontological independence all too easily borrows its force from these other notions, of local (or internal) ontological independence. Philosophers readily fail to distinguish the idea of an object independent of us, as experiencing beings, from that of an object-world which is independent of the form of experience manifested by any such beings. We introduce the ontological notion of a world globally independent of all experience, on the basis of evidence which in fact only sustains the weaker notion of local independence between items within the experienced object-world.

Without careful examination, from the observation of an object-world independent of *us* in a variety of subtle ways, a conclusion is drawn concerning a world ontologically independent of the form of all experience. In fact, however, there is no way of reaching the one from the other, either by logical entailment or on grounds of empirical inadequacy of the former without the latter (that is, through either transcendental or empirical deduction). It is merely that philosophers have not always appreciated the difference between the two. This shift, from objects independent of *us* – as experiencing beings – to objects independent of the form of all experience, might be referred to as the *ontological fallacy*.[9]

It is one thing to talk of a tree being ontologically independent of us, or indeed of the emergence of conscious life. It is another thing to talk of it being ontologically independent of the form of experience manifested in that conscious life (which itself might indeed not have emerged). The ontological fallacy is committed by regarding the facts which support the former, entirely coherent notion, as if they supported the latter. Making sense of a world independent of all contingent forms of experience which have emerged, we regard this as making sense of a world independent of the general structure which those contingent forms of experience exhibit. We note the independence of the object world given in experience, but confuse its local independence *of us*, as experiencing beings within the experienced

---

[9] It happens, as a matter of fact, to be more likely today that the slide into global ontological talk will commence from claims regarding ontological independence, which is why I have structured the present exposition accordingly. It should, however, be clear that the move from talk of an object's being dependent upon us in experience to its being dependent upon the very structure of object-directed experience would equally commit the ontological fallacy, thereby introducing the shift from local to global ontological talk. The symmetry between the shift from local to global talk in the cases of dependence and independence will be more evident when I return to explain the ontological fallacy in section 7.2 below.

5. The Need for Global Ontological Talk

world, for global independence of the form of all experience. Realists then proceed to affirm, and idealists to deny, that there is indeed some such globally independent reality.

The conclusions reached so far, even if acceptable, still leave work to be done. Perhaps local ontological talk is logically neutral with regard to global ontological talk. Perhaps it is not necessary to introduce global ontological talk in defence of our ordinary beliefs about the ontological status of the world. Perhaps such talk is indeed regularly introduced by way of a fallacy. Even accepting all this, the case against introducing such talk is still not complete. As long as the notion of a reality which might be – or not be – ontologically independent of the entire form of object-directed experience is accepted as coherent, there is no reason why global ontological talk should not be introduced for some reason other than to account for our common beliefs, and in some way which does not commit the ontological fallacy.[10]

The present chapter has attempted to argue only that our common-sense beliefs about the independence of the world around us can in fact be accommodated entirely within local (internal) ontological talk. This clears the way for an investigation of the coherence of global ontological talk, having shown how much of our ordinary beliefs would be left unchanged if such talk were to emerge as incoherent. In the next two chapters I will examine possible, though perhaps not conclusive arguments to the effect that global ontological talk is in fact not coherent.

---

[10] It might, for example, be suggested that although not needed to account for our ordinary beliefs about the ontological status of the world around us, global ontological talk has a theoretical use as a complement to our picture of the world. It could be introduced by way of something like a transcendental argument to the effect that it is needed to accommodate the kinds of assumptions necessary for certain plans and projects which we actually pursue within the cultural scheme to which we are committed. I am grateful to Anthony Grayling for raising this point.

6. Examining Global Ontological Talk: Verificationism

Having established that an internalist account in terms of local ontological talk is both logically neutral and empirically adequate to allow for the independence of the world around us, so that there is no obvious need to introduce global ontological talk of realism or idealism, we can now turn directly to an examination of such global ontological talk.

Recall what was said in the opening chapter (1.4) about the ontological claims of realism and idealism: For every realist position regarding a certain entity, there is a possible corresponding idealist position regarding that same entity. The realist asserts of some thing that it is ontologically independent of all experience and in doing so has identified an element of the real world. An idealist counterpart to this realist would deny that that element was indeed independent of all experience.

The present chapter will explore the possibility of arguing, in verificationist terms, against global ontological talk in a way that is meant to apply as much to a realist claim that there is a world independent of all experience as to an idealist claim that there is not one. The idea of any such argument is not to choose between two possibilities, but rather to reject both the realist assertion and the contradicting idealist assertion. The only way to avoid the see-saw of contradictories is to get off the see-saw. The question is, can this be done?

6.1 Carnap and verificationist arguments

Carnap's verificationist project leads him to attempt just such a move, away from realism and idealism, in his 'Pseudoproblems in Philosophy'.[1]

---

[1] In Rudolf Carnap, *The Logical Structure of the World*, translated by R.A. George, London, Routledge and Kegan Paul, 1967. All page references are to this edition.

6. Examining Global Ontological Talk: Verificationism

In the spirit of logical positivism, Carnap accepted the principle of verification, and regarded it as a *criterion* of *meaning*. Following what he took to be Wittgenstein's principle of verifiability, he asserted that a statement is meaningful if and only if it is in principle verifiable. It is a matter of relative insignificance for the present purposes that later, faced with the internal and external criticism of the Vienna Circle's verificationism, he exchanged the verifiability requirement for the weaker one of *confirmability*. The point of this was to leave room for inductive generalisations such as scientific laws and hypotheses which it is not possible to verify. Conceding this point to Popper, Carnap asserted that although scientific hypotheses can never be completely verified, they can be more or less confirmed (or disconfirmed) by appeal to evidence. A sentence was said to be confirmable when observation sentences could contribute to its confirmation or disconfirmation. Sentences that were in principle not confirmable were *meaningless*. However, all these reasonable qualifications notwithstanding, whether on his earlier or his later views, Carnap maintained his position that ontological claims regarding a reality independent of experience, being neither verifiable nor confirmable, are therefore meaningless.

Thus, in 'Pseudoproblems',

> a statement p is said to have 'factual content' if experiences which would support p or the contradictory of p are at least conceivable...[2]

Carnap goes on to say that:

> A (pseudo) statement which cannot in principle be supported by experience, and which therefore does not have any factual content, would not express any conceivable state of affairs and therefore would not be a statement, *but only a conglomeration of meaningless marks or noises*.[3]

He considers this to be a liberal criterion of meaning:

> We have not taken the strict viewpoint which requires of each statement that it should be supported or testable; rather, we consider statements meaningful even if they merely have factual content, but are neither supported nor testable. Hence we are using as liberal a criterion of meaningfulness as the most liberal-minded physicist or historian would use within his own science...[4]

Given this, Carnap proceeds on the assumption that experience in principle cannot lend support to any of the global ontological

---

[2] ibid., p. 327.
[3] ibid., p. 328, my italics.
[4] ibid., p. 328.

statements over their contradictories. In view of the discussion in the last chapter we might incline towards accepting this assumption. It then follows that these statements lack factual content, and hence that they are merely meaningless conglomerations of marks or noises. Far from having to determine which is true and which false, neither the realist's nor the idealist's statements are even meaningful.

However, this way of rejecting the very concern with any global ontological talk does rest, despite Carnap's assurances to the contrary, upon a view of meaningful statements that is rather stringent. For Carnap, as the above reveals, at least on the view in 'Pseudoproblems', the verificationist principle of meaning requires that every statement *taken on its own* should in principle be supported by experience. If it is not, it has no factual content and is then only a conglomeration of meaningless marks or noises. It is this atomistic view, whereby individual statements considered in isolation are the units of verification, that results in a particularly strong form of verificationism. And it is this somewhat doctrinaire view of meaningfulness that has, with justification, reduced the early verificationist project to its current level of disrepute. It could hardly be regarded today as providing an acceptable way of revealing all global ontological talk (realist or idealist) to be incoherent.

Quine, in 'Two Dogmas of Empiricism',[5] confronting the verification theory of meaning, rejects the 'supposition that each statement, taken in isolation from its fellows, can admit of confirmation or infirmation'. Rather, as he puts it, our statements about the external world face the tribunal of sense experience not individually but only as a corporate body.[6] Thus he says that 'what I am now urging is that even in taking the statement as unit we have drawn the grid too finely. The unit of empirical significance is the whole of science.'[7]

This provides a holistic form of verificationism which is far weaker than Carnap's atomistic view in 'Pseudoproblems'. It is only the language as a whole that must pass the test, must have empirical (or factual) content, not each and every sentence within it. This leaves room, in a way that the more programmatic atomistic form of verificationism does not, for there being some meaningful statements which are themselves not to be correlated with any specifiable experiences the occurrence of which would directly support or detract from the likelihood of that statement's being true.

As opposed to the stark atomistic verificationism of the Vienna Circle, as displayed in Carnap's 'Pseudoproblems', this more holistic form of

---

[5] op. cit.
[6] ibid., p. 41.
[7] ibid., p. 42.

6. Examining Global Ontological Talk: Verificationism

verificationism is altogether more reasonable.[8] However, it should be clear that once it is no longer required that any given statement itself be directly supported by experiences, but only that the whole of language be so supported, the verificationist theory of meaning can no longer be so readily used to reveal global ontological talk to be meaningless. For while it seems clear that for any statement of global ontological talk there is no experience which would directly support it or its contradictory, on the holistic view this no longer matters; it is not clear that such statements of global ontological talk could not be allowed in as parts of an entire language which as a whole did meet the verificationist's tests. Thus the weaker, holistic form of verificationism, while more acceptable, does not seem sufficiently strong to undermine all global ontological talk.

This holistic view of the verificationist theory of meaning has been taken up more recently by Dummett. As opposed to the view whereby a statement possesses an objective truth-value, independently of our means of knowing it, and is true or false in virtue of a reality existing independently of us, Dummett's anti-realist holds that

> the meanings of these statements [of the disputed class] are tied directly to what we count as evidence for them, in such a way that a statement of the disputed class, if true at all, can be true only in virtue of something of which we could know and which we should count as evidence for its truth.[9]

Or, in 'What is a Theory of Meaning (II)',

> On this account, an understanding of a statement consists in a capacity to recognise whatever is counted as verifying it, i.e. as conclusively establishing it as true. It is not necessary that we should have any means of deciding the truth or falsity of the statement, only that we be capable of recognising when its truth has been established.[10]

---

[8] It is interesting to note that Quine rightly sees this shift to a weaker holistic form of verificationism as 'issuing essentially from Carnap's doctrine of the physical world in the *Aufbau*' (ibid., p. 41). The atomistic verificationism which we find in 'Pseudoproblems' can perhaps be explained as due in part to Carnap's exposure to the Vienna Circle and Wittgenstein's work. Although published at roughly the same time, 'Pseudoproblems' was written after the *Aufbau*, in 1927, after Carnap had spent a year in Vienna and by his own testimony was more influenced by the programmatic verificationism of that Circle. (See. p. x of the Preface to the 2nd edition of *The Logical Structure of the World*, London, Routledge and Kegan Paul, 1967.)

[9] M. Dummett, 'Realism' in *Truth and Other Enigmas*, op. cit., p. 146. Similarly, he says a few pages later on that 'For the anti-realist, an understanding of such a statement consists in knowing what counts as evidence adequate for the assertion of the statement, and the truth of the statement can consist only in the existence of such evidence' (ibid., p. 155).

[10] M. Dummett, 'What is a Theory of Meaning (II)', in *Truth and Meaning*, (ed.) Evans and McDowell, Oxford, Clarendon Press, 1976, pp. 110-11.

In essence this clearly resembles the kind of verificationism advocated by Carnap in the spirit of logical positivism. But Dummett carefully avoids 'the logical positivist error of supposing that the verification of every sentence could be represented as the mere occurrence of a sequence of sense-experiences', and instead explicitly endorses Quine's holistic view of verificationism.[11] Dummett's verificationism thus involves accepting that only some sentences, those which in Quine's image lie on the periphery of the field, can be said to be verified merely by the occurrence of certain basic experiences. For any other sentences, closer to the centre of the field, 'our grasp of its meaning will take the form, not of a capacity to recognise which bare sense-experiences verify or falsify it, but of an apprehension of its inferential connections with other sentences linked to it in the articulated structure formed by the sentences of the language'.[12] This leaves room for the limiting case of a proof, as in mathematical theorems, which comprises verification by means of inference alone. Cases like this display very clearly the way in which such verificationism is significantly weaker than the earlier atomistic theory whereby a statement only had meaning to the extent that it itself had factual content, and so was in principle capable of direct empirical verification or falsification. And for just this reason, as we have seen, it is not clear whether in this weaker form verificationism could still exclude statements of global ontological talk.

Apart from this, it is of interest to note another respect in which Dummett is rather cautious in advocating an anti-realist theory of meaning. He does not insist programmatically that it is to be applied to all classes of statements. Rather, he accepts that for any disputed class of statements there is a question as to whether the meaning of those statements is to be given in terms of verification, or of truth conditions. This cautious approach of course suggests the question whether the verificationism involved in an anti-realist account of meaning is appropriate for the particular class of statements which comprise global ontological talk.

It is clear, however, that *if* accepted, and if the verificationist's *holism* is not taken so broadly as to encompass the whole of language, but only the whole of the relevant class of statements, such an account of meaning would undermine the concern with statements involving global ontological talk. Again, from what we have seen in the last chapter it would seem that, for any statement p involving global ontological talk, there can in principle be no evidence to distinguish between its being the case that p as opposed to not p. It follows, on the account being considered, that since we could not have any evidence

---

[11] 'What is a Theory of Meaning (II)', op. cit., p. 111.
[12] ibid.

6. Examining Global Ontological Talk: Verificationism 141

either for or against the realist's assertion that there is something independent of all experience, or for or against the idealist's assertion of the contradictory, neither statement is true. Furthermore, since we do not even know what would count as evidence, it also follows that neither is even meaningful. On this view then, there would be no room for either the realist or the idealist to assert their claims; we would have eliminated the see-saw of contradictories. There would similarly be no room for the sceptic to raise his corresponding questions.

But of course it would remain to say why this appealing application of verificationism to global ontological talk would not simply beg the question. After all, anyone intent on engaging in global ontological talk, whether realist, idealist or sceptic, is typically rejecting the pragmatist or anti-realist approach to the class of statements in question, and is assuming that the statements involved are meaningful, and are either true or false independently of our having, or knowing what, would count as *evidence* for them. We cannot therefore just opt for a verificationist account which replaces truth with something like warranted assertibility, and then proceed on *that* basis alone to legislate against the introduction of global talk.[13] We need to argue first that there is no room for the view that the statements of global ontological talk possess an objective truth-value, independently of our means of knowing it. It would then follow that nothing other than the anti-realist view is available with regard to them; and since that will not suffice to sustain global ontological talk, there would then be no room left for such talk.

However, in view of what we have already seen it would seem that showing *this* is precisely what requires some further argument for the incoherence of the central notion involved in talking about a globally independent world. Putnam, we have seen, argues against the metaphysical realist's epistemological thesis, and makes a strong case to show that our descriptions of the world are true only within the constraints imposed by our theories, rather than independently of all theories and of all evidence we can have for them. But this still leaves room, as we have seen, for the realist to affirm and the idealist to deny that there is some globally independent world, and leaves room for the sceptic to doubt whether that world is the way our best theories confirm it to be. This is because we are apparently still left with the

---

[13] Stroud makes a similar point in concluding his discussion of the verificationist response to scepticism about our knowledge of the external world: 'The point is that for anyone who finds the sceptical argument at all persuasive its very persuasiveness provides just as strong an argument against accepting the verifiability principle as that principle can provide against the meaningfulness of the sceptical conclusion.' (Barry Stroud, *The Significance of Philosophical Scepticism*, Oxford, Clarendon Press, 1984, p. 205.)

coherent notion of a real world, even if our reference to it is impoverished by the fact that we cannot say anything more about the way it is, over and above that it is that which exists independently of all experience. The relevant point here is that having once secured the possibility of this reference, however impoverished, it follows that we cannot simply legislate against the possibility of employing a model whereby the truth of a statement to the effect that there is some such world is determined independently of our evidence for it, solely by whether there *is* indeed some such world.

Furthermore, it is not in fact that we can say only that it might be the case that there is such a world, without unpacking this any further to suggest in what *way* it might be different from the way we experience it to be. In Chapter 3 we saw that it might be possible for BIVs to entertain the thought that they might be BIVs.[14] And if this argument is accepted, we can say that for all we know we might be BIVs, although we could never have any evidence for this being the case. Indeed we do not even know what would count as evidence for that being the case. We simply know what would count as its *being* the case, quite apart from any *evidence* we could conceivably have. To take another example, it might be suggested that the real world is different from the world as we experience it to be, in that it is, say, inhabited by certain organisms which are such that they only exist when unobserved, either directly or indirectly. Here too we do not know what would count as *evidence* for this being the case; yet it does not seem meaningless or without content.[15]

It thus appears that despite its initial appeal, any application of the verificationist theory of meaning to statements of global ontological talk will be question-begging as long as the basic notion of a globally independent or dependent world is still coherent. For as long as it is, there is no clear reason why the proponent of global ontological talk should not apply a truth-conditional account of meaning to the class of statements which comprises such ontological talk.

Thus verificationism of this form cannot simply be applied without further ado to the case of global ontological talk in any non-programmatic way. To anyone engaged in such talk the application to his case of this verificationist view will still seem to be doctrinaire, and insofar as this is so would not on its own seem to provide adequate grounds for the rejection of global ontological talk. On the other hand, if the basic notion of a globally independent (or

---

[14] See section 3.2.

[15] Although it might be conceded that it is without *scientific* content, and so is not a legitimate statement within a scientific theory. This concession will be taken up immediately below as the foundation for a final attempt at a less question-begging argument from verificationism.

6. Examining Global Ontological Talk: Verificationism 143

dependent) world were shown to be incoherent, there would no longer be any need to appeal to an argument from verificationism against global ontological talk at all.[16]

At this point it might be tempting to search for an even weaker form of verificationism, in the hope that we might thereby be able to come up with something sufficiently uncontentious to be accepted as a starting premiss even by someone engaged in global ontological talk, and which yet offers sufficient leverage to sustain a conclusion against such global ontological talk. One idea would be to concentrate on the fact that certain statements might be meaningful, and yet obviously be admitted to lack scientific content, just insofar as we do not know what could possibly count as evidence for them. That is, we might attempt to argue a case against the *legitimacy* of global ontological talk, without going so far as to claim that the assertions involved are meaningless. The principle involved would be something like the following:

> There is a legitimate assertion of a proposition p, only if it is possible to distinguish at least in principle between it being the case that p as opposed to *not-p*.

It is important to recognise how weak this principle is. In the first place, we should obviously not confuse legitimacy of assertion with warranted assertibility. By a *legitimate* assertion no more is meant than an assertion which is acceptable within a context of critical enquiry. This is not to say that its assertion is actually warranted. An assertion which is unwarranted might be legitimate within a critical context of enquiry. The above principle allows that only some of those statements whose assertion is legitimate within the critical context will be statements whose assertion is also warranted. This is because an assertion is legitimate in this sense just insofar as there *could* be evidence for it, and is warranted only if there actually is evidence for it.

Secondly, and more importantly, nothing about this weak principle commits us to either eliminating truth in favour of, or redefining it as, warranted assertibility. Indeed nothing at all is said about the truth of the statement, or of its meaningfulness. This consequently leaves the principle entirely devoid of any commitment to an anti-realist or pragmatist account. We can equally well apply this principle along with a view of truth as determined by what is objectively the case, independently of our means of knowing it, such that an assertion which it renders illegitimate within the context of a critical enquiry might none the less be independently true. The idea would simply be that since we have no evidence which can give us a grip on such statements, enabling us to distinguish between its being the case that

---

[16] Cf. Stroud, *The Significance of Philosophical Scepticism*, op. cit., pp. 207-8.

p rather than not *p*, they belong within some context other than that of critical enquiry. While verificationism in its more doctrinaire forms can attract scorn which we might consider justified, it is difficult to see what might be regarded as reproachable in this rather weak and straightforward principle. Indeed it is perhaps not quite right still to call it a 'verificationist principle'. Let us, therefore, see just how far we can go on this slender and uncontentious basis towards constructing an argument against global ontological talk. The question is whether the obviously weaker conclusion yielded by an argument based on this weak principle will still be strong enough to eliminate global ontological talk as required.

The argument might run along these lines: If experience did not, by its very form, require that a distinct object world be given, we might be in a position to establish whether or not there was an object-world which was ontologically independent of all such experience. However, since experience does involve – as a formal condition – being confronted with a distinct object world, it is impossible, either in practice or in principle, to tell whether that object-world presented in experience, or indeed some other, stands in ontological independence to the form of all experience [realism] or is merely ontologically dependent upon that form (i.e. is merely a feature thereof) [idealism]. Experience, just insofar as it is inconceivable without an object world being presented within it, is impervious, insensitive, to any fact of the matter regarding the global ontological dependence or independence of that object-world. Given the above weak principle, it would follow from this state of affairs that there can be no legitimate assertion that the world we experience is real, or not, since there would be no distinguishing between its being one or the other; independent of, or dependent upon, the form of all experience.

But how far does this conclusion take us? Earlier, metaphysical realism was seen to involve two theses, an ontological thesis to the effect that there is a real world, one which stands in global ontological independence of all experience, and an epistemological thesis to the effect that it is possible to know this world as it is. An argument against the epistemological claim regarding the absence of experiential colouring from our knowledge of the world still left the realist some room in which to find refuge, as long as he was willing to share it with the sceptic. It was thus emphasised (Chapter 3) that it is not enough to argue against the epistemological claim, since even without this the realist still had a leg to stand on, namely his ontological claim that there was something real, globally independent of all experience. A crude realist, who assimilates causal and ontological independence, could still assert *that* there was some epistemologically remote Kantian thing in itself; a more sophisticated realist could actually say

6. Examining Global Ontological Talk: Verificationism 145

that the real world (that which stands in global ontological independence of experience) is this very world with which we are in causal contact. He would merely have to give up his confidence about the epistemic *reliability* of this contact. Either way, as I have said, such ontological theses are basic to all forms of realism or idealism. It is the assertion of just such ontological theses that the present argument from verification would reveal to be illegitimate. Any ontological thesis – positive or negative – regarding a real world is one which we, given the structure of experience, cannot legitimately assert within the context of critical philosophy. Metaphorically, the distinct object-world of experience sets itself up as an anti-verificationist blanket over the *entire* realist and idealist framework.

To see this clearly, it will perhaps be of interest to recall here that the fact of being confronted with a distinct object-world, or indeed with one which exhibits local ontological independence or dependence, emerged in the last chapter to be neutral with regard to the introduction of global ontological talk. This neutrality was twofold; both between the possible positions within global ontological talk and with regard to the very question of whether or not to introduce any such talk in the first place. Having now added to the discussion the weak principle of verification – the very fact of the former type of neutrality (between realism and idealism) alters the latter neutrality (between introducing global ontological talk or not). Whereas without this principle the joint fact of a distinct object-world and of local ontological talk neither required nor denied the possibility of introducing some position of global ontological talk and in this sense was neutral, the possibility of introducing such talk is now denied. Given the present weak principle of verification, the neutrality of available evidence between realism and idealism means not merely that we need not introduce one or the other, but indeed that we may not; the introduction of either is excluded as illegitimate.

The argument from the weak principle can indeed take us this far; but unfortunately this is not far enough. It provides a sense in which we must avoid global ontological talk, but remains too weak to do all that is needed. The fact that our sceptic survives the demise – on the present weak verificationist grounds – of both the realist and the idealist can serve as evidence of this. (Again that philosophical compass.) It seemed, earlier, that an argument against the ontological thesis of realism would finally silence the sceptic who thrived in the situation in which the realist's epistemological thesis was rejected, while the ontological one was left intact. Yet it has now emerged that not any such argument will do.

All the weaker argument from verification shows is that we cannot legitimately assert that the object-world in our experience, let alone some other, is or is not ontologically independent of all experience. Although the argument thereby undermines the realist and idealist ontological *theses*, it is too weak to disallow the speculation that it might still be the case that there is (or is not) an independent reality, even though we could never find out. And this immediately lets in the sceptic. It is in this respect that the modified argument does not go far enough. It cannot lead us to reject *all* global ontological talk; merely that part of such ontological talk which results in assertions of ontological theses, positive or negative. Nothing has been shown to be wrong with the very *idea* of the global ontological independence or dependence of some world.

It should be noted, in contrast, that although Carnap's more programmatic verificationist argument in 'Pseudoproblems' also turns immediately on the *theses* of realism and idealism, the scope of that argument is not similarly restricted to those theses. Carnap uses the strong principle of verification to establish that, because they are not verifiable, such theses are *meaningless*.[17] Granting for the moment Carnap's view that the argument from verification establishes that the appropriate statements are meaningless (rather than merely illegitimate) within the given context – he rightly concludes from this that

> neither the thesis of realism that the external world is real, nor that of idealism that the external world is not real can be considered scientifically meaningful. This does not mean that the two theses are false; rather, they have no meaning at all, so that the question of their truth and falsity cannot even be posed.[18]

While this argument does indeed apply *directly* only to *statements*, it would seem to apply indirectly to any other form of ontological talk as well, precisely because ontological statements have been said to be *meaningless*. Their being meaningless renders the corresponding questions and speculations, which share the same propositional content, equally meaningless. Consequently Carnap holds that we can comfortably discard *all* concern over a 'metaphysical reality', and get on with our investigations of 'empirical reality'.[19]

However, this desirable extension of the argument rests on the programmatic use of the principle of verification. Having rejected any such programmatic lengths, the present more reasonable argument from verification applies only to those ontological theses towards which it was specifically directed. It shows that we cannot legitimately assert

---

[17] 'Pseudoproblems in Philosophy', op. cit., pp. 332-3.
[18] ibid., p. 334.
[19] Carnap defines these terms on pp. 273 and 281-4 (ibid.).

6. Examining Global Ontological Talk: Verificationism   147

ontological theses as the realist and idealist are wont to do, but does not attempt to establish that those theses are *meaningless*, or that they are neither true nor false. Consequently the conclusion of the weak argument cannot be so conveniently extended to apply to other forms of global ontological talk which, while assuming the coherence of these theses, and indeed *that* they are either true or false, do not try to assert them as true or as false. Questions and speculations involving global ontological dependence and independence thus remain perfectly acceptable forms of such ontological talk. Given a question, to which meaningful answers *can* be formulated, and which might be true or false, there is no reason to think that the question is rendered meaningless just because we cannot even in principle *verify* which of the formulated answers is the right one.

Even so, it might still be insisted that such questions are merely *pseudo*-questions; that, just insofar as the answers to them in principle cannot be legitimately asserted, they cannot themselves be *legitimate* as questions (even if they are coherent). However, this would again be to extend the scope of the conclusion in an unreasonable and doctrinaire way.

Perhaps it is reasonable to say of questions in the context of empirical science that they are only legitimate or relevant insofar as they can actually – or at least possibly – be answered. But not all critical contexts are of this sort. And it is surely the case that in the philosophical context a question might be legitimate simply because we know what kind of statement would count as an answer to it – even if it just so happens that that statement is such that we cannot, even merely in principle, offer any way of distinguishing between it rather than its opposite being the case. The statement is then indeed such that it cannot legitimately be asserted within the critical context, but a philosophical question surely does not have to be *answerable* to be legitimate. All that is needed are grounds for thinking that it does have an answer (even if we cannot know it), or that a coherent answer can be *formulated*.

Global ontological talk, beyond positive and negative assertions, involves such questions. The possible answers to them might perhaps belong in the domain of religion or in some other such area. But insofar as these answers can be coherently formulated the questions which prompted them remain philosophically relevant. Similarly such ontological talk involves speculation, talk of what might be the case. Thus it is not clear that the statement 'It is possible that there is no independent reality' is rendered either incoherent or illegitimate merely because we cannot make a legitimate assertion of the form 'There is a world which is ontologically independent of all experience'. On the contrary, the very fact that the latter is not verifiable only lends conviction to the previous speculation. This is brought out by the more forceful formulation of the same speculation: 'Consider the possiblity that there is no ontologically independent reality, although we could never legitimately judge this to be the case.'

Thus just showing that the assertion of global ontological theses is illegitimate does not show that *all* global ontological talk is illegitimate. And the above examples also show that such talk is far from philosophically trivial. The sceptic who wonders about the fact of there being, or about the nature of, an independent reality, does not make assertive judgments about the ontologically independent world, or ask questions which are only legitimate to the extent that they can be answered (i.e. questions of an empirical science). The sceptic merely ponders possibilities and points out that things might be one way or, perhaps, another way. He presupposes only that there *is* a truth of the matter, about which we would like to know. The fact that we cannot know, cannot establish a truth of the matter, far from making the sceptic's *question* meaningless or illegitimate, only adds to its force. The sceptic can now add to the possibility that there is no independent reality, or that the independent reality is not at all as we experience it to be, the addenda that since we could not tell that things were one way rather than another, we must simply refrain from *judgment* and accept the speculated possibility. Thus the weak argument only adds epistemological frustration to ontological scepticism.

It is one thing to have argued that all assertions of global ontological theses are illegitimate – thereby undermining the realist and the idealist; a further step is required to defuse the sceptic. For this a broader argument would be needed, not merely against the legitimacy of global ontological assertions (positive or negative) but quite generally against the coherence of all global ontological talk; assertions, questions, expressions of possibilities, speculations. The stronger and more programmatic verificationist arguments for this further conclusion are unacceptable, while the present modification, although acceptable, is again too weak.

A different approach might now be tried, an approach which finally confronts the very conception central to *any* form of global ontological talk, rather than one which concentrates on the verifiability of judgments which employ it.

Since this further argument would not involve verificationism, the attempt to deliver it should please those who are not inclined to accept verificationist arguments. And insofar as this line of argument turns directly to the coherence of the very conception upon which *any* form of global ontological talk is based, rather than applying directly only to asserted theses, it would differ in nature – and consequently in scope – from that of the verificationist approaches discussed in this section,

6. Examining Global Ontological Talk: Verificationism

overlooking the *programmatic* differences of scope between them. If the very notion central to global ontological independence or dependence were shown to be incoherent (although not necessarily devoid of emotive force), any such ontological talk, whether assertive or not, would be undermined even without the programmatic extensions of a verificationist argument.[20]

As will now be made clear, Carnap's general philosophical view in fact does suggest a path similar to the one we are about to follow.

6.2 Carnap's line of investigation in The Logical Structure of the World

While the argument in 'Pseudoproblems' is indeed directly concerned with statements, this is not true as a description of Carnap's concerns in general. Apart from his concern with verification as determining the meaningfulness of statements, he is also concerned to establish the meaningfulness of individual terms. Underlying the verificationist principle is a more general commitment to an empirical theory of meaning. According to this theory, individual concepts are meaningful only if they have either direct empirical reference, or are derivable from other concepts that do (in which case they have *indirect* empirical reference).

It would seem that in accordance with some such theory as this, a theory which examines individual concepts, the central conception involved in global ontological talk could be examined, and either established or undermined. If it were undermined, this would serve to take the argument against ontological talk beyond the applicability only to *assertions* of theses, to the required level of generality.

However, when Carnap himself attempts to provide his examination of concepts, in *The Logical Structure of the World*,[21] he is altogether too brief in disposing of the concept of a reality which is ontologically independent of all experience.

---

[20] It is of interest to recall here that at the end of the last chapter (p. 135 n. 10) it was mentioned that, even if global ontological talk is not needed to express our ordinary beliefs about the ontological status of the empirical world, it might be introduced as a theoretical underpinning to accommodate certain cultural projects to which our conceptual scheme commits us. In this role global ontological talk might be seen as no more than an explanatory device, employed with indifference to questions about whether such talk is *true* or *false*. Any such use of global ontological talk is very different from the employment of it which is of primary importance in this essay. Nevertheless it is worth noting that, while verificationist arguments – without unreasonable extension – would generally not affect this merely instrumental use of global ontological talk, an argument against the coherence of the central notion involved in such talk would have direct bearing on the use of it even as a mere theoretical prop.

[21] Rudolf Carnap, *The Logical Structure of the World*, op. cit. In what follows I will refer to this work by the abbreviation *TLSW*. All page references in this section are to this work.

The brevity of this discussion is in part a result of the intended emphasis of the entire book. Thus on p. 246, 'before going on to the clarification of some philosophical problems on the basis of construction theory', Carnap says:

> The problems we shall discuss are meant only as examples. In this book, the emphasis is put on construction theory itself, not upon its application; thus, we cannot give a detailed discussion of the individual problems. We must leave this for a separate discussion.

The brevity of the discussion might also derive in part from the fact that given the strength of the programmatic conclusion he is willing to draw from the argument in (the slightly later) 'Pseudoproblems',[22] Carnap does not consider that the case against all ontological talk remains incomplete until further argument has been provided against the very notion involved in any such talk. The full importance of further argument can be appreciated only when the unsatisfactory nature of the verificationist criterion of meaning is appreciated, and the conclusions of the argument which employs it are accordingly restricted in scope. Carnap himself did not believe the verificationist criterion to be unsatisfactory in a way which would require such restrictions. Consequently he did not think that very much turned on providing what to him seemed to be merely another argument for the same conclusion.

Nevertheless the concern in *TLSW* to examine the legitimacy of individual concepts rather than merely that of asserted statements coincides with the projected course of examination; so it remains to see to what extent our examination of concepts can proceed along the lines set out by Carnap in that work.

Carnap describes the aim of the *TLSW* at the outset:

> The present investigations aim to establish a 'constructional system', that is, an epistemic-logical system of objects or concepts.... Unlike other conceptual systems, a constructional system...attempts a step by step derivation or 'construction' of all concepts from certain fundamental concepts, so that a genealogy of concepts results in which each one has its definite place. It is the main thesis of construction theory that all concepts can in this way be derived from a few fundamental concepts, and it is in this respect that it differs from most other ontologies.[23]

---

[22] See n. 8 on p. 139 above.

[23] *TLSW*, p. 5. It should be noted that the word 'ontology' is used here as a translation of Carnap's 'Gegenstandtheorie'. This refers to those objects which a given theory posits as the objects which exist in the world. This is the sense in which Quine too uses the word. It should be clear by now that in this essay the primary concern is not with ontology as internal to a theory.

6. Examining Global Ontological Talk: Verificationism

His primary interest is in those concepts which form part of the constructed reality, by which he means *empirical* reality. (He emphasises that a 'constructed reality' is intended to be metaphysically neutral.) In particular he is concerned to show how concepts within empirical reality can be incorporated into a systematic account which demonstrates that, starting from a given class of fundamental concepts, other concepts which we employ in experience can be constructed. It is when Carnap comes to the question whether the concept of an ontologically independent reality can be constructed in this way that his treatment is too brief.

In contrast with *empirical* reality, with which science is concerned and of which Carnap attempts to outline a possible construction, there is a *metaphysical* concept of reality. The former is the only concept of reality which is of interest to Carnap. It does not contradict either realism or idealism (and in this sense is logically neutral between them). Yet the preoccupation with questions concerning empirical reality does not, as has been pointed out above, suffice to undermine the questions about a reality which exists independently of all experience. There remains a question (with regard to which we are not *intellectually* neutral) as to whether the empirical reality is also real in the metaphysical sense: that is, whether the reality which is distinct from and possibly ontologically independent of us in our experience is also ontologically independent of the form of that experience.

Carnap recognises that there *are* two senses of 'reality', the one neutral and homely and the other philosophically charged and metaphysical. He also recognises that the metaphysical notion of reality is common to both traditional idealists and realists – they agree in asserting that there is something real in the second, metaphysical, sense; they merely differ in their respective identifications of what it is that they hold to be metaphysically real. Thus Carnap says:

> The second [metaphysical] concept of reality (in the sense of independence from the cognizing subject) indicates the point where the schools of realism, idealism, and phenomenalism part company. These schools are distinguished from one another by the fact that they ascribe reality in the second sense to object domains of varying extent (within the field of the empirically real).[24]

There seems to be little doubt that the distinction Carnap makes between empirical and metaphysical reality coincides with the distinction between merely internal, or empirical, reality, and that which is said (either by traditional realists or idealists) to be ontologically independent of all experience.

[24] ibid., p. 282.

But Carnap does not clarify with sufficient care what he means by the metaphysical concept of reality. All he says is that it involves 'independence from the cognizing subject'. By now it should, I hope, be clear that this formulation is too vague. In the first place, Carnap talks of independence without explaining what sort of independence he has in mind. He does not adequately distinguish ontological from causal independence, and indeed does not seem to appreciate the importance of this distinction. As will immediately become apparent, the failure to make this distinction is the root of an error which renders his brief discussion of the matter altogether inadequate.

Furthermore to say that a metaphysical reality would be that which is independent of the cognizing subject leaves the matter open to multiple interpretations even once it is recognised that ontological independence need not involve the absence of causal relations. It could still mean either

(1) Some x is ontologically independent of any one cognizing subject, or
(2) Some x is ontologically independent of all cognizing persons, or
(3) Some x is ontologically independent of all experience, of the form of all experience.

Both (1) and (2) are perfectly legitimate, local and neutral forms of ontological independence. They apply within, and do not attempt to reach beyond, the experienced object-world. In contrast, (3) captures the notion which is central to the global kind of ontological talk against which we would wish to argue. It is only reasonable to assume that *this* is the concept which Carnap too has in mind: that is, that he would accept that (1) and (2) fall within the first concept of a constructed reality, whereas (3) goes beyond that to outline the concept of a metaphysical reality.

Thus (3) constitutes a more precise formulation of what Carnap might mean by the concept of a metaphysical reality. Now Carnap wishes to examine 'whether this second concept of reality can be constructed', i.e. whether it can be expressed through objects of the most important types which we have already considered...' (ibid.).

While this is precisely what Carnap needs to show, he does not in fact do so. His brief discussion of the issue on pp. 282-3 seems to miss the point, precisely because he has not been sufficiently careful in defining exactly what the concept of a metaphysical reality involves.

Carnap starts the discussion by saying that

> an object which has been constructed on the basis of my experience, will have to be called 'independent of my consciousness' if its constitution

6. Examining Global Ontological Talk: Verificationism

does not depend on my will, i.e. if an act of volition which aims at a change of the objects does not result in such a change.[25]

He goes on to suggest that, although this much can be constructed, it will not do as a concept of reality which either the realist or the idealist has in mind when the former ascribes it to, and the latter denies it of, physical bodies (p. 283). His reason for this is that on the definition just given a physical object in my hand is *not* real, insofar as an act of my volition can change it; whereas any physical object which lies outside our technological reach should be acknowledged as real, since it does not change if I carry out the appropriate act of will. The former conclusion is taken to contradict the position of realism; the latter is taken to contradict the position of idealism. Consequently this concept of reality cannot be the one either the realist or the idealist have in mind.

This, unfortunately, is not very impressive. Carnap has not shown that any attempt to construct the notion of a metaphysical reality must fail; it is not even the case that he has shown the failure of one particular attempt to construct it; he has, it seems, simply failed to identify which notion he was trying to construct.

Carnap has confused ontological independence with causal independence. He has managed to construct the notion of a reality which is in some (weak) sense causally independent of us ('an act of volition which aims at a change of the objects does not result in such a change'). It is hardly very interesting then to point out that this does not satisfy the requirements of the relevant notion of a metaphysical reality. There is no reason why it should. The fact that the successfully constructed weak notion of a causally independent reality does not satisfy either the realist's or the idealist's needs does not have any bearing on whether or not the relevant type of *ontological* independence can be constructed. This latter is not something Carnap has even attempted.

Nevertheless, satisfied with this apparently confused opening gambit, Carnap only goes on to assert that:

> One could try in various other ways to give a definition of reality (in the sense of independence of my consciousness) in such a way that the concept becomes constructable. However, one can show in each such case that the concept which is so defined does not agree with the concept as it is meant by realism as well as by idealism.[26]

And from this Carnap concludes that:

---

[25] ibid., p. 283
[26] ibid.

> The concept of reality (in the sense of independence from the cognizing consciousness)[27]... cannot be constructed in an experiential constructional system; this characterizes it as a nonrational, metaphysical concept.[28]

It is therefore said to belong not within (rational) science, but within metaphysics (p. 282).

By not considering carefully the sense of independence which he has in mind, Carnap has managed to take ontological independence as if it were simply causal independence. In so doing he is at most taking on the crude realist or idealist. What he says does not undermine the realist who claims – or the idealist who denies – that this very world to which our technology *does* apply is ontologically (yet obviously not causally) independent of us.

As was suggested above, it is possible that, because Carnap inclined towards the argument in 'Pseudoproblems', which was to establish the further-reaching conclusion to the effect that the entire concern with a metaphysical reality was *meaningless*, it seemed to him that there was no need to elaborate an argument for what he took to be a weaker conclusion. Indeed in the preface to *TLSW* he says quite explicitly that he considers the 'condemnation of all these theses about metaphysical reality (which is clearly distinguished from empirical reality) is more radical [in 'Pseudoproblems'] than that in the *Aufbau*, where such theses were merely excluded from the domain of science' (p. xi).

If the inadequacy of the proposed argument in *TLSW* against the constructability of the ontological notion resulted entirely from Carnap's conviction that the kind of argument in 'Pseudoproblems' could do all that was necessary, now that this has emerged not to be so the obvious task would be to complete the project Carnap outlined: namely, to provide an argument which showed that the central ontological notion was not one that could be constructed in terms of other more basic notions.

I will not, however, pursue this line of argument, for two reasons. The first is straightforward, and probably also explains why Carnap himself did not provide more than the blunt assurance that any other attempts – that is, any other than the brief and rather misguided first attempt to construct the metaphysical notion of reality – would fail. It is simply not at all clear how it is possible to establish the *impossibility* of constructing a given notion in terms of others. It is easy to show that a notion *can* be constructed in terms of others: by simply producing one possible construction of it. It is perhaps also relatively easy to point out that we have not yet managed to construct a given notion. But it is not

---

[27] ibid., p. 282.
[28] ibid., p. 283.

6. Examining Global Ontological Talk: Verificationism

at all easy to show that a certain notion *cannot* be constructed. (In fact the statement that '*x* is not a constructable notion' is not verifiable, and so by Carnap's own criterion should be deemed meaningless.)[29] It is of course possible to demonstrate how *difficult* the required construction is. But that would not show that it *could* not be provided, that *x* is not a constructable notion. The argument would simply not be strong enough. Thus, while the Carnapian strategy for showing that the ontological concept is not acceptable might at first seem promising, it in fact turns out to be impossible to provide a conclusive argument.

There is a second reason why Carnap's strategy is not well suited to provide the desired argument against the ontological notion. It is simply not clear what would count as the *basic concepts* in terms of which others could be constructed. Let us assume that Carnap had not confused *ontological* independence with other kinds, and had somehow proceeded to show that the concept of an ontologically independent reality cannot be constructed in terms of certain basic concepts. This in itself would not yet suffice to characterise it as a non-rational, non-critical concept. It might, after all, have been a *basic* concept itself. Indeed it is not clear why, should such construction fail, the ontological notion could not for that very reason be introduced as itself a basic notion.

Unlike the previous objection, this one does not pose a problem for Carnap. The problem arises only when the strategy of concept construction is prised apart from the rest of Carnap's philosophy. Carnap's work is embedded in the context of logical empiricism. For the logical empiricist there is a clear answer to the question as to which concepts are to be admitted as basic.

Carnap is involved in a step-by-step derivation of concepts on one level from those on a lower level, ultimately reaching down to the basic experience of the first level (pp. 5-6). The attempt is to show 'that it is in principle possible to reduce all concepts to the immediately given' (ibid., p. vi). In section 67 Carnap identifies quite definitely what is to count as a basic element for his constructional system. And any concept which is neither basic nor derivable from the basic level is excluded from the constructional, scientific framework.

Thus what excludes the possibility of introducing the ontological notion as itself basic is not Carnap's constructional theory as such, but rather the commitment to logical empiricism within which it is embedded. Within such a commitment to logical empiricism it is clear that the ontological notion cannot be introduced as basic. For the logical empiricist any basic concept must be sustained by direct

---

[29] It is to cope with such generalisations that Carnap was later forced to talk about confirmability rather than verification.

reference within experience – and it is indeed difficult to see how the concept of a reality that would be there even if there were no experience at all can be sustained by *direct* reference in experience. Given this, it follows that, if the ontological concept cannot be constructed *indirectly* in terms of other basic notions either (overlooking for now the difficulty involved in showing this construction to be impossible), Carnap can indeed conclude without further ado that it is not a critically sustained notion.

In the context of a constructional system which is not committed to logical empiricism, however, there is no reason to restrict the basic concepts to those sustained by raw experience, by direct reference to experience. Without the doctrinal underpinning of logical empiricism, I have no clear idea of what is to count as a basic concept. Consequently, even if the ontological notion cannot be constructed in terms of any other notions, this is not enough to lead to its rejection. No non-programmatic reason has been given to show why this notion should not then be introduced as itself a basic notion. Indeed, given this, the fact that it cannot be derived from other, supposedly more basic, notions, might easily be interpreted as providing all the more reason for accepting as basic the ontological notion of a world independent of experience; one which would exist even in the total absence of experience. While this is not a possibility that Carnap has to consider – given his marriage to logical empiricism – it is one that cannot, at least at present, be excluded from the present inquiry.

It thus becomes clear that, insofar as I am not so conveniently wedded to logical empiricism, Carnap's constructivist approach will not do. An argument against global ontological talk must examine its central terms more directly. If the central relation involved in global ontological talk were itself shown to be incoherent, the question of whether this ontological notion can be constructed in terms of other 'basic' notions would have become redundant. It would no longer matter whether it would have to be introduced as basic, or be derived from other notions. Either way, there would be no room for it.

7. The Terms of Global Ontological Talk

Let us, then, turn to examine more directly the terms of global ontological talk and the central relations involved in it.

Speaking quite generally, we have seen that any form of ontological talk involves a relation (in the simplest cases, a two-place relation) between objects, where 'object' is taken as broadly as possible, to cover any item which may function as the referent of a successfully referring term. Consequently, a presupposition for expressions of these relations being coherent is that the terms employed in any statement purporting to express such relations should each refer.[1]

However, the presupposition for the coherence of these ontological independence and dependence relations in general is only that the terms involved each refer, even if they refer to one and the same object. In contrast, when we narrowed our concern specifically to the global ontological relations involved in realist and idealist talk of something being or not being real, we specified that in those cases ontological relations must hold between *different* referents.[2] Consequently for global ontological talk there is a further presupposition. Here we have relations which presuppose not merely that the terms involved are successfully referring terms, but that they do not refer to one and the same object. That is, in these cases ontological relations hold only between referents x and y where x is not identical to y.

Given this it follows that any assertion of ontological dependence or independence which employs terms which do not refer will be incoherent as a form of ontological talk. And in particular it follows that any assertion which employs terms that either do not refer, or simply fail to refer to different objects, will be incoherent as an expression of global ontological talk of what is or is not real. In these cases, if the terms involved, on any coherent understanding of them, cannot deliver the referents as required, it will follow that talk of something being or not being real cannot be coherently set up. This is not to say that in these cases of presuppositional failure nothing would be thought, that the person's mind must be totally blank. It is simply

---

[1] See section 1.2.2 above.
[2] On the reasons for this see section 1.3 above.

that whatever thoughts we might have on those occasions, they could not be thoughts involving the global ontological relations relevant to talk of something being or not being real. And if this were shown to be necessarily the case with any global ontological talk, we would be released finally from the realist-idealist see-saw of contradictories.

A possible argument, in accordance with this strategy, will now be outlined.

7.1 A possible argument

Global ontological talk purports to assert independence or dependence between an object-world and the form of all experience. Before beginning, let us look at the two referring terms involved.

In considering the first term, the object-world, it will be reasonable to lay to one side those individuations of objects which are or might be the result of local cultural characteristics, and which might therefore differ from one cultural context to another. Rather, we might speak of the object-world simply as the lowest common denominator in virtue of which local individuations, despite divergences between them, are all alike individuations of an object-world. The present concern is not with the particular identification of the real world, but with the very identification of some object as being or not being real. We may therefore overlook all specific features of one particular identification of the 'real' over the other. Abstracting from the particular, we want now to talk about the general nature of an object-world, however identified.

The other term involved in global ontological relations is experience. Apart from the differences between one empirical form of experience and another, it is possible to identify the general form of experience which any individual experiencing beings, however different from one another, must embody. All conceivable experience, as we have seen,[3] takes the form of object-directedness. Abstracting from the particular, we are again talking now about the general form of any particular manifestation of experience.

This seems to equip us with a more or less clear idea of the two basic terms which function in the relations involved in all global ontological talk. Global ontological independence says of some object-world that it is independent of the form of all experience. Global ontological dependence says that the world – even that part of it which is locally independent of all experiencing beings – is still dependent upon the form of all experience. The question is, whether an argument can now

---

[3] See section 4.3 above.

7. The Terms of Global Ontological Talk 159

be provided to show that these two terms – despite appearances to the contrary – are not qualified to function in such relations of global ontological dependence and independence. I shall attempt to develop an argument to this effect, without introducing much supporting literature, in the hope that a stark presentation of the argument will facilitate an uncluttered view of its merits and shortcomings.

The exposition of the proposed argument may be separated into two strands, each of which takes up one of these two terms. The outcome of the entire argument will bear some resemblance to that of Davidson's attempt 'to urge that ... dualism of scheme and content, of organising system and something waiting to be organised, cannot be made intelligible and defensible'.[4] By a different route, concerned rather with the form of all experience and the object-world, we stand to reach a conclusion which converges with, and lends support to one aspect of, Davidson's call for the rejection of the scheme-content distinction (which he regards as the third dogma of empiricism).

(a) Let us turn back to the first term, the object-world, to consider the first strand of the proposed argument. This part of the argument may be stated briefly, before we consider its merit in greater detail. Whatever is said to be or not be real must, necessarily, be an object (of whatever kind). This is a precondition for the assertion or denial of reality. But being an object presupposes individuation. Individuation is essentially perspectival. Perspectival individuation does not necessarily presuppose experiencing beings, but does, at the very least, require the form of object-directedness. Object-directedness is the central feature of the form of all experience. From this it follows that to this extent the very conception of an object-world is bound up with the form of all experience.

It is important to clarify this intermediate conclusion before going over the argument for it in greater detail. In saying that the very conception of an object-world is bound up with experience, the idea is certainly not merely that the *act* of conceiving of that world – like all other acts – requires experience; but that that which is conceived *itself* requires experience of it, however rudimentary. The point is that *given* object-directed experience (in the absence of which we cannot conceive of anything at all) we cannot conceive of a world without conceiving of it as involving object-directed experience. Moreover, and more important, the point here is not simply that made by Berkeley in his famous tree argument, at least as that argument is readily interpreted.[5] The point is not merely that we cannot conceive of a world without *thereby*

---

[4] In 'On the Very Idea of a Conceptual Scheme', op. cit., p. 189.

[5] Berkeley, *The Principles of Human Knowledge*, sections 22-3. For a more charitable reading of Berkeley's argument, see A.C. Grayling, *Berkeley: The Central Arguments*, 1986, pp. 113-16

conceiving of it. Any argument which rests on this point will not, to say the least, seem very convincing. The present point, however, has to do with the role played by experience *in the object conceived*, not in the act of conceiving it. The world to which we are intentionally related is such as to have object-directedness built into it. Object-directed experience is introduced twice – once, trivially, in our consideration of the matter, and then again in the matter considered.

Let us turn back now to a more detailed consideration of the grounds for the central assertion, that all individuation is perspectival in the first place. We might start with the observation, from which we will work back, that insofar as individuation *is* perspectival, the belief about the independence of, say, mountains, interpreted along lines of global ontological independence, runs into trouble. In Chapter 5 it was shown that our common-sense beliefs about the independence of mountains could be accounted for in terms of local ontological independence, without having recourse to global ontological talk. However, this left open the possibility that, although not *needed*, global ontological independence of all experience *could* be introduced – albeit heavy-handedly – in support of those intuitions. If all individuation is indeed perspectival, however, it would appear that it is not merely, as was said in Chapter 5, that global ontological independence is not needed to account for those beliefs, but that indeed it cannot be used to account for them. To the extent that the individuation is perspectival it does not make sense to say of *mountains* that *they* would exist in the absence of the form of all experience, since the minimal perspectival element required for their individuation as mountains would then have been eliminated. It is difficult to maintain that this mountain would exist even if there were no experience, where this is interpreted to mean in the absence of the very form of experience which is required for its individuation as a mountain.

To the extent that all individuation is perspectival, it follows that, as soon as the absence of experience involved in global ontological independence is introduced, the belief concerning the independence of mountains seems, at best, to collapse into an entirely different, and by no means intuitive, belief. If, because individuation is perspectival, it is wrong to consider that this mountain would exist in the absence of all experience,[6] it would seem that the realist conviction could now be reformulated (thus no longer attempting to support our common-sense beliefs) to allow for this; *that*, whatever it is, which in experience we identify as a mountain, exists independently of all experience. Or more accurately, that that within which we identify a part as being a

---

[6] Recall that I use 'all experience' as shorthand for 'the form of all experience'.

7. The Terms of Global Ontological Talk   161

mountain, would exist even in the absence of all experience. Even if all our individuations are like secondary properties, so that we cannot identify something and say that *it* would exist in the absence of all experience, we can surely still have a coherent conception of *some* world – that same something which in experience is locally cut up[7] into various objects – which is totally non-perspectival, and so is independent of the form of all experience. But by way of this reformulation that which is real is pushed back – the belief concerning mountains having now been dissolved into one about some noumenal hard core underlying our perspectival individuations. The intuitive belief has evaporated, and in its place we now have, at best, a philosophical notion of an underlying world which is said to be independent of all experience. It would thus appear that the ontological fallacy identified above was all the more serious. It is not merely that our common-sense beliefs do not require, but that they cannot withstand, the move to introduce global ontological independence.

The realist thus becomes a transcendental idealist, and we find someone like Putnam saying:

> It is a property of the world itself, I claimed – i.e. a property of THE WORLD itself – that 'it admits of these different mappings'.
>
> The problem – as Nelson Goodman has been emphasising for many, many years – is that this story may retain THE WORLD but at the price of giving up any intelligible notion of *how* THE WORLD is.[8]

This retains ontological talk of a globally independent world, merely allowing it to recede to a noumenal status. But now consider further, that if we are to talk coherently about some such non-perspectival world surely that world must itself be individuated, just as much as the objects which were mapped onto it. And the question is whether *this* individuation could be any less bound up with the perspectival form of experience than that of mountains and valleys. It would seem that the same kind of consideration which might prevent us from saying that *mountains* would be individuated as such even in the absence of any appeal to the form of all experience shows that the very conception of a world (however noumenal) is equally bound up with object-directed experience (however residual).

There is, admittedly, a significant difference between mountains, tables, rabbits and valleys on the one hand and this noumenal world

---

[7] Which is not necessarily to say that *we* cut it up.

[8] 'Realism and Reason' in *Meaning and the Moral Sciences*, London, Routledge and Kegan Paul, 1978, p. 132.

onto which they are to be mapped on the other. The former objects are set apart from other objects. They are results of individuations within the object-world. The latter, however, is itself not set apart from some other object, but from the mere absence of one. It is the most general possible individuation of an object. Consequently there is no other thing which could be combined with it to form a different individuation; taken to the limit, there is no other way of cutting its contours. Thus the possibility of empirical relativism which is quite apparent in the case of mountains and valleys – viz. that they could have been valltains – does not apply in the case of this individuation of a bare world which is supposed to be such as would allow for global ontological independence.

To appreciate this, consider the attempt to say that rather than individuating between that bare world (something) and the absence of one (nothing), some other cultural group could cut across the two and individuate both as, say, 'nonething'. It is quite evident that this does not in fact manage to alter the distinction, but only its label. For consider that 'nonething' – to be individuated at all – must still be set apart from its absence. To make sense at all, to constitute a world, however devoid of qualities, 'nonething' must still be something, which is set apart from nothing. Yet this is just the initial individuation all over again.

However, the fact that the extreme generality of this individuation between something and nothing does not allow for empirical relativism, for perspectival variation, in the same way as the individuation between mountains and valleys did, does not in any way suffice to show that this individuation is not perspectival all the same. To see this, consider the following. Assume that no appeal can be made to object-directed experience at all, not even to the formal structure of such experience. Try now to assume that there is, however, something as opposed to the void in which it exists. In the absence of all experience, what possible individuation can there be between this something and the sheer absence of it? The only possible distinction would seem to be where one of the two (whichever) is or could be regarded as an object, and the other could not. However, this reintroduces the perspectival element of object-directedness, intentionality.

In the absence of reference to the object-directed form of all experience the very individuation of something as opposed to nothing thus collapses. There can be no non-perspectival individuation even of a mere something. Yet without the distinction between something and nothing, we cannot individuate a world. It thus appears impossible to individuate a world – however noumenal – except insofar as we assume object-directed experience of it. Wherever we conceive of reference to a world we are making sense of reference to a world which itself involves some such experience of it.

The element of object-directedness involved might indeed be residual, it might be temporally remote, it might even be merely that manifested by the formal structure of all experience. That is still enough to set the stage on which the individuation of a world – something – as opposed to the absence of one – nothing – can gain a foothold. But in the total absence of the form of all experience – its object-directedness – the distinction between *something* and *nothing* simply collapses.

I take this to show the sense in which the very individuation of an object as such is perspectival. And given that the very individuation of an object as such is perspectival, it should be all the more clear that individuation is perspectival at the level of more specific individuations, which rest on more obviously local perspectives. It is as if in talking about an object we overlook the fact that it is, in fact, an *experienced object-world* that we must have in mind if we are to talk of an object-world at all.

Perhaps there is room for some immediate amplification at this point. Saying that all individuation is perspectival is only meant to convey the idea that the individuation of an object presupposes at least the formal vantage point (object-directedness) implicit in the form of all experience. It should be emphasised that this can be accepted without fear of entailing a commitment to anything like radical relativism. Relativism would require accepting not merely that individuation is perspectival – itself an innocuous claim – but also that different individuations are available from different perspectives. In a sense, but not a philosophically charged one, this latter claim is in fact true. Differences of cultural individuations result from different *cultural* perspectives. This is what we saw above. We distinguish mountains and valleys; but elsewhere, in a different culture, the shared perspective might be such as to result in the individuation of valltains. Such relativism is, however, devoid of philosophical teeth. It is the consequence of cultural variation with which anthropologists and tourists are concerned. The point here is that, accepting the perspectival element involved in all individuation does not entail accepting metaphysical relativism, to the effect that beyond empirical and entirely translatable perspectives there can be radically different perspectives which deliver radically different individuations which cannot be translated into one another, or into a single larger perspective (unlike the way in which mountains and valltains can be translated). It is perfectly possible to reject *such* relativism while still maintaining that all individuation is perspectival. It could be that, empirical variation aside, there is a single over-arching perspective from which individuation can occur, and which accommodates within it the possibility of understanding regional variations.[9]

At this point it might be thought that, insofar as the notion of an object-world makes sense only given experience, if only in the limiting sense of the form of all experience, we can conclude that it is therefore dependent upon that form. This would amount to a form of idealism, minimally conceived as the idea that we cannot conceive of the world's existing independently of the form of all experience. However, as it stands the argument is only half delivered, and there is hope yet that its completion will eliminate this threat of idealism. Here we introduce the second strand of the argument.

(b) Note that to say that the world is dependent upon the form of experience we must be taking a view of experience, or indeed merely of the form of experience, whereby it is different from the object-world, in such a way that it is itself an object upon which the latter can be (or not be) ontologically dependent.[10] But there is reason to think that this view cannot be accepted, as will be seen if we now turn to examine this term more carefully, and appreciate that it is not merely that talk of 'the world' makes sense only given its involvement with the form of all experience, but equally that 'the form of all experience' makes sense only on the similar assumption of an object-world.

I have throughout appealed to the fact that we can coherently conceive of experience only as involving intentionality. To the extent that the very notion of experience involves directedness towards an object (world), it follows that we cannot conceive of referring distinctly to the form of experience in isolation from a world which is presented to it, however minimally. The conception of experience is such that it cannot be detached from the conception of an object-world which is presented to it.

It should be noted, however, that the mere fact of adding this second claim, that the form of experience involves being directed toward an object-world, to the first claim, that we cannot conceive of a world which is not experienced, is not in itself enough to block the possibility of idealism which arose so clearly when only the first claim had been introduced. There are, in our philosophical tradition, various ways of accommodating these two claims within a system of philosophical thought – ways which differ in their (mostly unnoticed) effects on the resulting philosophical position.

---

[9] This line of thought resembles that offered by Williams in 'The Truth in Relativism' (in *Moral Luck*, op. cit.) and in 'The Scientific and the Ethical' (in *Objectivity and Cultural Divergence*, ed. S.C. Brown, CUP, 1984); as also Davidson's line in 'On the Very Idea of a Conceptual Scheme', op. cit. I will return to this issue in Chapter 8.

[10] Recall the preconditions of global ontological talk set out in 7.1 above.

7. The Terms of Global Ontological Talk

There is a Kantian way of accommodating these joint facts, (a) that we cannot conceive of an object-world which is not minimally bound up with experience of it, and (b) that we cannot conceive of experience which is not bound up with an object-world. A Kantian strategy, to put it schematically, involves accommodating (a) and (b) in a layered, or two-stage, model. The first stage is concerned to settle global questions regarding an experience-transcendent reality. At this level we introduce the fact that we cannot conceive of an object-world which is not minimally bound up with experience; and in consequence formulate something like the doctrine of the noumenal world. This deals with our worries about the global issue. Having done so, we then leave the upper tier, the first stage, and proceed to the lower level, where we ask internal questions about the structure of our experience. On this second level we then introduce the second fact, that it is a condition of experience in general that we be directed towards outer objects; that it is impossible to conceive of experience which does not involve an object-world. This deals with the internal structure of experience. The two basic claims are thus segregated. In consequence we end up – although perhaps not quite as neatly as this suggests – with the positions of transcendental idealism (based on (a) at the level of global concerns) and empirical realism (based on (b) at the other level).

Most commentators on Kant have remained Kantian in that they have accepted (perhaps without identifying) this application of the two-tiered structure. Some, like Strawson, might wish to turn away from the discussion on the global level and find value in concentration on the other, empirical level. In contrast, I wish to confront these global issues. However, it is difficult to see what good reason there might be for adopting a compartmentalising strategy which allocates each of the two conceptual claims ((a) and (b)) to a separate section, the one global and the other local (internal). It is this strategy which determines the Kantian two-pronged outcome in the form of transcendental idealism and empirical realism. Once we avoid this strategy, we can consider the *joint* relevance to global ontological talk of both conceptual truths; that (a) we cannot conceive of a world which is not an object of experience (however minimally), just as (b) we cannot conceive of experience which is not directed towards an object-world (however rudimentary). It is in this that our investigation veers away from the Kantian approach.

Even when taken jointly, however, these two claims might be accommodated in such a way that their conjunction allows room for a kind of idealism. To the extent that the object-directedness inherent to the form of all experience can be set apart from the object-world which confronts us in experience, the possibility that the latter might be ontologically dependent upon that form remains unaffected by the claim that the form of experience itself cannot be detached from directedness towards an object-world. The attempt would be to segregate the form of experience, and the directedness to an object-world essentially involved in it, from the actual object-world which confronts us, and the experience involved in it.

It is of interest to note that any attempt to effect this separation would involve the introduction, again, of a two-level structure, albeit in a different application. The result would now be a Platonic model of two levels, the one being in some way transcendent, or external to the other. On a Platonic view the form of experience might be thought of as transcendent relative to the object-world which confronts us in experience, so that our relation to the latter can be said to fall under that form, to be dependent upon it. This is to turn the entire form of experience – object-directedness and all – into something akin to a Platonic Form, itself a separate object in a separate realm, which object is then said to be related to some other – empirical – object (i.e. the actual empirical world) in a way which can render the latter dependent upon the former. This is indeed the way the matter might seem if two realms are assumed, empirical and transcendent. However, this again is an unnecessary embellishment, and indeed one which readily issues forth a regress similar to that generated in Plato's *Parmenides* by the Third Man Argument, and for very much the same reasons, to do with the assumed transcendence of the Forms.[11]

The form of experience is being removed in objectualised form to a different level, at which Platonic heights it can function as something like a *transcendent* Berkeleyan God (cf. 4.3 above). Taken in this way we can ask whether it and the world are ontologically independent or dependent relatively to one another; but we can then also ask whether this objectual representation of the form of experience is itself real, dependent upon an intentional relation to it, just as it can be asked of Berkeley's God, occupying a transcendent realm, whether he is real, or merely exists insofar as he perceives himself. The only way to avoid this is to recognise that the problem arises from initially taking an objectual view of the form of experience, thereby making a model of that form, and mistaking this (once-removed) objectual model for the genuine thing, which is essentially object-directed rather than objectivised.[12] The point is not to ask whether the object-world is dependent upon some objectual representation of the form of

---

[11] Plato, *Parmenides*, 132a-133a.

[12] Insight into some of the issues relevant to this point might be gained from T. Nagel's 'Subjective and Objective', in *Mortal Questions*, CUP, 1979, despite Nagel's apology for the merely exploratory nature of that paper. See also his more recent *The View from Nowhere*, op. cit.

7. The Terms of Global Ontological Talk

experience – some wax-like effigy derived by objectivisation at Platonic heights – but whether it is dependent upon the very form of experience within which there is an intentional relation to that object-world (and to that objectual representation of the form itself).

Thus it is not appropriate to separate into a different ontological realm the form of all experience along with the object-world involved in that form. The Platonic separation renders an *objectual* view of what the form of experience is. This objectual view is unsatisfactory, since it renders impossible the individuation of any object, including itself: Individuation requires a perspective afforded only by an object-directed, not an object*ivised* form of experience. In conceiving of the form of experience we must in fact conceive of it in an Aristotelian way, as the form implicit in, and integral to, the experienced object-world. And this object-world is the very one which in turn could not be conceived of without the appeal to object-directed experience.

Where does this leave us? Once the nature of the terms is investigated, resulting in the dual claims that we cannot conceive of a world except as the object of experience (if only in the limiting sense), and that the form of experience involves being directed towards an object-world (if only in the rudimentary sense); and furthermore, once the discussion avoids the unwarranted (and untenable) assumption of a two-level superstructure which in one way or another introduces a convenient segregation into those two claims, we begin to realise that the conceptions of world and experience are separable only by abstraction. In conceiving of experience, even of the mere form of experience, we have in fact extracted that conception from that of the *experienced object-world*; in conceiving of an object-world we are similarly extracting our conception from that of the *experienced object-world*.

(c) It is at this point that the two strands of the argument come together in the required way, enabling us to complete the proposed argument.

The terms 'world' and 'experience' both seem to pick out, or make salient, different aspects of a *single* larger conception, the salience of the one being at the expense of the other. From the conception of an experienced object-world we derive by abstraction our conceptions both of experience and of an object-world. Yet for the most part we tend wholly to overlook the fact that if we are to talk of an object-world, or of experience, in both cases it is from the conception of an experienced object-world that we must commence. These conceptions, separable only as abstractions, rely on semantic opacity to secure apparent reference to two different referents; while in fact, once the sense of the terms is made transparent, as has been attempted in the foregoing analysis, both terms – experience and world – turn out to be abstracted from the larger conception, of the experienced object-world.[13]

Upon examination, two distinct terms which initially appeared to have different referents, such that the required ontological relations could hold between them, turn out to be derived by abstraction from a single third conception, which itself picks out only a single referent: the context of experienced objectivity. Under conditions of semantic opacity these two abstracted notions appear to have different referents. Rendered transparent, it turns out that they both pick out aspects of a third conception whose referent is different from either of the two putative referents suggested under conditions of opacity. The latter two prove to be impossible as referents, collapsing under conditions of transparency into that single common referent.

Any two (or more) terms of which this is true might be called referentially integrated terms. That is, such terms cannot be seen as referring terms which pick out two different referents, despite appearances under conditions of semantic opacity; but only as picking out different aspects of a single third referring term. In consequence any such terms converge on the same referent.

Precisely because the veil of opacity has hitherto remained largely undisturbed, experience and object-world being taken as picking out two different referents, the referent which both in fact share between them has no accepted label. I have referred to it variously as the experienced object-world, or as the context of experienced objectivity.[14] It is from the conception of this experienced object-world that we can then (either opaquely or transparently) abstract the notions of the object-world and of the form of experience.

So much by way of stating the core of the argument. However, the relation of referential integration introduced here requires some elucidation before we can appreciate the effect it has on the possibility of global ontological talk. Generally speaking, referential integration is a relation between referring terms and their referents. But this is not quite sufficient.

It is important to note that referentially integrated terms are said to pick out different aspects of a common conception, which is not the same as saying that they pick out different aspects of a common referent. For it would be difficult to maintain a distinction between terms referring to two different aspects (or sides) of the same object, as opposed to two different objects. The difficulty pertains to the

---

[13] As will become evident, the use of opacity and transparency here differs from, although clearly is related to, the established technical use of these terms.

[14] While no more need be said here, it should be noted that because of an obvious ambiguity and the less obvious conceptual tension in it, this latter phrase wears on its sleeve certain philosophically significant indicators, thereby making it particularly apt.

7. The Terms of Global Ontological Talk

distinction between an *aspect* and an *object*. (For example, would a surface be an *aspect* of a material body, or simply a different object?) Just insofar as we can refer to them, aspects of objects can themselves be seen as objects.[15] It would thus seem that there is not much distance between saying that two terms pick out different aspects of a single object and saying that they simply pick out different objects which are ontologically dependent upon one another. Consequently any attempt to insist on such a distinction for the present purposes would seem question-begging. And we would surely have to be wary of any attempt to argue that 'world' and 'the form of all experience' picked out different aspects of the experienced object-world, and that this undermined, rather than amounted to a form of, global ontological dependence between world and experience.

But this is not what has emerged from the above. If we could get so far as to say that 'world' and 'the form of all experience' pick out different aspects of the same referent, and could separate those two aspects sufficiently to refer to *them*, those aspects would indeed provide the required referents for global ontological talk. To insist then that they were nevertheless only aspects of a single referent rather than ontologically dependent objects would seem extremely tenuous. The problem that emerged, however, was that we could not get so far as to establish such reference in the first place, whether to aspects or to objects. For, in order to establish any referent for either of the terms, we needed first to conjoin it with the sense of the other term. And this resulted in the third, larger conception, which does not refer to one aspect rather than another, but to the entire context of experienced objectivity.

It is for this reason that referentially integrated terms were not said to pick out *two aspects of one referent* instead of two different referents. It was rather that they pick out *one single referent* between them, instead of two. Each term has a different sense. Understanding its sense reveals that term to be making salient an aspect of a larger conception which was previously opaque. The two terms jointly pick out aspects of that *conception*, which conception itself picks out a single referent, which is consequently the referent common to both terms.

To understand this more clearly it might be helpful to compare the particular case of referentially integrated terms with that of referentially convergent terms in general. The relation of referential integration might be said to constitute a special case of referentially convergent terms, i.e. terms with different senses and a single referent, as in the standard example of Hesperus and Phosphorus.

---

[15] Recall the definition in 1.2.2 above, whereby an object just is any item which may function as the referent of a properly referring term.

Under conditions of semantic opacity such referentially convergent terms might appear to have different referents; but they are revealed in semantically transparent contexts as referring to one and the same entity, merely differing in sense. This is just the case with referentially integrated terms. However, in the ordinary case of referentially convergent terms it is a matter of *a posteriori* discovery to reveal them as having a common referent, rather than two distinct referents corresponding to each of the two terms. This was, notoriously, the case regarding Hesperus and Phosphorus. In contrast, referentially integrated concepts form a special case, in which the concepts themselves are such that their senses, being abstractions from a common third sense, are linked, so that an a priori investigation reveals them to converge into that single larger conception, which itself has a single referent. It could not be otherwise, as it could in the case of Hesperus and Phosphorus, where it might have turned out that they had discrete referents. In the case of referentially integrated concepts this is ruled out by the very conditions for their having meaning in the first place. Apart from this difference, however, referentially integrated and convergent terms are alike insofar as they are only senses apart, and will be found to share a common referent.

Saying that referentially convergent terms in general, and referentially integrated ones in particular, share a single referent between them, rather than two different referents, brings out the need to provide the criterion for determining whether two or more terms refer to the same, or to different, objects. This is of course equally important in understanding the added requirement in the case of global ontological talk, that the referring terms should refer to different objects.[16] Clearly it is not possible to understand what it is to refer to two different objects without understanding what it is to refer to the same object. And this in turn cannot be explained fully without understanding what it is to be 'the same object'. The general issues involved here are large, and pertain to an extensive discussion which falls outside the scope of the present work. It is sufficient for our purposes to explain only how narrowly I am construing reference to the same object, leaving aside the adequate resolution of the general issues pertaining to an understanding of what it is to be the same object.

Two terms will be taken to refer to the same object only if their referents are qualitatively and numerically identical. I will not, for example, consider references to different parts of a whole as references to the same object. Referring to my desk-top, and to my desk-drawer, will not be taken to be two ways of referring also to the same object, the desk. The desk-top and the drawer are two different referents, two

---

[16] This issue was flagged in the first chapter; see n. 20 in section 1.3.

7. The Terms of Global Ontological Talk   171

objects which are parts of a larger and again different object, the desk. Nor will any successful reference by means of term A to a part or aspect of some larger unit, itself successfully referred to by means of term B, be taken to mean that A and B refer to the same object, whether to the part (A) or the whole (B).

This narrow understanding of what it is for something to refer to the same object is accommodated by the very wide reading that has been given to the term 'object', whereby the different aspects of an object, just insofar as they can be referred to, i.e. can serve as referents, are themselves objects. This means that there is no need to look to any larger whole in which that referent is a part, in order to discover which object it refers to. The reason for construing 'object' so widely, and reference to the same object so narrowly, is that it is important to make sure that in turning to examine ontological talk we have not, simply by convenient definition, already precluded the possibility of certain ontological relations holding between *different* objects.

We might capture the above narrow definition of what it is to refer to the same object by saying that 'x' and 'y' (and any other 'z') refer to the same object if by fixing the reference of one term we converge upon the precise referent of the other(s). Conversely, any two or more terms would refer to different objects if in fixing the reference of the one we do not thereby converge upon the precise referents of the others. Some further examples might make this clearer.

In fixing the reference of 'colour' (that into which transparent light can be decomposed) we do not converge upon the precise referent of 'extension'; and vice versa, in fixing the reference of 'extension' (any spatial structure in two or more dimensions) we do not converge upon the precise referent of 'colour'. In referring to colour and to extension we are therefore referring to two different objects. It is, of course, precisely because the two referents are different that in discovering that colour cannot exist without extension we have an interesting case of ontological dependence, rather than merely the self-reflexive case of an object being dependent upon itself. In contrast, in fixing the reference of Phosphorus we do converge upon the precise referent of Hesperus and, of course, vice versa. Thus in this case we have two terms which refer to the same object.[17] It is for this reason that in the assertion that Hesperus is ontologically dependent on Phosphorus we do not have a very interesting case of such dependence; it amounts to no more than the dependence of an object upon itself. And the case is

---

[17] Note that any two synonymous referring terms, e.g. bird and feathered-biped, will refer to the same object; but I have thought it useful to regard such terms as simply co-referential, reserving 'referential convergence' for those terms which converge on the same referent but differ in sense, in a way that ordinary referring synonyms, for example, do not.

similar when we move from referentially convergent terms, to the special case of referentially integrated terms, insofar as here too the terms converge on a single referent, and so refer to the same object.

Given this, we can now turn to the effect of referential integration on the possibility of global ontological talk. Ontological dependence and independence relations *in general* required only that the terms involved refer, without stipulating that they should refer to different objects. This was designed to avoid the arbitrary denial of the obvious – if trivial – ontological dependence relation which holds between any object and itself, namely that it could not exist in its own absence. It is true of every object that it is ontologically dependent upon itself; false that it is independent of itself. It is consequently clear that the mere fact that two terms have been shown to be referentially integrated, and so pick out only one referent between them, is not in itself sufficient to preclude all ontological talk.

Accordingly, to the extent that the concepts of world and all experience, despite being referentially integrated, are made to serve in statements expressing ontological dependence and independence, the result is not quite as intended, but is nevertheless a coherent form of ontological talk. Once the cover of semantic opacity is removed from the referentially integrated terms, it emerges that the referent of both terms is one and the same – the context of experienced objectivity. Consequently, upon the elimination of semantic opacity, the assertion that the object-domain is independent of the form of all experience emerges as an assertion that the context of experienced objectivity is independent of itself. The other assertion, that the world is dependent upon the form of all experience, becomes an assertion that the context of experienced objectivity is ontologically dependent upon itself. And there is no doubt that both these forms of ontological talk are coherent; the latter claim is as analytically true as the former opposing claim is analytically false.

But this is *all* that can be salvaged by way of coherent ontological talk from the intended global ontological talk, in the face of the referential integration of its terms. And this does not constitute global ontological talk. It is hardly relevant to the concerns of the realist, the idealist or the sceptic to establish that every object, including the context of experienced objectivity, is ontologically dependent upon itself rather than independent of it.

In the particular application of ontological relations involved in talk of what is or is not real it was found necessary to admit the formal requirement that the referring terms used in asserting those relations must refer to different objects. Accordingly the presuppositions of the coherent expression of any statement of *global* ontological dependence or independence were that the terms involved should not only be

7. The Terms of Global Ontological Talk 173

successfully referring expressions, but also refer to different objects.[18] In consequence of this added presupposition, however, expressions of global relations cannot employ referentially integrated terms. In the case of referentially integrated terms there is no room for the required reference to two different objects, since both terms are revealed under conditions of transparency to converge on one and the same referent.

Consequently, as referentially integrated terms, 'world' and 'form of all experience' do not satisfy one of the formal requirements for the coherence of the global ontological talk which they are supposed to constitute. Insofar as the concepts of world and the form of all experience are referentially integrated, and cannot be understood in any other way, the question as to whether their presumed different referents are ontologically dependent upon or independent of one another cannot be posed at all. They do not *have* different referents corresponding to the terms 'world' and 'form of all experience' which would enable us to raise questions pertaining to global ontological relations. Given the loss of the required referential distinctness due to referential integration, a relation of global ontological independence or dependence cannot even be set up.

The required terms for global ontological talk – of world and experience which are not referentially integrated, i.e. which pick out different referents – are not available. On the other hand, those which are available – those which emerge under conditions of semantic transparency – emerge as having a single common referent, and insofar as they converge on the same referent they are not suited to function as terms in a relation of global ontological dependence or independence. To the extent that it is based on the assumption of notions which are in fact unavailable – i.e. notions of a world and the form of all experience which are not referentially integrated, and so do not converge on a single referent – global ontological talk is altogether empty. Based on the available notions, which are referentially integrated, it is seen to fall foul of its own presuppositions. The result can at best be transformed into the entirely different, trivial form of reflexive ontological relations which no longer constitute global ontological talk at all.

The attempt to express statements specifically of global ontological dependence and independence thus appears to emerge as incoherent. I shall treat statements which purport, impossibly, to express global ontological relations, as instances of presuppositional failure and hence as not being either true or false. A full account of the semantic issues raised by these statements, although obviously important, would extend beyond the limits of the present work, and in the absence

---

[18] See 7.1 and 1.3 above.

of a more detailed discussion I would not wish to commit myself further than I have to any one view of them over the other. Neither is it necessary for the present purposes to do so. The point here is only that, due to presuppositional failure, such ontological talk seems to have proved impossible. It should be noted, however, that what we have is not merely the failure on a particular occasion of a significant sentence to express a statement which is either true or false. The presuppositional failure is such that these sentences *could not* be used to assert statements of global ontological talk which were either true or false. It is *this* that brings into question the very significance of such sentences.[19]

Referential integration between terms precludes us from setting up relations of either global ontological independence or dependence, insofar as further examination of the nature of such talk has revealed that it stands in contradiction to one of the required conditions of its coherence. In this way an argument from referential integration suggests one way of getting off the realist/idealist see-saw of contradictories: or rather, the impossibility of getting onto that see-saw in the first place.

So much as a statement of the argument designed to show the incoherence of the desired form of ontological talk. The question is whether this argument is satisfactory. Before turning to some objections, it will be of interest to recall the ontological fallacy identified above.

7.2 The ontological fallacy again

In the light of this suggested argument from referential integration against global ontological talk, the ontological fallacy identified in Chapter 5 now seems to be of increased importance.

The ontological fallacy involves any transition from talk of something's being or not being independent of *us*[20] in the context of the experienced object-world, to talk of something's being or not being independent of the form of all experience inherent to that context. Or, more succinctly, it involves a slide from something's being or not being independent of all forms of experience, to its being or not being independent of the form of all experience. In particular, we have seen that the fallacy most readily occurs when evidence for independence in the former sense is mistakenly taken to support a claim of

---

[19] Compare Strawson, 'On Referring', in *Logico-Linguistic Papers*, London, Methuen, 1974, pp. 9-12.

[20] Again, taken broadly, in the Wittgensteinian sense, to mean any conceivable experiencer, however remote from us-humans.

7. The Terms of Global Ontological Talk

independence in the latter sense. We can now see that there is in fact more than this involved in the ontological fallacy. The move from local 'dependence or independence of us' to global 'dependence or independence of the form of all experience' also requires a shift in the interpretation of that which is said to be either dependent or independent.

The shift from local ontological relations between an item and ourselves, to global ontological relations between that item – qua part of the object-world – and the form of all experience presumes a shift from the notion of an object world which might well be referentially integrated with the form of experience to the notion of one which is not so integrated.

Upon further investigation, however, the incoherence of this conception of an object-world and experience which are not referentially integrated seems to have emerged. Given that this is the case, there is no room to apply global ontological dependence or independence. Thus we see that, insofar as the foregoing argument is accepted, the import of the ontological fallacy is not merely that by way of it an otherwise coherent conception is incoherently introduced. That would merely require that we be more cautious in introducing it. The fallacy does not consist merely in an erroneous move – it involves an erroneous move to an incoherent notion. By way of the ontological fallacy we move from the general application of ontological dependence and independence within the context in which they function coherently as contradictories, to an incoherent specific application of them.[21]

It thus becomes clear that talk of global ontological independence or dependence could not be introduced except by way of some such fallacy. The incoherence of the required reference to a world and to the form of all experience can then pass undetected precisely *because* the purported reference is introduced by way of a fallacy, by way of the easy slip from talk of an object-world independent of us in the context of experienced objectivity to talk of an object-world independent of the form of all experience. The evidence for the former simply makes the latter seem so intuitive that it appears not to merit the further investigation which would reveal its added complexity, and ultimately its incoherence.

By way of the ontological fallacy the realist, idealist and importantly also the sceptic mistake the perfectly acceptable notion of a world referentially integrated with the form of object-directed experience, compatible with local ontological talk, for the notion of a world which is not referentially integrated with the form of such experience,

---

[21] The incoherence being the result of the unsatisfied extra presupposition in these cases, viz. that the terms involved refer *to different objects*.

appropriate to global ontological talk. The realist then asserts that there is some globally independent world, the idealist that there isn't, while the sceptic worries that such a world might be very different from the way we experience it to be. None of them notices that this notion of a world which is not referentially integrated with experience is, if the argument above is accepted, in fact incoherent; that it results from setting up global ontological talk under conditions of semantic opacity, in which it is not apparent that the terms employed are in fact referentially integrated and so share a single referent between them. They mistakenly think they have a grip on a coherent notion of a world and experience in the absence of referential integration, thereby making it possible to consider the question of global ontological dependence or independence, when in fact all they have is a coherent grip on the notion of a world which is referentially integrated with the form of experience, and which therefore cannot be taken up into the relations of global ontological talk at all.

Once the ontological fallacy is avoided, and to the extent that the argument for the incoherence of the required form of global ontological talk is accepted, neither the ontological realist's assertion that there is some globally independent world, nor the ontological idealist's corresponding denial, nor even the sceptic's worry that there might be a disturbingly alien one, can get off the ground. All alike – despite the very different things they say in employing them – accept as coherent the relations of global ontological talk. Revealing the incoherence of these relations promises to take the case against global ontological talk beyond the application to asserted ontological theses, which is all the acceptable form of verificationist argument could sustain, to the required level of generality.

7.3 Objections and clarifications

However, some important objections to the above argument might be raised.

One obvious question is whether the referential integration between world and experience is not tantamount to an assertion that the one could not exist without the other – in which case we have a claim of reciprocal ontological dependence between the two. We could hardly hope to reveal the incoherence of all global ontological talk while resting our argument on a notion of referential integration which itself turns out to appeal to global ontological talk.

However, I believe that the reasons for thinking that referential integration does not in fact involve any global ontological talk should already be clear. To the extent that referential integration entails

7. The Terms of Global Ontological Talk

some form of reciprocal dependence between its terms, this cannot be a relation of global ontological dependence, just insofar as such relations hold between different referents, and these terms have, according to the argument, only a single referent between them – the context of experienced objectivity. Whatever dependence might hold in the case of referentially integrated terms, it cannot be a relation of global ontological dependence.

This leaves open the possibility that the terms of global ontological talk are *conceptually* dependent upon one another. While the required ontological relation holds between different referents (and in this case there is only one common referent), conceptual dependence can hold between abstractions (of which there are indeed two). And surely, it might be objected, such conceptual dependence between the referring terms could not in itself suffice to establish referential integration, i.e. a single referent for the two concepts. It would seem possible for each of the conceptually dependent terms to have a different referent, and so for those referents to stand in relations of ontological dependence or independence relative to one another, regardless of the conceptual dependence which holds between those referring terms.

But this objection rests on a misunderstanding. The argument did not in fact move from conceptual dependence of two terms to their referential integration. The conceptual link between the two terms was closer than mere conceptual dependence. Rather than two primitive concepts dependent upon one another, they turned out to be abstractions – from a third conception, with a single referent – under conditions of opacity which established them as apparently both primitive concepts and discretely referring expressions. In fact any conceptual dependence would therefore have to hold between the conception of an experienced object-world and each of the two abstractions from it – experience, and object-world. It is then clear that it is not the case of two primary referring concepts which are conceptually dependent upon one another, in which case it would indeed still be possible to consider relations of ontological dependence or independence between their referents.

Taking a broader view, both these objections might be said to stem from a basic error which has typified traditional philosophical thought on these matters and which will continue to do so as long as the blanket of opacity is left intact. As long as it is assumed that we can start with the world and the form of all experience as two primitive terms, it seems to make sense to ask whether they are conceptually dependent, or whether their presumed different referents are ontologically dependent upon one another. We start from two presumed primitive terms and regard the relation between them as being in need of clarification. The point of the argument from referential integration is to effect a reversal of the traditional approach. Rather than regarding the terms 'world' and 'experience' as primitive, we should see them as secondary or derivative. It is not that we might as well reverse matters in this way, but that we are compelled to do so once the semantic opacity is removed and the concepts of world and experience are recognised to have meaning only insofar as their single common source is the context of experienced objectivity, from which those two terms are derived as secondary concepts.

The idea is that traditional thinking on these matters might simply have got things the wrong way around. What we start from is the context of experienced objectivity. From that primary context, by a process of abstraction, we can then distill the secondary conceptions of an object-world, and of object-directed experience, each of which has no unique referent, but rather a single common referent between them. It is only when, under conditions of opacity, this is overlooked, that we are induced to ask about the global ontological dependence or independence of their presumed referents. That is, questions of global ontological talk all arise because we start with the abstractions rather than with the primitive unified context from which those two terms are abstracted. And given this, the attempt to search for discrete referents for world and the form of all experience, and to ask about their ontological dependence and independence is bound to prove illusory.

It is perhaps of some value to note that starting from the context of experienced objectivity might provide an effective way of accommodating a variant of neutral monism. It was noted earlier (in Chapter 4) that the attempt by neutral monists to construct the categories of the mental and the material from neutral elements left open the possibility, indeed strongly suggested, that those neutral elements might be real. Starting from the context of experienced objectivity the neutral monist might now restate his case, talking of deriving the mental and the material by abstraction from the context of experienced objectivity (rather than by construction from elements possibly independent of the two), thereby equally well dissolving the old problem of how the one can effect the other. This avoids the suggestion that the neutral source from which constitution was to commence might constitute a globally independent, noumenal reality.

Nevertheless saying that the form of experience and object-world are secondary conceptions derived by abstraction from the context of experienced objectivity does not in itself commit us to this particular view, or indeed preclude us from identifying experiencing subjects (either persons or pure mental entities) and material objects as basic and underived particulars within the context of experienced objectivity. And it should be noted that, insofar as we would not wish to

7. The Terms of Global Ontological Talk 179

preclude this possibility, it is significant that reference to experiencing subjects and material objects alone, which would allow for local ontological talk, would not suffice to constitute global ontological talk.

A further objection might be raised. Consider that the argument given in this chapter bears some resemblance to Putnam's attempt to argue that it cannot be that we are BIVs because if we were we could not even formulate the possibility; the same words would then, in effect, express the quite different hypothesis that we are notional-brains in notional-vats. Similarly here, in trying to formulate global ontological talk, we cannot get our words to mean what we would need them to mean, whereas what they do mean turns out – once the semantic opacity is removed – to be unsuitable for expressing the realist and idealist positions, or indeed for inclusion in any other form of global ontological talk.

This comparison immediately suggests an extension. It will be recalled that I argued against Putnam,[22] that BIVs could consider that they might be BIVs, essentially by referring locally to BIVs in their experience and saying that they might be like that. It is significant that there is in fact no parallel move here. The *most* we can do is take some particular object which confronts us and suggest that *it* might be globally independent of or dependent upon the form of all experience. But since the form of all experience is referentially integrated with the object-world in which that particular item is (perspectivally) individuated, we would in fact be asserting that that item was ontologically independent of or dependent upon the experienced object-world of which it is itself a part. This is no longer a form of global ontological talk between world and all experience. What we have here are ontological relations between a given item, and the single referent common to *both* terms of that purported global ontological talk. Of course any item is ontologically dependent on, rather than independent of, the experienced object-world of which it is a part. But this is merely a variant of the trivial ontological dependence that holds between that experienced object-world and itself. It simply says that no part of the experienced object-world could exist in the absence of that experienced object-world. This is as interesting, and as neutral regarding realism and idealism, as any statement to the effect that no item in the universe could exist in the absence of the universe.

One final, illuminating objection might be mentioned. I have argued that world and the form of all experience are referentially integrated and in consequence have a single referent which for the most part remains hidden behind a veil of opacity. Whatever this common referent is, the objection runs, surely *it* is assumed to be something real, indeed

[22] See section 3.2 above.

the ultimate reality.

The experienced object-world, the context of experienced objectivity, is indeed basic, ultimate, primitive. It is all of that, but nothing about the argument could suggest, or indeed allow saying, that it is or is not real. For in asserting that it is real we would be asserting that the context of experienced objectivity is ontologically independent of the form of all experience. But it seems evident that there can be no room to ask of that entire context of experienced objectivity whether it is ontologically independent of, or dependent upon, a feature which, although essential to it, can only be abstracted from it as a secondary concept, in such a way as to have no referent other than that context of experienced objectivity itself. The attempt to say that the context of experienced objectivity is real thus collapses, again, into the trivial assertion that it is ontologically dependent on itself. No such assertion can amount to a form of ontological talk that is relevant to realism, idealism or scepticism.

In this sense the assertion is indeed trivial. Yet in another it is perhaps of some significance. We can talk of the context of experienced objectivity as being ontologically dependent on itself, and on nothing other than itself, and can say that we cannot go any further than this in search of an understanding of its ontological status. In this we come to rest at what there basically is; and find ourselves converging on the traditional idea of *substance*. Yet there is no room left for talk of this, the context of experienced objectivity, being real in the sense required for setting up global ontological talk of realism, idealism and scepticism. We thus appear to have managed to prise apart our traditional conception of what is most fundamental from our misconception (in terms of a reality as that which is independent of all experience) which traditionally gave rise to realism, idealism or scepticism about the world.[23]

Thus the context of experienced objectivity is basic and primitive; from it concepts of world and experience can be derived as secondary conceptions by way of abstraction; and within it relations of local ontological talk come into play. While all this is the case, this context of experienced objectivity with which we are left is itself outside the scope of ontological talk (except in the residual sense that the context of experienced objectivity can be said to be ontologically dependent on itself, or that any part is dependent on the whole). Global ontological talk, pertaining to the world and the form of all experience, seems to have proved impossible, and in this sense if the present argument is accepted we end up well removed from realism, idealism and

---

[23] Of course, this is not to deny that there remain other forms of scepticism which will persist in taxing the philosopher. Clearly not all forms of scepticism rest on this basis. I have been concerned only with one particularly central form of scepticism here.

7. The Terms of Global Ontological Talk

scepticism about the external world (except of the local, empirical forms, within the experienced object-world).

As anticipated at the outset of this chapter, the argument from referential integration can be seen as offering a way of bringing about the demise of a distinction akin to that between scheme and content to which Davidson addressed himself. And to the extent that it, or some more adequate reworking of the argument, is right, it follows that Stroud's Challenge mentioned at the outset (see 2.1 and 2.5 above) will finally have been met. The sceptic who wonders whether the real world – that which is globally independent of all experience – is as we experience it to be is then finally silenced, along with the realist and the idealist. Recall that this sceptic was not silenced by the argument against the metaphysical realist's *epistemological* thesis in Chapter 3, or by the Goodmanian relativism in Chapter 4, or by the acceptable arguments from verification in Chapter 6. In this way the sceptic has served as a philosophical compass, forcing a discussion of the central notion involved in any global ontological talk. By revealing the incoherence of such talk this sceptic stands finally to be excluded. Not by leaving his seemingly still potent question conveniently unanswered, as Rorty, Strawson, Quine, Putnam and Goodman did, but by showing his question to be empty, insofar as it rests on an incoherent application of ontological talk. As an incoherent question it surely would deserve to be left unattended, as it is by Strawson after his rejection of Kant's transcendental idealism. It is in this defusing of the sceptic's question that Stroud's Challenge would be met. Stroud stressed in 'The Significance of Scepticism':[24]

> We must come to understand in detail just what is faulty or incoherent in the traditional question about knowledge, or in the way it arises and is given its special force. We need to understand why we have at most an *illusion* of raising a real question when we ask it.[25]

If the argument proposed above is accepted, then having once revealed the ontological fallacy and the referential integration of the terms involved in global ontological talk we would in fact be in a position to explain not just the incoherence involved in the question, but also how the illusion might arise; that is, to explain why talk of there being a

---

[24] op. cit., p. 293.
[25] The same challenge, elaborated and more forceful, is re-issued in his more recent book, *The Significance of Philosophical Scepticism*, op. cit. Thus, in the concluding lines of the book he writes: 'The challenge is to reveal the incoherence of the traditional conception, and perhaps even to supply an alternative we can understand, without falling once again into a form of idealism that conflicts with what we already know about the independence of the world or denies the intelligibility of the kind of objectivity we already make very good sense of.' (p. 274) Regarding the latter, see Chapter 5 above.

real world might appear so intuitive in the first place. It would seem that this might be the result of the ontological fallacy, by means of which we slip from the obvious local independence of the world around us (on which realists and idealists typically agree) to the relevant global use of ontological talk. The latter is then charged with all the intuitiveness gleaned from, and properly belonging to, the former. This fallacious importation might itself sustain a confidence in global ontological talk which diverts us from a more direct examination of it which would, by removing the semantic opacity involved, reveal that far from being intuitive such global ontological talk is in fact incoherent. The idea is that this incoherence is commonly concealed by the veil of semantic opacity which is itself kept in place, protected from examination, by the apparently intuitive force added to global ontological talk by way of the easy slide into it through the ontological fallacy.

Stroud concludes his paper with the suggestion that, although it might by then have lost its appeal,

> Having reached that point we could perhaps appreciate how a fully naturalistic account could give us *all there is* for us to understand about human knowledge...[26]

Indeed in the absence of global ontological talk there is no option other than to fall back on the radically internalist perspective outlined in Chapter 4. This leaves room for the merely local forms of such ontological talk, which do not attempt to apply ontological independence and dependence relations beyond the context of experienced objectivity in which they can function coherently as contradictories.

To have shown that there is no coherent way of stepping beyond the merely internalist position in the way that philosophers – unaware of the ontological fallacy – have supposed possible in the past, to some extent basing their positions on just this fallacy, would thus be of some significance. We would be left with no possibility of stepping beyond the integration of world and experience to the coherent formulation of questions or speculations (let alone assertions) of global independence or dependence between world and all experience. There would no longer be any room to talk coherently of what is or is not real; independent of the form of all experience. The integration of world and experience is all we would have – which is not to say that it falls short of anything. We could not even say in what way we might have less than we can coherently conceive of having.

Having undermined as incoherent all global ontological talk, it

[26] 'The Significance of Scepticism', op. cit., p. 294

7. The Terms of Global Ontological Talk

would remain to work our way around, with more or less reflective curiosity, within the context of experienced objectivity. The resulting internalist position will inevitably be coloured by the recognition of the necessary perspectival element, the importance of which, once recognised, cannot be overlooked. This forces us away from a simple empirical realist view, and yet, as we will see shortly, does not lead us into anything like the quicksands of empirical idealism.

8. Conclusion

It is now time to assess where all this leaves us. Whether the argument offered in the last chapter, to the effect that global ontological talk is incoherent, is right is a matter I would not wish to pronounce on without a good deal more discussion. Further objections to the proposed argument can and surely must be raised. I choose for now to let matters rest as they are. To the extent that the argument is accepted, there remains no room to assert (with the ontological realist) that there is a world which is ontologically independent of the form of all experience, or to assert (with the ontological idealist) that there is only a world which is dependent upon the form of all experience, or to doubt (with the sceptic) whether there is a globally independent world, or indeed whether that world is as we experience it to be. To return to the metaphor employed in the second chapter – the philosophical map will have been cut down to size: it will have emerged that there is no room on it for anything other than an internalist account within the context of the experienced object-world.

However, even if the argument of the last chapter is not adequate to force the move away from global ontological talk by revealing it to be incoherent, we have, I believe, seen a strong case showing that while all the philosophers discussed (in Chapters 2-4) do still waver and leave room for global ontological talk, if only in their willingness to accept a possible commitment to a noumenal world, there is in fact good reason to be altogether less accommodating. It is not only that a thoroughgoing internalist position is sufficient – that the local ontological talk involved in such a position is both empirically adequate to accommodate our common-sense beliefs about the independence of the world, and logically neutral with regard to global ontological talk, so that there is no reason why the former should require a move to the introduction of the latter. We have also seen further, in Chapter 5, that the introduction of global ontological talk is most commonly the result of fallacious reasoning (allowing for the moment that we might not want to accept the further argument from referential integration, whereupon global ontological talk could be introduced *only* by way of the ontological fallacy). And, once introduced, global ontological talk would, at best, constitute an

8. Conclusion

unnecessarily heavy-handed way of accounting for the independence and dependence relations manifested in the world around us.

The deflationary attempt to tidy up the philosophical superstructure thus, at the very least, enables us to adopt a position of internalism within the context of experienced objectivity, altogether devoid of global ontological talk. It will rightly be asked, immediately, in opposition to what this can be called a position of 'internalism', if the further argument is accepted, to the effect that no other position is coherent. I suggest that the use of this term might merely provide oblique reference to the misguided philosophical concern in opposition to which this position is formulated: the concern to raise chimerical questions which attempt to reach 'out', beyond the integrated context of experienced objectivity. This oblique reference is intended to flag the contrast between the present position and those which still commit the ontological fallacy and thereby concern themselves with purported external issues concerning what there is or is not independent of all experience. However, apart from this textual reference to a different and incoherent philosophical approach, internalism does not involve acceptance of the legitimacy of such issues.

It seems that the task we are left with is to investigate internally the way we move around within a given context, and the way of the world given in that context. But this still leaves entirely open the nature of the investigation. It is at this point, having so far only cleared the ground, that more positive work might begin. For the present purposes, however, it will perhaps suffice to provide some general and reassuring orientation.

Clearly, one way of conducting this investigation, but by no means the only or indeed the most fruitful way, is that demonstrated in the writings of the later Wittgenstein. Indeed to some extent the argument presented here is reflective of what I take to be the philosophical temperament of the *Investigations*.

The sciences provide a rather different way of conducting such an investigation; concentrating on causal dependence and independence relations. The only constraint imposed on such scientific investigation so far is entirely negative. The scientific investigation of the world cannot be associated with the assumption that this world or some other is or is not ontologically independent of the form of all experience.

Either way, it should be noted how much is in fact left unchanged by this confinement to navigation within the context of experienced objectivity. The present rather vague outline of possible internalist concerns might sound reminiscent of Rorty's view[1] that all we can

---

[1] In *Philosophy and the Mirror of Nature*, Oxford, Blackwell, 1980.

claim is a point of view located 'within the conversation of mankind'. To a certain extent – insofar as this excludes appeal to a globally independent reality – this comparison is acceptable.

Importantly, however, saying that all we can have is a point of view located 'within the conversation of mankind' also seems to imply that we are in some way confined to *conversation*, to *texts*. This is something that Rorty, following Derrida, apparently accepts. However, there is nothing about the argument in this essay which forces us to accept either Rortean conversationalism or Derridean textuality. The present case against global ontological talk has not aimed to establish, nor has it eventuated in our confinement to language. In this respect, then, it is wrong to describe the present account as leaving us merely with a position within the conversation of mankind. The framework provided allows us to reach out of language to an object-world; indeed to both subjects and objects which are often locally independent of one another.

Consequently the internalist position with which we are left by the present discussion need not give up the metaphor of knowledge as a mirror of nature, which is what Rorty would have us do. Rather, we only have to give up a certain interpretation of the ontological status of the nature that is mirrored. An internalist approach is free to consider that we do mirror nature, it is merely that the nature mirrored is at most one given as locally independent of us within the context of the experienced object-world.

Giving up the mirror of nature threatens to leave it unclear what it is that scientific explanation does, and seems indeed to reduce all voices in the conversation of mankind to mere chatter in the confinement of a cell of words. This criticism of Rorty has been voiced, for example, by Bernard Williams.[2] It is therefore important that this book intersects with Rorty's position in claiming that all we have is an internal point of view; and yet because the argument is not directed against the epistemological model of the mirror of nature, but only against the ontological status of that nature, it can nevertheless allow for a position which avoids this criticism. Indeed, once the mirror-of-nature view is accommodated within the internalist account, pared of the ontological extravagance which has possibly emerged as incoherent, it might well be quite harmless and immune to the objections Rorty levels against the model.

The resulting account amounts to something like the naturalistic account Stroud anticipates in 'The Significance of Scepticism'.[3] Still more clearly it coincides with Davidson's concluding remark to his 'On the Very Idea of a Conceptual Scheme':

[2] 'Auto-da-Fe' in *The New York Review of Books*, 28 April 1983, pp. 33-6.
[3] op. cit. See quote in 7.3 above.

8. Conclusion

> In giving up dependence [i.e. reliance] on the concept of an uninterpreted reality, something outside all schemes and science, we do not relinquish the notion of objective truth – quite the contrary.[4]

It does not follow from this, however, that we might secure a grip on objective *non-perspectival* truth about the world. Davidson says that, in 'giving up the dualism of scheme and world, we do not give up the world, but re-establish unmediated touch with the familiar objects whose antics make our sentences and opinions true or false'.[5] This is perhaps so, but it can no longer be taken to mean that we can simply resort to the straightforward empirical realist or positivist account of those objects. The antics of those objects are more complex than that account allows. Insofar as we are confined to the context of *experienced objectivity*, we cannot hope to represent the world non-perspectivally. Nor, indeed, is there any reason to be tempted to do so.

Note that it is not merely that we cannot secure a non-perspectival view of the world; but that we cannot secure a view of a non-perspectival world.[6] The point is that it is not a limitation of ours that we are confined to perspectival views of a globally independent world – which would collapse us back into epistemological idealism. It is simply in the nature of the context of experienced objectivity that we can make sense only of describing a perspectival world. Nevertheless this still leaves room for objectivity.

In our desire for objectivity, it is necessary to draw back from the more local perspectives to the widest perspective possible, which encompasses and explains the more local perspectives. This resembles what Bernard Williams has called 'the absolute conception of the world'.[7] I do not mean to imply that internalism demands a commitment to the absolute conception of the world. The point here is, again, only that this conception can in fact be prised apart from a realist view and contained entirely within an internalist position divorced from global ontological talk. We step back in search for the least perspectival description possible, while recognising that, confined as we are to the context of experienced objectivity, there is no room for

[4] op. cit., p. 198.
[5] ibid.
[6] Herein lies the danger of committing the ontological fallacy in a different form.
[7] See B. Williams, *Descartes: The Project of Pure Enquiry*, op. cit. Unfortunately Williams there seems to regard this conception as firmly wedded to a form of realism which appears to appeal to a globally independent world. In a more recent paper, however, 'The Scientific and the Ethical', in *Objectivity and Cultural Divergence*, (ed.) S.C. Brown, CUP, 1984, Williams seems more sensitive to this matter but even so continues to talk of 'the world as it is independently of our experience' (p. 215), or as 'already there' (p. 214), without going into further discussion of what this might mean, thereby failing to separate the absolute conception of the world from global ontological talk.

the ideal that we might achieve a totally non-perspectival description.[8] In the recognition that the most objective description possible will be the least locally perspectival, or, perhaps better, that the least locally perspectival will be the most objective possible, we might find some new currency for Sidgwick's metaphor of 'the point of view of the universe'. In this we might also begin to glimpse the significance of the tension contained in the phrase 'the context of *experienced objectivity*'.

It should be noted, finally, that internalist explanation within the context of experienced objectivity is also sufficiently powerful to exclude relativism of different conceptual schemes (while allowing, fortunately, for mere cultural variation). To the extent that such relativism rests, as Davidson shows it might, on the concept of a globally independent reality external to all schemes, it should be clear that accepting the conclusion of the last chapter would undermine philosophical relativism. But even without that conclusion we can at least conceive of eliminating philosophical relativism by way of what we might call *perspectival ascent*, ultimately ascending to that absolute 'point of view of the universe'.

However, all this is mentioned as a mere pointer. The sole task of this book has been to investigate that global ontological talk upon which central forms of realism, idealism and scepticism all rest. Understanding the nature of the internalist account within the context of experienced objectivity with which we are left, and the various philosophical questions it raises, would belong in a different enquiry.

---

[8] Williams, in his paper 'The Scientific and the Ethical', op. cit., leaves it unclear to what extent he accepts that any description will be minimally perspectival, even in the scientific domain which he separates sharply from the ethical. In places he talks of features of our world-picture which represent the world 'in a way that is to the maximum degree independent of our perspective' (p. 214), but then in others talks of the absolute conception 'consisting of non-perspectival materials' (p. 216).

Bibliography

Anscombe, G.E.M., 'The First Person', in *Mind and Language*, (ed.) S. Guttenplan. Oxford: Clarendon Press, 1975.
Armstrong, D.M., *A Materialist Theory of Mind*. London: Routledge and Kegan Paul, 1968.
Austin, J.L., *Philosophical Papers*. Oxford: Clarendon Press, 1961.
Austin, J.L., *Sense and Sensibilia*. Oxford: Clarendon Press, 1962.
Ayer, A.J., *Language, Truth and Logic*. London: Gollancz, 1936.
Bennett, J., *Kant's Analytic*. Cambridge University Press, 1966.
Bennett, J., *Kant's Dialectic*. Cambridge University Press, 1974.
Berkeley, G., *The Principles of Human Knowledge: With Other Writings*. Edited with an introduction by G.J. Warnock. London, Fontana, 1962.
Bieri, P., Horstmann, R-P. and Kruger, L., *Transcendental Argument*. Dordrecht: Reidel, 1979.
Blackburn, S., *Spreading the Word*. Oxford: Clarendon Press, 1984.
Bradley, F.H., *Appearance and Reality: A Metaphysical Essay*. London: Allen and Unwin, 1893.
Brown, S.C., (ed.) *Objectivity and Cultural Divergence*, Royal Institute of Philosophy Lecture Series, 17. Cambridge University Press, 1984.
Burnyeat, M., (ed.) *The Skeptical Tradition*. Berkeley: California University Press, 1983.
Carnap, R., *The Logical Structure of the World*. London: Routledge and Kegan Paul, 1937.
Carnap, R., 'Pseudoproblems in Philosophy', in *The Logical Structure of the World*, op. cit.
Chisholm, R., *Perceiving: A Philosophical Study*. Ithaca: Cornell University Press, 1957.
Chisholm, R., *Person and Object: A Metaphysical Study*. London: Allen and Unwin, 1976.
Clarke, T., 'The Legacy of Scepticism', in *Journal of Philosophy*, vol. 69 (1972), pp. 754-769.
Davidson, D., 'Radical Interpretation', in *Dialectica*, 27 (1973), pp. 313-328. Reprinted in *Inquiries into Truth and Interpretation*, op. cit.
Davidson, D., 'On the Very Idea of a Conceptual Scheme', in *Proceedings and Addresses of the American Philosophical Association*, 1973-4, vol. XLVII (1974), pp. 5-20. Reprinted in *Inquiries into Truth and Interpretation*, op. cit.
Davidson, D., *Inquiries into Truth and Interpretation*. Oxford: Clarendon Press, 1984.

Davidson, D. and Hintikka, J., (eds.) *Words and Objections – Essays on the Work of W. V. Quine*. Dordrecht: Reidel, 1969.

Dennett, D.C., *Brainstorms: Philosophical Essays on Mind and Psychology*. Hassocks: Harvester Press, 1978.

Dennett, D.C., *Content and Consciousness*. London: Routledge and Kegan Paul, 1969.

Dennett, D.C., and Hofstadter, D.R., *The Mind's Eye*. Hassocks: Harvester Press, 1981.

Dennett, D.C., 'Beyond Belief', in *Thought and Object – Essays on Intentionality*, (ed.) Andrew Woodfield, op. cit.

Descartes, R., 'A discourse on Method', 'Meditations on First Philosophy', 'The Principles of Philosophy' in *The Philosophical Works of Descartes* (translated by E.S. Haldane and G.R.T. Ross). In two volumes. Cambridge University Press, 1931.

Dummett, M., *Truth and Other Enigmas*. London: Duckworth, 1978.

Dummett, M., 'What is a Theory of Meaning (II)', in *Truth and Meaning* (ed.) Evans and McDowell, op. cit.

Evans, G., *The Varieties of Reference*, (ed.) John McDowell, Oxford: Clarendon Press, 1982.

Evans, G. and McDowell, J., (eds.) *Truth and Meaning*. Oxford: Clarendon Press, 1976.

Fraassen, B.C.v., *The Scientific Image*. Oxford: Clarendon Press, 1980.

Frege, G., 'Thoughts', in his *Logical Investigations*, (ed.) P.T. Geach. Translated by P.T. Geach and R.H. Stoothoff. Oxford: Blackwell, 1977, pp. 1-30.

Frege, G., *Foundations of Arithmetic* (translated by J.L. Austin). Oxford: Blackwell, 1978.

Geach, P.T., 'Good and Evil', in *Analysis*, vol. 17 (1956), pp. 33-42.

Geach, P.T., *Mental Acts*. London: Routledge and Kegan Paul, 1957.

Geach, P.T., *Reference and Generality*. Ithaca: Cornell University Press, 1962.

Goodman, N., *The Structure of Appearance*. Indianapolis: Bobbs-Merrill, 1951. Also published by – Dordrecht: Reidel, 1977.

Goodman, N., *Fact, Fiction and Forecast*. London: Athlone Press, 1954; Indianapolis: Bobbs-Merrill, 2nd edition, 1965; Hassocks: Harvester Press, 1979.

Goodman, N., *Ways of Worldmaking*. Hassocks: Harvester Press, 1978.

Gombrich, E.H. *Art and Illusion: A Study in the Psychology of Pictorial Representation*. London: Phaidon Press, 4th ed., 1972.

Gregory, R.L. and Gombrich, E.H. *Illusion in Nature and Art*. London: Duckworth, 1973.

Grayling, A.C., *The Refutation of Scepticism*. London: Duckworth, 1985.

Grayling, A.C., *Berkeley: The Central Arguments*. London: Duckworth, 1986.

Grice, H.P. and Strawson, P.F., 'In Defense of a Dogma', in *Philosophical Review*, vol. 65 (1956) pp. 141-158.

Guttenplan, S., (ed.) *Mind and Language*, Wolfson College Lectures, 1974. Oxford: Clarendon Press, 1975.

Haack, S., *Philosophy of Logics*. Cambridge University Press, 1978.

Hacking, I., *Why does Language Matter to Philosophy?*. Cambridge University Press, 1975.

Hacking, I., 'Is the End in Sight for Epistemology?', in *The Journal of*

Philosophy, vol. 87, no. 10 (1980), pp. 579-588.
Harman, G. and Davidson, D., (eds.) *Semantics of Natural Language*. Dordrecht: Reidel, 1972.
Harrison, T.R., *On What There Must Be*. Oxford: Clarendon Press, 1974.
Harrison, T.R., 'Transcendental Arguments and Idealism', in *Idealism Past and Present*, (ed.) G. Vesey, op. cit.
Hintikka, J., '*Cogito, ergo sum*: Inference or Performance?', in *Philosophical Review*, vol. 71 (1962), pp. 3-32.
Hintikka, J. and Davidson, D., (eds.) *Words and Objections*. See Davidson and Hintikka, above.
Holtzman, S.H. and Leich, C.M., (eds.) *Wittgenstein: to Follow a Rule*. London: Routledge and Kegan Paul, 1981.
Hume, D., *A Treatise of Human Nature*, (ed.) L.A. Selby-Bigge. Oxford: Clarendon Press, 1888.
Hume, D., *Enquiries Concerning the Human Understanding and Concerning the Principles of Morals*, (ed.) L.A. Selby-Bigge. Oxford: Clarendon Press, 2nd edition, 1902.
Ishiguro, H., *Leibniz's Philosophy of Logic and Language*. London: Duckworth, 1972.
James, W., *Essays in Radical Empiricism*. London: Longmans, Green, 1912; Harvard University Press, 1976.
Kant, I., *Critique of Pure Reason*, translated by Norman Kemp Smith. London: Macmillan, 1929.
Kant, I., *Prolegomena to Any Future Metaphysics*, translated and edited by Peter G. Lucas. Manchester University Press, 1953. Also published by – Indianapolis: Bobbs-Merrill, 1950.
Kaplan, D., 'Dthat', in P. Cole (ed.) *Syntax and Semantics 9: Pragmatics*. New York: Academic Press, 1978, pp. 221-243.
Kaplan, D., 'Quantifying In', in D. Davidson and J. Hintikka (eds.) *Word and Objections: Essays on the Work of W.V. Quine*. op. cit., pp. 206-242. Also in L. Linsky, (ed.) *Reference and Modality*. New York: Oxford University Press, 1971, pp. 112-144.
Kim, J., 'Rorty on the Possibility of Philosophy', in *Journal of Philosophy*, vol. 77, no. 10 (1980), pp. 588-597.
Korner, S., *Categorial Frameworks*. Oxford: Blackwell, 1970.
Kripke, S.A., *Naming and Necessity*. Oxford: Blackwell, 1980. Originally published in Harman and Davidson (eds.) *Semantics and Natural Language*, op. cit. pp. 253- 355.
Kripke, S.A., *Wittgenstein On Rules and Private Language*. Oxford: Blackwell, 1982.
Lear, J., 'Leaving the World Alone', in *Journal of Philosophy*, vol. 79 (1982), pp. 382-403.
Lear, J., 'The Disappearing "We" ', in *Proceedings of the Aristotelian Society, Supplementary Volume* LVIII (1984), pp. 219-242.
Leibniz, G.W., 'Monadology' in *Philosophical Writings*. London: Dent, 1973.
Lewis, D., *Counterfactuals*. Oxford: Blackwell, 1973.
Lewis, D., *Philosophical Papers*, vol. 1. Oxford University Press, 1983.
Linsky, L., *Referring*. London: Routledge and Kegan Paul, 1967.
Linsky, L., 'Reference and Referents' in *Semantics*, (ed.) D. Steinberg and L.A. Jakobovits. Cambridge University Press, 1971.

Locke, J., *An Essay Concerning Human Understanding*, (ed.) P. H. Nidditch. Oxford: Clarendon, 1975.
Mackie, J., *Problems from Locke*. Oxford: Clarendon Press, 1976.
Margolis, J., *Knowledge and Existence*. Oxford University Press, 1973.
Mates, B., *Skeptical Essays*. University of Chicago Press, 1981.
Moore, G.E., 'Is Existence a Predicate?', in *Proceedings of the Aristotelian Society, Supplementary Volume* XV (1936), pp. 175-188. Reprinted in *Philosophical Papers*, op. cit.
Moore, G.E., 'Proof of an External World' Annual Philosophical Lecture, British Academy, 1939. Published in *Proceedings of the British Academy*, vol. XXV, pp. 273-300. Reprinted in *Philosophical Papers*, op. cit.
Moore, G.E., *Philosophical Papers*. London: George Allen & Unwin, 1959.
Nagel, T., 'What is it Like to be a Bat?', in *Philosophical Review*, vol. 83 (1974), pp. 435-450. Also in *Mortal Questions*, op. cit.
Nagel, T., *Mortal Questions*. Cambridge University Press, 1979.
Nagel, T., 'Subjective and Objective', in *Mortal Questions*, op. cit.
Nagel, T., *The View From Nowhere*. Oxford University Press, 1986.
Nozick, R., *Philosophical Explanations*. Oxford: Clarendon Press, 1981.
Piaget, J., *Psychology and Epistemology*. London: Viking Press, 1971; Harmondsworth: Penguin, 1977.
Pitcher, G., *A Theory of Perception*. Princeton University Press, 1971.
Platts, M., (ed.) *Reference, Truth and Reality*. London: Routledge and Kegan Paul, 1980.
Popper, K., *Conjectures and Refutations*. London: Routledge and Kegan Paul, 1963.
Popper, K., *Objective Knowledge*. Oxford: Clarendon Press, 1972; 1979.
Putnam, H., 'It Ain't Necessarily So', in *Journal of Philosophy*, 59, 22 (1962), pp. 658-671. Also in *Mind, Language and Reality*, op. cit.
Putnam, H., 'Robots: Machines or Artificially Created Life?', in *Journal of Philosophy*, vol. 61, no. 21 (1964) pp. 668-691.
Putnam, H., 'The Meaning of "Meaning"', in K. Gunderson (ed.) *Minnesota Studies in the Philosophy of Science VII: Language, Mind and Knowledge*. Minneapolis: University of Minnesota Press, 1975. Also in *Mind, Language and Reality*, op. cit.
Putnam, H., *Mathematics Matter and Method – Philosophical Papers* vol. I. Cambridge University Press, 1975.
Putnam, H., *Mind, Language and Reality – Philosophical Papers* vol. II. Cambridge University Press, 1975.
Putnam, H., *Meaning and the Moral Sciences*. London: Routledge and Kegan Paul, 1978.
Putnam, H., 'Reference and Understanding', in *Meaning and the Moral Sciences*, op. cit.
Putnam, H., 'Realism and Reason' in *Meaning and the Moral Sciences*, op. cit.
Putnam, H., *Reason, Truth and History*. Cambridge University Press, 1981.
Putnam, H., 'Why There Isn't a Ready-Made World', in *Synthese* vol. 51, no. 2 (1982), pp. 141-167.
Putnam, H., 'Why Reason Can't be Naturalized', in *Synthese* vol. 52, no. 1 (1982), pp. 3-23.
Putnam, H., *Realism and Reason – Philosophical Papers*, vol. III. Cambridge University Press, 1983.

Quine, W.V., *From a Logical Point of View*. Harvard University Press, 1953; 2nd edition 1980.
Quine, W.V., 'On What There Is', in *From a Logical Point of View*, op. cit., pp. 1-19.
Quine, W.V., *Word and Object*. Cambridge, Mass.: M.I.T. Press, 1960.
Quine, W.V., *The Ways of Paradox*. New York: Random House, 1966.
Quine, W.V., *Ontological Relativity and Other Essays*. New York: Columbia University Press, 1969.
Quinton, A., *The Nature of Things*. London: Routledge and Kegan Paul, 1973.
Rorty, R., 'Verificationist and Transcendental Arguments', in *Nous*, vol. 5 (1971), pp. 3-15.
Rorty, R., 'The World Well Lost' in *Journal of Philosophy*, vol. 69 (1972), pp. 645-665 (-669).
Rorty, R., *Philosophy and the Mirror of Nature*. Oxford: Blackwell, 1980.
Rorty, R., *Consequences of Pragmatism*. Hassocks: Harvester Press, 1982.
Russell, B., 'On Denoting', *Mind*, vol. 14, 1905, pp. 479-493. Reprinted in *Logic and Knowledge*, op. cit.
Russell, B., *Our Knowledge of the External World*. London: Allen and Unwin, 1914.
Russell, B., *The Analysis of Mind*. London: Allen and Unwin, 1921.
Russell, B., *The Analysis of Matter*. London: Routledge and Kegan Paul, 1927.
Russell, B., *Sceptical Essays*. London: Allen and Unwin, 1928.
Russell, B., *Logic and Knowledge – Essays 1914 – 1950*. London: Allen and Unwin, 1956.
Ryle, G., 'Imaginary Objects', in *Proceedings of the Aristotelian Society, Supplementary Volume* XII (1933), pp. 18-43. Reprinted in *Collected Papers*, vol. II, op. cit.
Ryle, G., 'Philosophical Arguments'. An Inaugural Lecture – 30 October 1945. Oxford: Clarendon Press, 1945. Reprinted in *Collected Papers*, vol. II, op. cit.
Ryle, G., *The Concept of Mind*. London: Hutchinson, 1949.
Ryle, G., *Dilemmas*. Cambridge University Press, 1954.
Ryle, G., *Collected Papers*, vols. I and II. London: Hutchinson, 1971.
Salmon, N., 'How *Not* to Derive Essentialism from the Theory of Reference', in *Journal of Philosophy*, vol. 76, (December 1979), pp. 703-725.
Salmon, N., *Reference and Essence*. Oxford: Blackwell, 1982.
Schofield, M., Burnyeat, M. and Barnes, J.,(eds.) *Doubt and Dogmatism: Studies in Hellenistic Epistemology*. Oxford: Clarendon Press, 1980.
Schwartz, S., (ed.) *Naming, Necessity and Natural Kinds*. Ithaca: Cornell University Press, 1977.
Sellars, W., *Science, Perception and Reality*. London: Routledge and Kegan Paul, 1964.
Shoemaker, S., *Self-Knowledge and Self-Identity*. Ithaca: Cornell University Press, 1963.
Smart, J.J.C., *Philosophy and Scientific Realism*. London: Routledge and Kegan Paul, 1963.
Strawson, P.F., 'On Referring', in *Mind* vol. 59 n.s. (1950) pp. 320-344. Also in *Logico-Linguistic Papers*, op. cit.
Strawson, P.F., *Individuals – An Essay in Descriptive Metaphysics* London: Methuen, 1959. Reprinted 1961, 1977.

Strawson, P.F., *The Bounds of Sense*. London: Methuen, 1966. Reprinted 1968, 1975.
Strawson, P.F., *Logico-Linguistic Papers*. London: Methuen, 1971.
Strawson, P.F. and Grice, H.P., 'In Defense of a Dogma', op. cit.; see Grice and Strawson.
Stroud, B., 'Transcendental Arguments', in *Journal of Philosophy*, vol. 65 (1968), pp. 241-256.
Stroud, B., 'Transcendental Arguments and Epistemological Naturalism', in *Philosophical Studies*, 31 (1977), pp. 105-115.
Stroud, B., 'The Significance of Scepticism', in Bieri et al, op. cit. pp. 277-297.
Stroud, B., 'Kant and Skepticism', in *The Skeptical Tradition* (ed.) Burnyeat, op. cit., pp. 413-434.
Stroud, B., *The Significance of Philosophical Scepticism*. Oxford University Press, 1984.
Stroud, B., 'The Allure of Idealism', in *Proceedings of the Aristotelian Society, Supplementary Volume* LVIII (1984), pp. 243-258.
Vesey, G., (ed.) *Idealism Past and Present*, Royal Institute of Philosophy Lecture Series, 13. Cambridge University Press, 1982.
Wiggins, D., *Sameness and Substance*. Oxford: Blackwell, 1980.
Williams, B.A.O., 'Wittgenstein and Idealism', in *Understanding Wittgenstein*, Royal Institute of Philosophy Lectures, 7, 1972-73 (pp. 76-95). London: MacMillan, 1974. Also in *Moral Luck*, op. cit.
Williams, B.A.O., 'Strawson on Individuals', in *Philosophy*, vol. 36, (1961), pp. 309-332. Also in *Problems of the Self*, op. cit.
Williams, B.A.O., 'The Truth in Relativism', in *Proceedings of the Aristotelian Society*, LXXV (1974-75), pp. 215-228. Also in *Moral Luck*, op. cit.
Williams, B.A.O., *Problems of the Self*. Cambridge University Press, 1973.
Williams, B.A.O., *Descartes – The Project of Pure Enquiry*. Harmondsworth: Penguin, 1978.
Williams, B.A.O., *Moral Luck*. Cambridge University Press, 1981.
Williams, B.A.O., 'The Scientific and the Ethical', in *Objectivity and Cultural Divergence*, (ed.) S.C. Brown, op. cit., pp. 209-228.
Wittgenstein, L., *Philosophical Investigations*. Oxford: Blackwell, 1953 (3rd edition, 1967).
Wollheim, R., *F.H. Bradley*. Harmondsworth: Penguin, 1959.
Woodfield, A., (ed.) *Thought and Object – Essays on Intentionality*. Oxford: Clarendon Press, 1982.

Index

absolute conception of the world, 102, 187
adjectives, attributive and predicative, 3, 4, 6
anti-realist theory of meaning, 139-41
appearance and reality, ix, 23, 26-7, 44, 80, 83
artifacts, 7, 9-11, 68, 129
Austin, J.L., 2-6

Bennett, J., 31n4
Bergson, H., 102
Berkeley, G., 15n21, 19, 19n28, 111, 112, 132, 133, 159, 159n5, 166
Blackburn, S., ix
brains in a vat (BIVs), ch. 3 *passim*, 109-10, 120, 142, 179
Brown, S.C., 102n14, 164n9

Carnap, R., viii, 2, 22, 54, 122n3, 123, 123n4, ch. 6 *passim*
Cartesian, 47, 49
causal independence/dependence relations, 7-10, 26, 119, 152-4, 185
Clarke, T., 115n36
co-referential terms, 171n17
cogito, 17-18, 47
Cole, P., 68n12
conceptual dependence, 177
conceptual framework, 94
conceptual scheme, 34-5, 48-51, 54, 188
construction theory, 150, 155-6
context of experienced objectivity, 168-9, 172, 175, 177-8, 180, 182-3, 185, 187-8
contradictories, 6-7, 14, 20-1, 116, 138, 182
  see-saw of, 20, 136, 141, 158, 174
conversation of mankind, 186

Craig, E., ix
cultural variation, 163, 188
  see also relativism

Davidson, D., 36, 39n19, 101-2, 115n36, 159, 164n9, 181, 186, 188
dependence, ontological vs. referential, 49-51
Derrida, J., 186
Descartes, R., 17-18, 109
Donnellan, K., 63
dreams, 120, 123
Dummett, M., 84n22, 139-40

empirical adequacy, 117, § 5.2 (122-31), 184
experience, 6, 10, § 1.2.3 and *passim*
  form of, 12-13, 104-15, and *passim*
  disembodied, 49
experienced object-world, 110-12, 123, 128, 130-1, 152, 163, 167-8, 174, 177, 179-81, 184, 186

factual content, 137-8
Ferrari, G., x
Frege, G., 63, 65, 68
functionalism, 44, 49

Geach, P., 3
God, 4-5, 17, 19, 82, 111-12, 127n5, 132-3, 166
Goehr, L., x
Goodman, N., viii, 39, 42, 94-104, 115, 181
Grayling, A., ix, 135n10, 159n5
green/grue, 22-3, 95

Harrison, R., ix
Heyd, D., x
Hintikka, J., 18n27

Index

Holt, E.B., 114
Hume, D., 31, 94

idealism and realism, traditional, 16-19, 44, 113, 131, 151
idealism, vii, viii, 15
  empirical, 15-17, 26, 29, 31, 55, 82, 110-12, 125, 183
  transcendental, 16, 28-32, 35-6, 38, 43, 47, 52, 55, 63, 76, 80, 82, 87, 96-7, 161, 165, 181
  Berkeleyan, 17
  epistemological, 15, 28, 76, 187
  ontological, 15-21, 28-9, 76, 99-100, 112-16, 131-2, 176, 184
individuation, 158
  perspectival, 159-63
inputs
  sensory, 79
  experiential, 80-1, 91
  conceptually contaminated, 79-80, 90-2
inscrutability of reference, 46
intentional objects, 18, 66, 69, 70, 113, 125
intentional existence, 123
intentionality, 11, 46-7, 109, 112-13, 162, 164, 167
internal, 112, 115, 135
internal questions, 165
internalism, viii, ix, 61, 74, 79-83, 85-7, 91-2, 103-4, 114-15, 117, § 5.1 *passim*, 122n3, 130-1, 133, 136, 182-8
  radically internalist, 182
  internalist account, 116
  neutral, 114-15, 123
irrealism, 94, 98-101, 103-4, 115

James, W., 114, 115n35

Kant, I., viii, 15-16, 23n29, § 2.1 (25-32), 32, 38, 43-4, 47, 52, 54n37, 76, 80, 82-4, 87-9, 97, 103, 105, 119, 165, 181
Kantian, 35, 42-3, 45-6, 52, 63, 76, 80-1, 83, 95, 105-6, 118, 144, 165
Kaplan, D., 68, 68n12

Kripke, S., 8, 63, 65-6, 68
Kuhn, T., 102

Leffers, E.W., x
legitimacy, principle of, 143-5
Leibniz, W., 124, 128n6
Linsky, L., 63
Lloyd, G.E.R., ix
Locke, J., 94
logical empiricism, 122n3, 155-6
logical positivism, 137

materialism, 44, 114
Meinong, A., 18
Mill, J.S., 63
mirror of nature, 186
Moore, G.E., 36

Nagel, T., 47n23, 108n21, 166n12
naturalistic accounts, 182, 186
neutral monism, 114-15, 178
neutrality, 114-16, 119, 121, 145, 152
  logical, 113-15, 117-18, 122, 135-6, 151, 184
  intellectual, 122, 151
notional objects (brain, vat), 58-9, 69, 69n14, 70-1, 73, 179
notional world, 57-8, 63, 66-7
noumena(l), 30, 35-6, 38, 40, 42-3, 45, 80-5, 87-92, 96-8, 118-19, 161-2, 165, 178, 184

O'Brien, L., x
object-directed experience, 11, 17, 22, 25, 45-6, 48, 104-7, 109, 111, 113-14, 119, 130-1, 134-5, 158-66, 175, 178
Ockham's Razor, 1, 18
Ockhamism, 98
ontological dependence and independence relations, vii, viii, § 1.2.2 (6-11) *passim*, § 1.3 (13-15), 21, 110-11, 152-4, 157, 172
ontological dependence
  local, 113-15, 117, 122-3, 145
  global, 112-15, 118, 121-3, 128, 132, 146, 149, 158, 159, 172-9, 182
ontological fallacy, the, 134-5, 161, 174-6, 181, 182, 184-5
ontological independence

local, 112-15, 117-18, 120-2, 125, 128, 130-4, 145, 152, 182, 186
global, 111-15, 118-28, 130-5, 145-6, 149, 158-60, 162, 172-6, 178-9, 181-2, 187-8
ontological relativity, 34, 46, 96
ontological talk, viii, 1, 17, 21, 24, 31-5, 45, 51-2, 54-5, 77, 93, 100-1, 103-4, 110-11, 146-7, 149-50, 157, 171-2, 174, 180-2
local, viii, 21, 110-14 and *passim*
global, viii, 21, 111-16 and *passim*
opacity, veil of, 179, 182

perceptions, bundles of, 94
persons, § 2.4.1 (48ff.)
perspective (perspectival), 102, 159-63, 183, 187, 188
perspectival variation, 162, 163
cultural perspectives, 163
perspectival ascent, 95n4, 188
physicalism, 44, 49
Platonic, 166-7
Platonic Forms, 127n5, 166
point of view of the universe, 188
Popper, K., 137
presuppositions, 13-14, 20-1, 157, 172-3
presuppositional failure, 6-7, 157, 173-4
Pseudoproblems, 136-8, 139n8, 146, 149-50, 154
Putnam, H., viii, ix, 36n14, § 2.3 (37-46), 52, 54-5, ch. 3 *passim*, 95-7, 103, 141, 161, 179, 181

qualities, secondary and primary, 83-4, 94
Quine, W., § 2.2 (32-7), 39, 43, 45-6, 50, 52, 54, 79-80, 96-7, 102-4, 138, 139n8, 140, 150n23, 181

raw-experience, 34-7, 45, 79, 102, 108 (raw sensations), 156
ready-made world, 88-92, 95, 98
real, §§ 1.2.1, 1.3 and *passim*
empirically, 29, 46, 47
transcendentally, 46
realism, vii, viii, 15
empirical, 2, 16-17, 26-8, 30, 35, 38, 41, 47-8, 51-2, 55, 63, 66-7, 72, 76, 78, 80, 82-3, 86-7, 110-11, 118, 165, 183, 187
internal, 2, 27-8, 30-1, 38, 41, 44-5, 55, 57, 62, 91, 97, 111
transcendental, 26, 27
metaphysical, 38, 40-4, 54, 55n39, 56, 59, 62, 80, 87-9, 90, 92, 95, 98, 141
external, 27, 44, 54, 72, 79
epistemological, 15-16, 29, 39-44, 92, 141, 144-5, 181
ontological, 15-21, 28, 39-44, 92, 97, 99-100, 113-16, 131-2, 144-5, 176, 184
realist, traditional, 18-19
see idealism and realism, traditional
reality, empirical, 27, 146, 151, 154
metaphysical, 146, 151-4
reference
causal (direct) theory of, 57-8, 62-6, 68-9, 71-2
traditional (descriptive) theory of, 58, 63-5, 72
magical theory of, 40-1, 58, 58n2, 62-3, 71
puzzle about, 57, 59, 60-2, 72, 74
referential integration, 168-70, 172-9, 181, 184
referentially integrated terms, 168-70, 172-3, 177
referentially convergent terms, 169-70, 171n17, 172
relativism, 35, 39, 40-1, 44, 90-2, 94-5, 95n4, 99-101, 103-4, 115n36, 181, 188
empirical, 102, 162-3
metaphysical, 163
radical, 95, 101-2, 163
Rorty, R., 54, 54n38, 98-100, 181, 185-6
Rosen, L., x
Russell, B., 114

Salmon, N., 8, 68n11,
sceptic/scepticism, vii, viii, ix, 24, 29, 31-2, 38, 43, 52-7, 59-61, 73-93, 103, 115n36, 116, 141, 144-6, 148, 172, 175-6, 180-1, 184, 188

scheme/content distinction, 36, 159, 181, 187
Searle, J., 63
Secada, G., 96n5
semantic opacity and transparency, 167-8, 168n13
　semantic opacity, 172, 176-9, 182
　semantic transparency, 173
　semantically transparent/opaque contexts, 170
Sidgwick, H., 188
Smith, B., x
souls, 17, 127n5
Strawson, P.F., 7n9, 31n4, §§ 2.4-2.5 (46-55) *passim*, 87, 103, 105-6, 108n20, 165, 174n19, 181
Stroud, B., 36, 36n14, 36n15, 53, 141n13, 143n16, 181-2, 186
Stroud's Challenge, 32, 53-5, 181
subject-object distinction, 46-9, 114, 120
substance, 47, 94, 180

Tanner, T., x
textuality, 186

thing-in-itself, 26-32, 37, 43-5, 52, 77, 80, 82-3, 85, 90, 95, 97-9, 144
third man argument, 166
transcendental arguments, 61-2, 117, § 5.1, 135n10
translation, 46, 102
tree argument, 159

verification, 22, 44, 58
verificationism, viii, 38-41, 122n3, ch. 6 *passim*, 176, 181
　verificationist principle of meaning, 137-8, 150
　atomistic vs. holistic, 138-40
versions, 94-6, 100-2, 104
Vienna Circle, 137-8, 139n8

Wallach, R., x
Whorf, B.L., 102
Williams, B., x, 12, 39n19, 50-1, 102, 115n36, 164n9, 186-7, 188n8
Wittgenstein, L., 12, 12n16, 137, 139n8, 185
Wittgensteinian, 12, 118, 174

DATE DUE

HIGHSMITH   # 45220